CUISINES OF THE
AXIS OF EVIL
AND OTHER IRRITATING STATES

"*Cuisines of the Axis of Evil* is laugh-out-loud-funny; a shrewd primer on some of the more unsavory regimes the world has to offer, and a savory rendering of their cookery. Chris Fair by turns channels Richard Holbrooke, Steven Colbert, and Elizabeth David as she whisks up up a truly original contribution in the field of international relations and cookbooks."

—Peter Bergen, author of *The Osama bin Laden I Know*

CUISINES OF THE
AXIS OF EVIL
AND OTHER IRRITATING STATES

A DINNER PARTY
APPROACH TO INTERNATIONAL RELATIONS

CHRIS FAIR

Guilford, Connecticut

To buy books in quantity for corporate use
or incentives, call **(800) 962–0973**
or e-mail **premiums@GlobePequot.com.**

Cover and interior illustrations: James Polisky (www.jamespolisky.com)
Text design: Casey Shain

Library of Congress Cataloging-in-Publication Data
Fair, Chris.
  Cuisines of the axis of evil and other irritating states : a dinner party approach to international relations / Chris Fair.
    p. cm.
  Includes bibliographical references and index.
  ISBN 978-1-59921-286-9 (alk. paper)
  1. Cookery, International. 2. International relations. I. Title.
  TX725.A1F273 2008
  641.59—dc22

                                                    2008012814

Printed in the United States of America

10 9 8 7 6 5 4 3 2 1

To everyone who is hungry
for justice, peace, and security.

CONTENTS

ACKNOWLEDGMENTS

Where does one begin thanking everyone who needs to be thanked for a project like this—without endangering or disgracing them? There are folks like Scott and Mariam and Glenn who provided loads of help but who don't want to be identified for fear their reputations may be ruined. They know who they are, and I owe them dinner. Peter Bergen is owed a honkin' heap of *fesanjan,* as he put me in touch with my guardian angel in publishing, Svetlana Katz, who believed in this project and kept beating on doors despite complaints about the inclusion of certain countries. Many shukrans, gracias, and dhanyavads also go to the patient and adventurous folks at Globe Pequot Press. Kaleena Cote kept this one-wing bird in the air, Amy Paradysz wrestled the Foot Note monster to the ground, and John Spalding never spent a day in the box, much less thinking in one.

Throughout the years there have been many a folk who have eaten at my house as I experimented with this stuff and have given me frank advice. There is the LA crew of Mike, Seema, Ian, Libra Brad, and many others who came and drank without my knowing who they were exactly. Then there was the DC crowd, which often included neighbors, colleagues, and random dates from the Internet. In the civilized (read: married) phase of this project, I bestow mounds of gratitude upon my husband Jeff, Hannah, Meagan D., Ry and Annie, Dave and Ellen, Jack and Anne, Chris C., Polly, John, and Anne Marie and other neighbors on whom I pawned off "test desserts." I thank dog daily for my "spouse Jefferson," my brothers (Joe and Pork), their wives (Whitney and Ashley), and their children (Mallory and Logan) who have long cowered at my culinary offerings. Fearing some Iraqi rendition of the American Thanksgiving feast, they called ahead to check on the menu. I am also grateful to Dawn C. who found me and Bob and Bug, who, at long last, welcomed me as kin. I hope they don't change their minds after reading this!

I owe so many thanks to everyone else who schlepped over for various iterations of this grub and gave honest feedback on which recipes worked and which did not. I also owe debts of gratitude to friends (some of whom may become foes) who read various chapters of this volume and gave me the straight advice on why they stank.

I am also thankful to colleagues who advised against ruining my career with this project. I hope they will consider me when they need a dog walker or a cat sitter in the future. I can also water plants and shovel snow.

INTRODUCTION

I am not the most obvious author of the gustatory castigation you are perusing. I grew up in Huntertown, Indiana, a town of no particular distinction. When my mom re-optimized her spousal situation, we moved from Huntertown to the comparatively metropolitan Fort Wayne, Indiana—a town that some of you may have heard of. Actually, "The Fort," as we call it back home, *is* big enough now to feature in national meteorological reports, which is surely a signifier of progress. It is also home to the Roller Dome, a high-value terrorist target according to the Department of Homeland Security. In fact, my home state of Indiana apparently has the largest number of terrorist targets in the entire country.[1] Having fled Fort Wayne to take up my studies at the University of Chicago, I now have a career that takes me to some of the most interesting—and some would say dangerous—places in the world. (Or at least I *had* such a job before I wrote this book.)

In the course of studying, doing research, living, and working abroad, I've eaten cold frog curry in Burma, lapped up fresh strawberry ice cream as it dripped upon my *hejab* one hot day in Tehran, and ate fresh olives out of malodorous barrels in Damascus. I sipped salted Kashmiri tea at the height of the insurgency from the "luxury" of the roof of a ratty houseboat in Srinagar, and savored the lovely cardamom tea (that I imagine the Taliban quaffing in their caves) above Peshawar's bustling thieves' market. I've dined with soldiers in the Khyber Pass and socialized with a Nepali prostitute in Delhi and eunuchs in Lahore. I rummaged for delicious lunch packets of curried fish and rice from the bombed-out bazaars of Jaffna city, the epicenter of Tamil Tiger violence. I avoided assiduously the dog restaurants of Vietnam, which reportedly are shacks poised atop kennels with the hapless dogs howling away while diners above nibble on sausages made of their littermates. The constant feature of snake dishes on Vietnamese restaurant menus also served as powerful appetite suppressants.

Throughout the course of these travels, I have seen things that make me want to holler. All around the world *right now* folks are starving, living in horrid conditions, and deprived access to justice, security, and basic rights that the readers of this book likely take for granted. While non-state actors (read: terrorists, insurgents, criminals, traffickers, and the like) get most of the grief, many states addressed herein are doing some pretty nasty things to their own populations and to polities of other states. To my dismay, while the U.S. government opines about the nefarious evildoers such as terrorists and autocrats running countries enshrined in collectives such as the "Axis of Evil" or "Outposts of Tyranny," in truth U.S. foreign policy has contributed to or subsidized some pretty odious deeds across the world and has done so for decades. This makes me sad—and hopping mad. These policies not only endanger others, they also endanger *us*.

Yet, despite our strength and wealth, I think most Americans seem insouciant about U.S. foreign policies and their implications for the billions of folks who are not lucky enough to have been born in America—or at least in Europe, Australia, New Zealand, or a few other outposts of decent economies and democracies. I have no illusions that the average American (from, say, my hometown of Huntertown, Indiana) will bother reading a book about why Iran is included in the Axis of Evil but Israel or China isn't. Similarly, many Americans cannot find Afghanistan or Iraq on a map despite the fact that our soldiers have been fighting and dying there since October 2001 and March 2003, respectively.

Bringing the World to Your Lazy Susan

Since 80 percent of the American citizenry and 30 percent of U.S. congresspersons don't even have passports,[2] it is unlikely that Americans are going to get out and see for themselves the countries in the Axis of Evil or other irritating states. In some cases, warfare and/or sanctions actually preclude safe and/or legal travel for Americans, even with a passport. So even though it is high time for Americans to get out and see the world, I am not betting on such a development any time soon. However, given our ever-expanding appetites and waistlines, we can bring the world to America's dinner table. Thus, the time is right for a dinner party approach to foreign policy and international relations.

Cynics may allege that this is just an angry, grouchy, eccentric chick using the vehicle—nay, *excuse*—of the cookbook genre to say things that she couldn't in any other kind of book. There may be truckloads of truth in that assertion, but we all know that food and politics are as intimately related as eating and, for example, toilet paper. What amazes me is that given all the verbal projectiles flying about at your average dinner party—especially family dinners—friendships and families weather the gratuitous stumping on well-worn positions about god, the lack thereof, or politics. No matter what one says, friendships are not typically ruined, families are not shattered in disgust, and spouses still drive home together—even if one is strapped to the ski rack while driving through hail, sleet, and snow. Sitting around the table eating and—when not prohibited by law or religious belief—drinking, everyone gets a free pass at speaking their mind, even if he or she doesn't actually have one.

Leaving aside the obvious intimacy of the dinner setting to lay out any number of social and political positions, food has always been connected to larger political issues. At the most palpable level, autocratic regimes are notorious for their paucity of food security while the bellies of global hegemons bloat with their successes. Culinary habits of countries with imperial or colonial legacies almost always bare the imprint of those pasts. The only decent food worth eating while visiting the United Kingdom can be had from the ubiquitous curry shacks that form edible archipelagos across that island country. In the Netherlands, folks nosh on Indonesian food in vast quantities. The French munch their North African tagines in ample amounts as well as Levantine delicacies, while in Japan the fast ethnic food of choice is Korean. And in the United States, the analogue to all of these is Mexican food. What the preceding examples have in common is the fact that these fast ethnic foods are *cheap* and undervalued, embodying the past or present *political* relationship of these countries to that of the diner.

Conversely, when you travel to places that had been formerly occupied or colonized, it is often the height of sophistication to serve guests the food of the former imperial master. I can't count the times that I have been served some horrid version of British food on the South Asian subcontinent. The Vietnamese love to serve up French delicacies at home and abroad, and, mercifully for those of us who tire of snake-based entrees, the French baguette can be bought from vendors purveying the tasty stuff from large bags saddling their bicycles. Similarly in the United States, if you want to pretend to be sophisticated, you plop down some serious change at a fancy hotel and treat yourself to "high tea," in a forgotten nod to our colonial masters across the great pond.

One need only look at the fast-food landscape to see the "culinary" imprint of global hegemons. While American chain restaurants and coffee outlets have popped up everywhere—including war zones—what "foreign" fast-food competitors have infested the United States on such a scale? American chains have even gone to great lengths to *pretend* to be foreign: Outback Steakhouse is not, to the best of my knowledge, in any way, shape, or form connected to Australia. Naturally, the public culture of eating in the United States (and other countries such as Cuba, France, Britain, the Netherlands, and Australia) reflects the migration history of the nation's vastly varied population and introduced domesticated versions of, among others, Chinese, Italian, Vietnamese, Indian, and Arab foodstuffs, all of which often bear little resemblance to that of cuisine back in the "homeland."

Even the fundamentals of culinary civilizations stand witness to histories of mercantilism, missionaries, and militarism. It is impossible to think of Indian foods without the tomato, potato, and chili. However, these decidedly "New World" foods did not appear in India until the Portuguese showed up. Polenta is a dish that we all think of as distinctly Italian, yet the base of that food—corn—never germinated a pod in Europe before Columbus brought his flotilla (and germs) to the Americas . . . and returned. In addition, while the Belgians may have cornered the market with their chocolates, cacao was also native to Latin America, and, in fact, the plants died when they were first brought to Europe by missionaries. Reflecting the spread of various Muslim empires, biryanis and kebabs are found throughout the Middle East, Central and South Asia, and beyond, as are the rice dish *pullow* and *manto* (a meat dumpling). Samosas, or sambosas (fried dough stuffed with meat and or veggies), exist in Ethiopian and Eritrean cuisines as well as those of Central and South Asia.

The cuisines of countries engaging in colonizing enterprises embraced new spices and culinary concepts and even invented a few "back home." While we all talk of "curry powder" as if it were a common staple of South Asian fare, in truth this is very much a British colonial invention meant to cater to the tastes of those who had developed a fondness for the food while out in the bush serving Her Majesty in the Raj. Until quite recently, curry powder per se did not have a place in Indian cooking. The dishes that are frequently called "curries" are made by frying (in a fairly regular sequence) chili powder, cumin, and turmeric, to which other items can be added. Much like the American pizza, which was re-imported to Italy, curry powder is now used by middle-class Indian housewives pressed for time between domestic duties and outside employment.[3]

Chew on That Thought

While most folks recognize the power of food to bring people together, I notice most its power to divide. Many religions enshrine various forms of commensalism, or rules that govern with whom you can eat and with whom you cannot. In Hinduism, high-caste persons can't eat in the presence of those who are low caste, whose very shadow defiles the former. Many religions specify not only the animals that can be eaten but the ways in which those animals must be killed as a precondition for eating them and the means by which they must be prepared. This can seriously limit the number of people one can eat with.

Cuisines also yield some insights into the social structure of countries in question. Indian food is time-intensive and requires either a platoon of servants or a daughter-in-law. Women can spend hours of their day slicing and dicing up tiny vegetables, slaving over an open gas burner with little or no ventilation, and, in some cases, cooking up their family victuals over a fire made of desiccated cow dung! And as housewives everywhere hang up their apron for a computer or a real estate license, food slopped to their families changes accordingly. Yet despite the obvious centrality of women in food production and preparation, in many parts of the world, men and women are socially barred from eating together. More disturbing, while women do all the heavy lifting and cooking of those meals, in some places those same women are resigned to eat whatever scraps their menfolk have left for them.

In other words, eating structures power and social relations in ways that most of us have internalized without much thought. Because food is important to me and because my pre-marriage dating list resembled the roll call of the U.N. General Assembly, I've had to abandon relationships with men who were Jewish, Muslim, or Hindu simply because of their eating rules. I eat pork, drink booze, and think vegetarian cuisine is best left for ruminates. I found their eating issues to be bigger hindrances than their various religious commitments, because food—in its preparation and in its consumption—is one of the most fundamental things that we as humans share, and these rules critically create groups who can be included or alternatively excluded in this most primal act.

Food also encapsulates differences in social mores between and within cultures. For example, Americans flinch at those Chinese, Vietnamese, and Koreans who eat dog and cat—man's best and passable friends, respectively. Some Hindus in India are disgusted that we love eating our cows, with whom they share their own spiritual affections. While Americans think of their beloved horses as being akin to big dogs, folks in Central Asia love their horses too—formed into spicy sausages and gracing a fatty *pullov*. My Chinese colleagues and friends have pointed out how wasteful Americans are when we only eat part of the animal and discard the rest. They are correct to ask, why is a beef steak delicious but a brazed ox penis is repugnant?

Similarly, folks in many Muslim countries are obsessed with various animal parts with alleged properties conferring sexual prowess upon its consumers. For instance, in several places in the Muslim world, it is a delicacy to eat the "egg of lamb," which, as you may have guessed, is the poor animal's family jewels. As you stroll through the meat bazaars of the Muslim world, you are greeted by elegant piles of elaborately arranged organ meat, kept glistening by the efforts of the shopkeepers who sprinkle them with water dotingly. Often they are decorated with garlands of chili peppers, sliced tomatoes, and red onions.   Pakistanis love their brain curry and their spicy stew of goat head and feet. The latter, *sir paya,* is particularly disconcerting, with at least one *whole* goat head staring up at you blankly from the pot. I flee from this dish when I see it, but I have to ask myself why I find these offerings to be vile while I am perfectly happy eating other parts of that same goat in curries or as kebabs. Similarly, why do most Americans find the Asian culinary custom of eating cockroaches disgusting when most of us eat shrimp and lobster, which are little more than the cockroaches of the sea? Clearly these value judgments of what is or is not edible reflect cultural values that we rarely consider—until we are confronted with one of these affronting delicacies.

Only the foolish would underestimate the social and political importance of food when, in fact, every aspect of what we put into our mouths is burdened with social, political, religious, and even militarized baggage even though most of us remain woefully unaware of the same. It seems to me that cuisine is a perfectly defensible lens through which to look at the countries examined herein and U.S. policies toward the same, and I hope you will agree.

Who Is Included in this Culinary Castigation?

This book takes to task *ten* countries, expositing their various perfidies and providing a culinary overview and a detailed dinner-party battle plan for each one. I also share some peculiar—if disturbing—trivia on these countries. The ten singled out for their various deceits and misconduct in the global arena are:

The Charter Members of the Axis of Evil: North Korea, Iran, and Iraq

Despite being signatories to the Nuclear Nonproliferation Treaty (NPT), these three are known proliferators of nuclear technology and, depending on the evidentiary standard of your choosing, are dallying in other weapons of mass destruction technologies and supporting terrorism as well. In addition, they are nondemocratic regimes with numerous human rights violations.

The NPT+3 States: Israel, India, and Pakistan

While these three countries are not signatories to the NPT, they have all acquired nuclear weapon technologies in spite of the internationally accepted global nonproliferation regime. In addition, Israel, India, and Pakistan possess or are acquiring the necessary platforms (such as air, sea, and ground) to deliver their bombs. All three states also have dubious human rights records, and all three rightly stand accused of bullying their neighbors. These three countries are by any objective standard "irritating," even if they have all enjoyed at times special relationships with the United States that buy them immunity from being called so publicly—until now.

The Dashers of Democracy: Cuba, Burma (or Myanmar, if you despise freedom), and China

Most of the world thinks of Cuba, Burma, and China as being democracy-free zones where their citizenry languish under the oppressive thumbs of the noxious regimes. Indeed, these impressions are not ill-founded. Cuba, until early 2008, was run by the ailing hirsute despot Fidel Castro, who could talk his polity into submission. His almost-as-geezerly brother, Raúl Castro, is in charge now. The Burmese chafe under the tyranny of khaki-clad Buddhist generals who have recently rounded up the country's hapless monks and beat them and shot them. And then there's China, with a raft of unsavory policies mostly at home but a few abroad as well. Despite the opprobrium it rightly deserves, China gets a free pass because it virtually owns the U.S. economy. If you are going to be a repressor state, you better have some bucks and a seat on the United Nations Security Council to stay out of trouble! These countries don't have freedom, but they have great food!

The United States of America

This will be controversial and an inconvenient truth, but most of the world *is* irritated by the U.S. of A., and there is a wealth of poll data to support this contention. Welcome to the Great Satan Barbecue—bring your own beer!

This book is not intended to tell the reader everything there is to know about the cuisine of the miscreant country in question, nor is it intended to tell everything there is to know about the various ignominies that merit inclusion in this gustatory castigation. However, this is a serious book about entertaining and about understanding some of the hardest-to-understand countries on the planet—through the lexicon of the dinner party, which is just plain fun. Who, after all, doesn't like a dinner party?

Some Warnings and Disclaimers

First, I'm Not Your Typical Culinary Expert

Growing up, my mother didn't cook very much at all, and when she did, whatever was prepared was to be generally avoided. My mom unloaded semitrailers for a living, among other jobs, and with biceps like hers, it was not considered prudent to complain about her peculiar concoctions. When I left home for college, I had to use Jiffy mix to make biscuits and had no clue how to boil an egg. Oddly, I first learned to cook from an ill-tempered Indian woman who could have been—but mercifully was not—my mother-in-law. While I am thankful that I dodged that marital bullet, that crazy termagant was the first person who in earnest taught me how to cook, and for that I will always be oddly grateful. Since my two-week tenure in her "housewife boot camp" in 1995, I have been eating and cooking my way through some of the world's most fascinating cuisines.

Second—and This Is Good News for You, I Think— I Don't Have a Fancy Kitchen

I don't have expensive knives or a collection of high-end doodads and thingamajoobers to make food defy gravity, take on peculiar shapes, or magically cook itself. The upshot of this is, *if I can make this exotic fare, so can you.* In fact, once you have mastered the gastronomical challenges of the world's craziest countries, you are, in effect, a culinary colonial master—or mistress, if you prefer. World domination can be achieved in your very own kitchen with some degree of dedication and the assistance of modern domestic technologies such as the food processor or, as previously mentioned, a daughter-in-law.

Third: There Can Be Dangers and Other Nuisances

Aside from the thousands of Indian women who die mysteriously in "kitchen fires," I nearly cut my finger off with an immersion blender working on the Iraq chapter. Be careful out there! "Don't drink and blend" would be my advice to you—and don't run with sharp objects, either. Also be careful throwing things into hot oil. Hell, be careful *making* oil hot—the stuff can catch on fire. Always use caution when handling anything over a flame or anything hot enough to cause you grief.

I've thrown in some ideas as to where you can find things if your small town in Iowa doesn't offer up a bevy of international markets, but since vendors change and so have scruples, I can't vouch for them. Thus, as always, use your smarts when shopping on the Internet. There are nasty predators out there just waiting for you and your credit card information.

The next thing you should know is that while I have been to many—maybe even most—of the countries in this book, I haven't been to all of them. If I get some things wrong, I hope you'll forgive me. I've asked friends and colleagues to read some of the chapters for errors and advice. Despite their best efforts, I still may have made egregious mistakes for which I am ultimately responsible and grumbling for your generous consideration. I've done my darndest to not be wrong, but I am but a mere simian with an opposable thumb. These recipes are a combination of my efforts to eat and cook and peruse cookbooks until I figure out how to make a particular dish for which I have developed a hankering or a fondness. It's been trial and error, and my friends, family, and spouse have been patient and tolerant guinea pigs in this adventure. I have also asked waiters and cooks for their secrets or to explain why my efforts fail, and I am grateful for their various pieces of advice, often whispered out of earshot of their managers.

Finally, I probably have a few opinions with which you won't agree. And, if you haven't guessed it, the tone of this volume is sardonic, satiric, grouchy, and hopefully humorous, with a heaping serving of hyperbole. My goal in writing this book is twofold: to get folks to think about the world from what is at first blush a safe vantage point—cuisine—and to make people think about food and its various levels of culinary and nonculinary import more than they did before.

PART 1

The Charter Members
of the Axis of Evil:
North Korea, Iran, and Iraq

THE CHARTER MEMBERS
OF THE AXIS OF EVIL

O n January 29, 2002, I was hanging out with my best friend, Michael, at a diner in Santa Monica. As we ate our pancakes and sausages, we watched The Shrub[4] deliver his State of the Union speech with the same fascination that one might watch sea monkeys. Much of the speech was laudable, albeit imbricated with gratuitous efforts to milk the heinous events of 9/11 for all they were worth to buttress his shaky presidency. As he wound his way through various platitudes, he mapped out a so-called national strategy for the post-9/11 United States. He declared:

> Our second goal is to prevent regimes that sponsor terror from threatening America or our friends and allies with weapons of mass destruction. Some of these regimes have been pretty quiet since September the 11th. But we know their true nature. North Korea is a regime arming with missiles and weapons of mass destruction, while starving its citizens.
>
> Iran aggressively pursues these weapons and exports terror, while an unelected few repress the Iranian people's hope for freedom.
>
> Iraq continues to flaunt its hostility toward America and to support terror. The Iraqi regime has plotted to develop anthrax, and nerve gas, and nuclear weapons for over a decade. This is a regime that has already used poison gas to murder thousands of its own citizens—leaving the bodies of mothers huddled over their dead children. This is a regime that agreed to international inspections—then kicked out the inspectors. This is a regime that has something to hide from the civilized world.
>
> States like these, and their terrorist allies, constitute an axis of evil, arming to threaten the peace of the world. By seeking weapons

of mass destruction, these regimes pose a grave and growing danger. They could provide these arms to terrorists, giving them the means to match their hatred. They could attack our allies or attempt to blackmail the United States. In any of these cases, the price of indifference would be catastrophic.[5]

In many ways, this was a declaration of war on countries that had absolutely *nothing* to do with 9/11. I felt ill: I knew my brothers would go to fight some war that would doubtless increase our national insecurity and squander the moral support the USA received in the wake of 9/11.

While I began joking about the cuisines of the Axis of Evil almost immediately and hosting what evolved into "AoE" dinner parties, everything was wrong with the speech. Iran was at the time actually helping the United States in Afghanistan, and the speech soured Tehran's appetite to engage constructively in that effort.

We now know that the "Axis of Evil" phrase was tossed into the speech by a Canadian White House speech writer with the same insouciance as one might toss a tomato into a salad. This exercise of informational improvisation and misjudgment revealed the writer's historical and geometrical ignorance. As Peter Galbraith has pointed out—and which any seventh-grade geometry student immediately understood—an axis is a straight line between two points. As such, the phrase, while captivating the American public and horrifying the world, simply made no sense, as North Korea, Iran, and Iraq could not possibly form such an axis. The historical analogy was also inept. The World War II "Axis" derived from the *alliance* between Germany and Italy, or the so-called Berlin-Rome Axis.[6] However, there is no—and was no—alliance among these three dubious regimes. Until the Bushies destroyed Iraq, Iran and Iraq were bitter foes, and North Korea had nothing to do with either.

A Cookbook Is Born!

By September 2002 both my brothers were called up involuntarily. As they were in the National Guard, this was unprecedented and rent the illusion that the Bush folks were pursuing diplomatic solutions in earnest. War was imminent, and many Americans had bought the canard that Saddam was behind 9/11. My brothers were among the first in and, thankfully, among the first out. It was during this, the worst year of my life, that the idea of this cookbook was born. I dedicate a plate of *fesanjan* to my brothers—something they may not welcome all that much, given their aversion to the stuff.

None of what follows in this gustatory castigation is intended to exculpate these dubious regimes. But what is clear is that the Iraq war has worsened the United States's strategic position vis-à-vis Iran and North Korea—both of whom were and are much more dangerous than Iraq was in 2003. The Iraq war gave Iran a strategic victory it did not earn, and it now runs the cards at the table in Iraq. While Iran benefited from the United States routing the Taliban and initially supported the United States, now Iran is, in some debatable measure, backing the Taliban in Afghanistan in effort to hurt the Americans in that theater too. In fact, Iran is in the enviable position of grabbing the United States by the crotch in both theaters simultaneously while doing whatever the hell it wants—because it can. Buoyed by its success in Iraq and in Afghanistan, and aided by Israeli incompetence, Iran snatched another victory in Lebanon in 2006 through its proxy, Hezbollah. With the United States bogged down in Iraq and unable to do a damned thing about it, both Iran and North Korea have engaged in a nuclear game of chicken, and the United States has had no option but to blink.

In the meantime, ladies and gentlemen, sharpen your knives and start your blenders!

Dossier of North Korean Perfidy

Korea, alas, had been an independent kingdom for much of its history until the Japanese occupied it in 1905 following the Russo-Japanese War. In 1910 Japan formally appropriated the entire Korean peninsula, during which time the Japanese did some vicious and inhumane things to the Koreans—a fact that persists as an irritant in Japan's relations with both Koreas. After World War II, when Japan was vanquished, Korea was split into two portions divided by the 38th parallel. The Koreans' aspiration to found an independent Korean state was scuttled by American meddling in the south and Soviet occupation of the north.

In November 1947 the United Nations General Assembly (UNGA) called for a general election under the auspices of the UN, but the pitiless Soviets flat out refused to let the UN in. So the UN drafted another resolution calling for elections in those areas that the UN could get into. In May 1948 Korea had its first elections in the area south of the 38th parallel, giving rise to the Republic of Korea, which was formally inaugurated later that year in August. A commie regime was decreed up in the north under the leadership of its founding Stalinist, "President Kim Il Song," who gave shape to the crazy country that befuddles and beguiles the world today.[7]

Despite the persistent and pervasive NoKo propaganda to the contrary, Kim Il Song was an "uneducated guerilla who transformed himself into a quasi-divine emperor known as the 'Great Leader.'"[8] Great Leader (or GL) molded North Korea into a Stalinist dictatorship and ran the place for fifty years. In 1950 he unsuccessfully prosecuted the Korean War to seize U.S.-sponsored southern Korea. By the time the war ended in 1953, more than a million were dead. The GL exercised absolute power over his tattered nation, and he ruthlessly murdered or incarcerated real and fabricated foes alike. He was an insatiable, egotistical nut job who erected tens of thousands of monuments to himself and plastered his photograph on every crevice of public space. He even had folks pin his portrait to their clothing—over their hearts, of course. Places that graced his bum, such as benches, were sealed in glass and rendered into odd relics to the strange man.[9]

North Korea officially refers to the GL as "Eternal President," as established in the preface of the North Korean constitution. (Yes, they do have one!) He died in 1994 and was succeeded by his short, stout, bouffant-sporting, platform-heel-donning son, Kim Jong Il, whom the GL dubbed "Dear Leader"—as distinguished from his "Great Leader" self. The father declared his son to be a "genius of 10,000 talents." Despite the obstacles to leadership that death poses, the GL's mummified corpse continues to reign as President for Eternity.[10]

The lore of Dear Leader's nascence is shrouded in absurdity. Officially, he is said to have been born in 1942 in a log cabin nestled idyllically on North Korea's sacred Mount Paekdu. A bright star and rainbow manifested in the sky, and a bird (reportedly a swallow) flew down from heaven to mark the birth of a "general who will rule the world." Of course, this romanticized tale is ridiculous. The short, stocky Elvis impersonator's parturition took place in an army camp in Siberia, where his screwy father had absconded with a ragtag group of commie guerilas to escape the Japanese—who, as noted, were not kind to Koreans.[11]

North Korea Today

Today, North Korea—aka the Democratic People's Republic of Korea (DPRK)—is a northeast Asian state of twenty-three million folks subjected to the maniacal rule of the Courvoisier-quaffing henchman in chief "President Kim Il Song." Under his leadership, this country is indeed a reckless menace that, unlike Iraq in 2002, keeps me awake at night. As President Bush's notorious Axis of Evil speech attests, North Korea was included in this geometrical and historical confabulation because it's "a regime arming with missiles and weapons of mass destruction, while starving its citizens." In fact, North Korea's dossier of perfidy is much more robust than Arbusto's missives suggest.

Indeed, the NoKos want to acquire—and in good measure have already acquired—nuclear weapons. The DPRK began dabbling in nuclear know-how in the 1960s when, in cahoots with the Soviet Union, it established a large-scale atomic energy research complex in Yongbyon some fifty-six miles north of Pyongyang. While it continued pursuing various aspects of nuclear technology throughout the 1970s, its weapons program began in the 1980s. U.S. intelligence officials first announced in 1985 that they had evidence that North Korea was building a secret nuclear reactor near Yongbyon. While North Korea acceded to the Nuclear Nonproliferation Treaty (NPT) in 1985, it refused to sign a safeguards agreement as required by its NPT commitment. Since then, it has been busy with various proliferant pursuits. While the NoKos have been very clear about their nuclear intentions, curiously no one seemed willing to believe they meant what they said. That may be because the North Korean government lies so much.[13]

But its actions have backed up its noxious rhetoric. In January 2003 it withdrew from the NPT without any real fallout. North Korea was the first—and thus far only—state to jettison the framework, and many worry that this consequence-free caper may set a precedent for other countries (read: Iran) to do the same. The brain-dead could be forgiven for not understanding that withdrawing from a treaty that commits a country to civilian nuclear technology *might* signal intent to acquire nuclear weapons. For those that did not pick up on that rather obvious clue, on October 3, 2006, the NoKo Foreign Ministry issued a "clarification statement" that averred Pyongyang's intention to test a nuclear device. Just as they said they would, on October 9 they indeed blew one up. It was not a terribly impressive blast—really more of a bout of nuclear flatulence—with an estimated yield of less than one kiloton. In case you don't know what that means (I didn't), that's about 3 to 4 percent of the explosive power of the American atomic bomb dropped on Nagasaki.[14]

While that may have been a wee nuclear squirt, the NoKos had been leading up to what nonproliferation devotees call "nuclear breakout" for years, as their withdrawal from the NPT in 2003 attests. In fact, the NoKos had been threatening to leave the NPT as early as *1993*. To placate and appease Pyongyang and temper its intemperate nuclear outburst, the United States and North Korea penned an "Agreed Framework" in October 1994. This framework rewarded the North Koreans handsomely for their contumely conduct and nuclear cupidity in that it recompensed them for doing that which they were *obliged* to do under the NPT. They magnanimously agreed to halt operation and construction of dubious nuclear reactors involved in their clandestine nuclear program. In exchange, they were to receive two "light-water" nuclear reactors that were not proliferation risks. Washington tossed in some

. . . And a Hare-Brained Scheme

An older East German chap, a Mr. Szmolinsky, breeds monster rabbits the size of BIG dogs (twenty-four pounds and up), each of which produces about fifteen pounds of delicious meat that can easily feed eight hungry folks—and probably many more protein-deprived North Koreans. Pyongyang solicited his services to set up a breeding facility for his beasts in North Korea, presumably hoping to feed its starving masses. Silly Mr. S dispatched twelve of his Monster Bunnies to North Korea, where he foolishly believed they were in a "petting zoo." Without a shred of irony, he was asked to come to North Korea on Easter to help them set up a farm to breed his leviathan leporids. When his trip was suddenly called off, Mr. S suspected foul play. He now believes that his rabbits were feasted upon by party officials. No more bunnies for Pyongyang![15]

fuel oil for the new facilities for good measure. An international consortium—the Korean Peninsula Energy Development Organization (KEDO)—was formed to implement this defeasance masquerading as a "diplomatic break-through," proroguing Pyongyang's eighteen-month-long temper tantrum.[16]

Keeping with North Korea's long-worn track record of improbity, in 2002 U.S. intelligence reported that the NoKos had been stealthily enriching uranium for weapons in violation of the much-lauded "Agreed Framework." The only thing that was surprising was that it was so surprising. In response, KEDO suspended the oil shipments. The NoKos retaliated by resuming their proliferation and kicking out the nuclear inspectors from the International Atomic Energy Agency (IAEA) on December 31, 2002. The next day it dumped the NPT.[17]

Not only were Pyongyang's nuclear intentions as obvious as a K Street hooker, so was the fact that North Korea was, sub rosa, in cahoots with Pakistan in its nuclear quest. U.S. intelligence types are pretty convinced by now that Pakistan was a key supplier of nuclear enrichment technology to Pyongyang, and speculation is rife that Islamabad pimped out its centrifuge enrichment technology to the North Koreans for help in advancing its medium-range missile, which can target cities nestled within India far from Pakistan's reach. Indeed, one of the missiles capable of striking deep within Ms. India is the Ghauri—a clone of the North Korean missile risibly named the "No Dong."

Timing is everything. In the 1980s, just as North Korea began exporting ballistic missile know-how, Pakistan figured out how to produce weapons-grade uranium at the "Khan Research Laboratory," run by Pakistan's infamous nuclear black marketer, A. Q. Khan. As one analyst with the U.S. Congressional Research Service notes, "By the time Pakistan probably needed to pay North Korea for its purchases of medium-range *No Dong* missiles in the mid-1990s . . . Pakistan's cash reserves were low. Pakistan could offer North Korea a route to nuclear weapons using HEU [highly enriched uranium] that could circumvent the plutonium-focused 1994 Agreed Framework and be difficult to detect."[18]

In fact, Islamabad and Pyongyang have been engaging in nuclear and missile foreplay for more than *thirty* years. Indeed, their (d)alliance was solidified during the Iran-Iraq war, during which both helped *Iran*. (Remember that during that time, Pakistan was purportedly a *U.S.* ally.) U.S. analysts believe that Pakistani ballistic missile engineers forged relationships with their NoKo counterparts during this period. Some analysts have suggested that the remarkable resemblance between Iran's Shahab missile and Pakistan's NoDong-cum-Ghauri is probative of developmental coordination between Iran, Pakistan, and North Korea that may have begun in 1993. From the mid to late 1990s, planes were spotted jetting back and forth between North Korea and Pakistan ferrying high-level officials, scientists, and missiles and their components. This cooperation may have gone both ways, with Pakistan helping their NoKo pals to develop solid fuel technology, which is needed for more stable missiles. Reportedly, both Iranians and Pakistanis were present when the Taepo Dong I did its test flight in 1998.[19]

To bastardize a famous aphorism of the notorious nuclear theoretician Herman Kahn, policy wonks seem incapable of thinking the unthinkable, or perhaps are just inclined to substitute wishful thinking for a meaningful policy approach to compel the NoKos to cease and desist their nuclear follies. As Jonathan Pollack has no doubt rightly noted, "there is virtually no possibility that North Korea will irrevocably yield the totality of these capabilities."[20] One such example of wishful thinking is the so-called Six Party Talks, which is composed of the United States, North Korea, China, South Korea, Japan, and Russia. Don't let the long list of actors deceive: It is primarily a U.S-NoKo show but the United States wants the others around to deny Pyongyang's longing for a tête-à-tête with Washington, which churlishly refuses to deal with North Korea because its knickers are still in a twist over the NoKos' breach of the 1994 agreement.[21]

In February 2007 the "Six Party" participants prematurely boasted a victory of sorts when six men clad in the obligatory dark suits happily shook hands and smiled following high-level wrangling in Beijing. *The Economist* gushed about this breakthrough after more than three years of "negotiations" and North Korean "bolshiness." Ostensibly, North Korea agreed to close its nuclear plants within sixty days in return for aid and other enticements. In some measure "this breakthrough" *could* pave the way for the return of nuclear watchdogs and *could* facilitate the "longer-term goals of dismantling the North's nuclear facilities, establishing normal relations between North Korea and America and securing a permanent peace on the Korean peninsula, where the war of 1950–1953 is not yet officially over."[22]

In fact, there were more than a few skeptics about the North Koreans' trustworthiness. Gary Samore (who has much experience negotiating with

Pyongyang over its nuclear deceit) published a memo from the chief NoKo negotiator at the Six Party Talks. Its author, Kim Gwe Gwan, writes to Dear Leader in hopes of securing his approval of the deal tabled in Beijing. The note is dated one day before the celebrated Beijing shindig.

Dear Leader:

Once again we are victorious. The ruthless Chinese thought they could stop us, but we tested right in their faces . . . The arrogant Americans thought they could take your money and squeeze us to abandon our nuclear deterrent. Instead, they are forced to give back some money and accept a freeze that keeps our vital nuclear assets untouched. The brazen Japanese thought they could hold a nuclear deal hostage to their missing people, but they ended up all by themselves. Thank goodness our generous but gullible Korean brothers keep sending cash and food no matter what we do.

The draft agreement . . . is a sweet deal. All we have to do is shut down and seal the Yongbyon facilities under IAEA supervision within 60 days. To make sure the IAEA doesn't try any of its old tricks to investigate our past activities, we have ensured that the agreement specifies that necessary motoring and verification measures must be "agreed between the IAEA and DPRK." As you know Dear Leader, shutting down the 5 MW reactor is no big loss. We already have enough plutonium for our national deterrent . . .

[And] this time, we have not specified how long the shutdown lasts . . . If the Americans do not accept our demands, such as completion of the light water reactor project, we can always threaten to turn the 5 MW reactor back on and reprocess the spent fuel unless we get another 50,000 tons of oil. The south will pay to keep the peace.

However, if the Americans offer us enough compensation, we could decide to "disable" the 5 MW reactor, depending on what "disable" means. "disable" is a much better word for us then "dismantlement," which we had to accept in the 1994 agreement. We will work with chief engineer Li to design disablement measures that could be reversed in a pinch . . .

In conclusion, Dear Leader, I respectfully request that you approve the draft agreement. We give up very little and leave all our options open. If the Americans misbehave again, we can restart the nuclear program and even test again. Maybe our scientists will get it right the next time. If the payoff is generous enough, we can decide to disable the 5 MW reactor and declare our enrichment shopping list. Or, we can just stall for two years and wait for the next U.S. President. In any event, we have drawn the venom from the Bush Administration. They are too weak and distracted to hurt us. In the meantime, we can look forward to the six Party Ministerial meeting in Beijing and meeting secretary Rice.

Break out the snake liquor![23] [Emphasis added to illuminate the odd Korean beverage comprised of an actual snake pickled in booze.]

Additional sardonic commentary by this author is obviated by that missive. In the intervening months since February 2007, North Korea had (surprise) reneged on its promises to shut down the reactor by April 14 and to let IAEA inspectors back in. By September 2007 the Koreans had again promised to do the right thing in exchange for more goodies. However, we would be wise to note the words of Jonathan Pollack, who has presciently argued, "It would not be prudent . . . to anticipate an early end to Pyongyang's program or to the dangers this program poses both for security in East Asia and for the future viability of the nonproliferation regime."[24]

Regrettably, North Korea is a grotesque human rights trampler as well. In November 2005 the UNGA adopted a resolution expressing its grave concerns about the "systematic, widespread and grave violations of human rights" in North Korea. This came in the wake of numerous resolutions by the UN Commission on Human Rights. Since no one takes UNGA resolutions very seriously—and North Korea is no exception—it continues to deny its citizens standard-issue rights such as "freedom of information, association, movement, and religion, nor organized political opposition, labor activism, or independent civil society. Arbitrary arrests, torture, lack of due process and fair trials, and executions remain of grave concern. Collective punishment of entire families for 'political crimes' remains the norm."[25] It's difficult to get visibility on these issues because Pyongyang doesn't let international human rights organizations in to see what's going on.

And if that's not enough, North Korea has even engaged in terrorism. In 1983 it tried to assassinate the president of South Korea, Chun Doo Hwan, when he traveled to Rangoon, Burma, for a state visit. The president was supposed to attend the opening ceremony held at the Martyr's Mausoleum at the National Cemetery, and narrowly escaped the assassination attempt because he arrived late. When the talented South Korean ambassador showed up before the president, the North Korean army major Zin Mo thought he was the president and detonated the bombs planted by two NoKo army captains two days before. The powerful blast killed four members of the South Korean cabinet, two senior presidential advisors, and the ambassador. Notably, at that time Kim Jong Il was in charge of clandestine foreign operations. The DPRK had previously tried to whack the South Korean president while he was on another state visit in Gabon.[26]

The DPRK is also responsible for the bombing of Korean Air Flight 858 on November 29, 1987, which killed all 115 on board. In 1988 the United States designated North Korea as a state that sponsors terrorism; however, the U.S. Department of State acknowledges that the DPRK is not known to have sponsored subsequent acts of terrorism. North Korea continues to howl, whine, and beg Washington to take it off that ignominious list. Thus far, Washington has resisted its pleas.[27]

The DPRK also squanders tons of cash to maintain Dear Leader's absurdly lavish lifestyle and to permit him to ply his minions with luxury goods and fete friends and foes alike with preposterously over-the-top soirees while defying the international community on its nuclear program and funneling resources into an enormous military. In the meantime, the average Korean starves.[28] In fact, in the 1990s rural North Koreans were left to subsist on bark and grass. Pyongyang's persistent and perilous pursuit of its portfolio of perfidious policies has further imperiled the food security of the vulnerable segments of its population. Demonstrative of its callousness toward its masses, North Korea banned individuals from buying or selling grains at farmers' mar-

Dear Leader, "The Artiste" and Connoisseur

DPRK lore contends that when Dear Leader was at (predictably) Kim Il Sung University, he penned over 1,500 books. That's about a book a day for those who care to do the math. He also created a racy, private dance troupe to gyrate about to the discomfort of party types who have to watch the show in disgust. In addition, he claims to have written and directed several films, although that is likely a load of nonsense. Nonetheless, Kim Jong Il has amassed more than 10,000 videos and boasted to a U.S. diplomat that he owns every Oscar-winning flick.[29]

kets and announced that it would revive the odious Public Distribution System. Under this draconian program, the state has the sole right to distribute grain. When the government used this system in the 1990s, between one and two million people died of starvation and many more millions endured severe malnutrition.[30]

Shortages All Around

In 2006 North Korea was wracked by floods that worsened its chronic food shortages. According to the World Food Programme, NoKo is short some 800,000 tons of food. These shortfalls are being felt by North Korea's most vulnerable—the old and infirm, children, and pregnant and nursing women. As one may guess, Pyongyang has an unsavory track record of feeding its elite first, which include military brass, intelligence operatives, police, and other law-enforcement goons. The table scraps—often less than the minimum amount of calories needed for sustenance—is doled out to the general population. Further adding to these food woes, South Korea—which is the largest food donor of recent years—suspended its food aid to protest North Korea's afore noted nuclear test.[31]

Tens of thousands—if not more—North Koreans have fled the country to escape pervasive hunger and political repression. Many are thought to be hiding in China, South Korea, Japan, Europe, the United States, and anywhere else they can flee to and avoid repatriation. Leaving the North Korean nuthouse without permission is an act of treason, so if the poor folks are so ill-fated as to be repatriated, harsh punishments and even executions await them. Not surprisingly, the Chicoms are the enemy of freedom, relentlessly hunting down NoKo fugitives who left the "worker's paradise."

But the Chicoms's cruelty does not end with hunting down escaped North Koreans. Indeed, the Chinese even harass aid workers trying to help the poor sons of bitches. To avoid China, a small number of North Koreans are bold enough to plot their escape by taking long and arduous journeys to Cambodia, Laos, Mongolia, Thailand, and Vietnam, all in an effort to reach the prized destination of South Korea. Hundreds are detained in these various transit countries.[32]

Another odd crime that North Korea has perfected is abduction. Kim Jong Il has become quite notorious for absconding with perfectly innocent folks to whom he has taken a shining. Fancying himself a cinemaphile and director, Kim looked high and low for a North Korean director to fulfill his cinematographic dream of a socialist *Godzilla* flick. Having conceded the failure of these efforts, he did the next best thing: In 1978 he kidnapped the Orson Welles of South Korea, Shin Sang-ok, and his hottie actress wife, Choi Eun-hee. The spouses were held for five years without knowledge of each other's whereabouts.[33]

In 1983 Kim held one of his notorious banquets in which the two were reunited and even begged for their forgiveness. In the end, Shin became the propagandist of the regime and Choi became the star. They "agreed" to this arrangement, and Kim settled them in a lovely luxurious home and gifted them his and hers Mercedes. A year later, while in Europe, the couple ditched their guards in Vienna and escaped to the U.S. Embassy. After laying low in a CIA safe house for two years, they penned a book about their tenure in NoKo under the thumb of the world's strangest and most dangerous dictator.[34]

While this is one of the more famous abductions, the South Korea–based Korea Institute for National Unification claims that some 3,800 South Koreans were whisked away to North Korea between 1953 and 1995, several hundred of whom remain in detention. Many of these unfortunates were used in (no doubt unconvincing) propaganda broadcasts to the south, while others have been used to train NoKo spooks, which is a very unsettling thought. The

Booze, Boobs, Bling, and Bobbles

Kim Jong II is reputed to drink the blood of virgins to stay young, throw drunken orgies, and import sultry Scandinavian hotties to sate his lusts. When he was a young letch, he created "pleasure teams" to "service" him and his dad. He enjoys throwing lavish parties festooned with women in his seven-story pleasure palace. Dear Leader also imbibes Hennessy VOP (over $630 a pop) in such quantities that in 1994 the company declared him the world's biggest buyer of the brew two years in a row. He famously owns numerous S-class Mercedes (around $100,000 each) and imports French china, Swiss watches, and European food delicacies (and chefs and fancy Italian pizza kitchens), as well as sporting goods and mink coats. In fact, at the height of the famine, the DPRK imported some $24 million worth of this fancy crap. Between 2000 and 2004, the Germans claim that the NoKos bought $12 million in luxury goods from Germany alone.[35] All this while his people forage in public parks for bark.

NoKos remain recalcitrant and unmoved by the repeated requests of the South Korean government and families alike to confirm the detainees' existence, let them go, or, in the event of death, repatriate their remains. They even seized a dozen or so Japanese to teach the NoKos the Japanese language. Indeed, the North Korean officials have hearts of coprolite.

Given all this nuclear-backed perfidy, it is empirically verifiable (read: friggin' obvious) that of the three charter members of the Axis of Evil, North Korea is clearly the most pressing menace to regional and global security. Iran, as argued elsewhere in this grouchy volume, runs a close second. Yet the Bushies decided to invade Iraq, which was hardly a menace by 2002 when the White House began quivering its saber. Maybe that's because of the three countries in the Axis of Evil, Iraq was the one that *didn't* have nuclear weapons. I don't think one has to be a Kojak to figure this out—but I would like a lollipop if you have one to spare.

Let Them Eat Bark (Donated by China and South Korea)

In the late 1990s, between one and two million North Koreans starved to death while Dear Leader, Kim Jong Il, dispatched his personal chef, Kenji Fujimoto, all the way to Copenhagen to pick up some bacon and to Paris for the finest wines and cognacs. (Dear Leader also likes more pedestrian brews like Johnnie Walker scotch and Hennessy XO cognac.) Fujimoto frequently jet-setted across the globe to keep his boss properly feted and feasted. He'd schlep melons from China and caviar from Iran and Uzbekistan, and, of course, he sojourned to Japan's Tsukji fish market to purloin the world's finest sushi-quality fish. Before absconding from Pyongyang, Fujimoto fed the gourmand beast for more than a decade. In his "cook-and-tell" memoir, he "spills the beans" on his freakish taskmasker. In one telling tale, Fujimoto described Kim as an ultimate gastronome, a sushi chef's dream client: "He particularly enjoyed sashimi so fresh that he could start eating the fish as its mouth is still gasping and the tail is still thrashing . . . I sliced the fish so as not to puncture any of its vital organs, so of course it was still moving. Kim Jong Il was delighted. He would eat it with gusto."[36]

In another bestial display of disregard for his starving subjects in the famine of the 1990s, the dumpy despot ensured that his wasteful waistline would not dwindle. In 1999 his agents "recruited" two Italian chefs and consigned them to Pyongyang and later to an unnamed seaside location where they established a sophisticated pizza kitchen. One of the Italians, Ermanno Furlanis, wrote his own cook-and-tell exposition titled *I Made Pizza for Kim Jong Il*.[37] Once ensconced, he and the other chef were tasked with teaching three of Dear Leader's cooks—all of whom were in the army—the delicate art of pizza making. After being ordered to whip up a pizza, Furlanis began carrying out his preparations under the watchful eyes of his pupils, who noted in great detail the proceedings. One of them even asked him to provide the exact number of olives used and distance between them. Furlanis witnessed the comings and goings of couriers bearing decadent French delicacies. When Furlanis, being an Italian, objected to these Francophile offerings, he was soon placated with the arrival of a shipment of Barolo [a dark, dry red wine from the Piedmont region of Italy].[38]

While Kim Jong Il feasted on freaky delicacies of still-quivering fish and obscenely high-end Italian and French specialties, his masses would starve if the international community didn't feed them. His response to the famine was outright insouciance, although he executed his agriculture secretary to show he cared. Curiously, while Dear Leader never promised to feed his people, he *did* promise to feed to his million-man army—and that is what he did. He justified this by the chimera of a U.S. invasion: "If the U.S. imperialists know that we do not have rice for the military . . . then they would immediately invade us."[39]

In my rare occasions to dine upon North Korean food (i.e., a NoKo restaurant in Beijing and restaurants elsewhere that folks unreliably whisper to be North Korean), I could not detect any significant difference from South Korean food. Experts on the Koreas that I have quizzed have told me that the main difference is that in North Korea people are starving and rely upon the Chinese, South Koreans, and others for basic sustenance, but if they had food to cook, their preparations are very reminiscent of SoKo victuals. Others claimed that as you go north, the food becomes less spicy. A typical Korean meal involves several side dishes (*mit banchan*), loads of rice (*bap*), and the main dishes. Koreans are not big dessert eaters. After eating, they typically drink tea with whatever fresh fruit is around. (Don't worry: I've found a dessert for you.) Koreans don't typically serve beverages with meals either. They instead make sure that everyone has a bowl of soup or watery kimchi, but we will deviate from authenticity here too.

The Plan of Attack

As with all of this book's dinner parties, this one assumes a crowd of eight voracious diners. Adjust accordingly. We are going to serve four side dishes, two of which should be prepared in advance of the party (not the cucumber dish—it doesn't last long in the fridge). We are also going to make two barbecue entrees, which should be marinated at least one full day in advance of the soiree, in addition to a noodle dish that needs to be served immediately, although all of the chopping can be done in advance. We will serve a poached pear for dessert, and throughout our meal we will have barley tea (*bori cha*) or if you prefer, ice water infused with the barley tea. There is also a variety of booze options, including *soju* (sweet potato liquor), fruit liqueurs, and beers.

Side dishes

- *Baech'u Kimchi.* (pickled Nappa cabbage). Store bought.
- *Mu Saengch'ae* (pickled radish)
- *Oi Namul Muchim* (spicy cucumber)
- *Sang Meenari Muchim* (seasoned watercress)

Main course

- *Bulkogee* (fire beef)
- *Dwaeji Bulkogee* (spicy pork)
- *Jap Chai* (sweet potato noodles with beef and vegetables)
- Medium-grain white rice in ample quantities

Dessert

- *Paesuk* (pears poached in rice wine)

Beverages

- Korean sweet potato liquor (*soju*). If you can't find this, the Japanese rice wine, sake, will suffice as an acceptable substitute.
- Koreans love beer (*mek-chu*). Since you are not likely to get a real North Korean beer and since the Chinese and Japanese bail the Koreans out of starvation, you could just as easily go with the Chinese Tsingtao or the Japanese Kirin or Sapporo.

- There are a number of fruit liqueurs available at Korean markets that are quite delicious, including one made of blackberries and strawberries. You'll have to ask your nearby Korean grocer. Mine pointed me in the direction of a lovely fruity number that is "lady oriented." He encouraged me to stick to the *soju* for my manly diners.
- *Bori cha* (barley tea). Your guests can drink this beverage hot or refreshingly cold. Many Korean restaurants serve cold water flavored with barley tea using a ration of two parts water and one part tea.

PREPARATION

SIDE DISHES

Baech'u Kimchi *(Pickled Nappa Cabbage)*

Buy this from your Asian supermarket. To serve, put in small bowls and garnish with roasted sesame seeds.

Mu Saengch'ae *(Pickled Radish)*

Use Korean, Japanese (daikon), or Chinese radishes, which are widely available in many supermarkets catering to Asians. Do not use the ubiquitous red radish! Korean radishes are torpedo-like in shape and are white on the bottom and green on the top. Daikon radishes are white and slender, and Chinese radishes are white and fat. *Mu saengch'ae* itself can also be purchased in many Asian supermarkets.

Ingredients

1 tablespoon red chili powder (If you don't want this to be as spicy as is traditional, you can drop this down to 1 teaspoon.)

1 tablespoon soy sauce

3 tablespoons rice vinegar

1 tablespoon rice wine

1 tablespoon sugar

2 cloves garlic, finely chopped or crushed

1 tablespoon finely chopped ginger

2½ tablespoons sesame oil

1 tablespoon sea salt

⅛ teaspoon freshly ground black pepper

1 pound Korean, daikon, or Chinese radish cut into thin strips

For garnish:

1 teaspoon red pepper flakes (more if desired)

1 tablespoon roasted sesame seeds

Let's get cooking

1. Mix all the ingredients except the radish and garnish in a large bowl. Whisk well to incorporate.
2. Toss in radish pieces and mix well to thoroughly coat.
3. Refrigerate for several hours before serving. (It is best to let this marinate overnight.) Put portions in several small bowls and garnish with red pepper flakes and sesame seeds before serving. This stores well in the fridge for several days.

Oi Namul Muchim *(Spicy Cucumber)*

Ingredients

1 pound seedless cucumbers (You can use the long and thin "English cucumber," which is grown in a greenhouse and shrink-wrapped. It is also known as European seedless, hothouse, and greenhouse cucumber. You can also use seedless Kirby cucumbers.)

2 teaspoons sea salt

1 scallion, thinly sliced (white and pale parts only)

½ teaspoon red pepper flakes (more if desired)

1 tablespoon rice vinegar

1 teaspoon rice wine

1 teaspoon sugar

1 clove garlic, crushed

2 teaspoons sesame oil

For garnish:

1 teaspoon red pepper flakes (more if desired)

1 tablespoon roasted sesame seeds

Let's get cooking

1. Trim the ends from the cucumbers. (If you want, with a lemon zester, remove a few strips of skin down their lengths to make a design.) Slice the cucumbers into near paper-thin slices. Place them in a bowl, sprinkle with sea salt, and let them sit for 20 minutes to draw the water out. Turn onto paper towels and blot dry, or put them in a salad spinner to spin out the water.
2. In a large bowl, whisk together all the ingredients except the garnish and the cucumber.
3. Toss the cucumber into the dressing and refrigerate for several hours before serving. Serve either cold or at room temperature in small bowls, garnished with red pepper flakes and sesame seeds.

Sang Meenari Muchim *(Seasoned Watercress)*

Ingredients

2 bunches watercress

1 tablespoon sesame oil

2 cloves garlic, minced

1½ tablespoons cider vinegar

3 tablespoons soy sauce

2 scallions, finely chopped (Chop off the roots and the dry green tops. You can use the rest of the bulb and the green part of the stem.)

1 teaspoon sea salt

For garnish:

1 teaspoon red pepper flakes (more if desired)

1 tablespoon roasted sesame seeds

Let's get cooking

1. Wash the watercress and cut the main stem and other stems that connect the sprigs. If the sprigs are small enough, leave intact. If not, cut in half. If you don't do this, it will be difficult to eat later.
2. Blanch the watercress in boiling water (about 1 minute). Quickly remove and rinse with very cold water to stop the cooking process.
3. In a small skillet, heat the oil and fry the garlic. Remove from heat.
4. Toss the watercress with the garlic and oil, vinegar, soy sauce, chopped scallion, and sea salt. Serve at room temperature in small bowls, garnished with red pepper flakes and sesame seeds. (If you make this in advance, store in the refrigerator and garnish immediately before serving.)

MAIN COURSE

Bulkogee *(Fire Beef)*

Bulkogee, despite its translated name, is not spicy. It's a sweet and richly flavored dish that draws from soy sauce, garlic, honey, and pear. It is typically served in leaves of romaine lettuce with spiced scallions. The recipe calls for ⅛-inch slices of beef. I don't know about you, but *I* can't slice beef this thin. I go to a Korean grocer that sells *bulkogee* cuts, but you can also use the "fajita" cuts found in many markets, although it is thicker than is preferable. You could also ask your butcher, if you're lucky enough to have one. Finally, if you absolutely can't get it this thin, you will lose points for style but it will still taste good, although the thinner the beef, the better the marinade soaks in. Venison is a delicious substitute for beef, if you are looking for new recipes for all that deer you get next season.

Ingredients

1 Asian pear, grated, with the peel but not the core (If you can't find an Asian pear, any ripe pear will do. A Bartlett is a good substitute.)
⅓ cup soy sauce
⅓ cup honey
⅓ cup rice wine
4 cloves garlic, pressed

3 scallions, finely sliced (You can use most of the scallion, except for the
   nasty roots and scraggly, dry green ends.)
2 tablespoons sesame oil
¼ teaspoon freshly ground black pepper
⅛ teaspoon sea salt
2 pounds thinly sliced beef (try sirloin), preferably ⅛ inch thick

For garnish:
Sesame seeds
Scallions, halved lengthwise and cut in 2-inch pieces
Clean leaves of romaine lettuce

Let's get cooking

1. In a large ziplock bag or plastic bowl, whisk together the grated pear and
   all of the seasoning ingredients. (Pick a bag or bowl that is big enough to
   comfortably accommodate the meat.)
2. Add the meat and toss to thoroughly coat with the marinade. Let the meat
   marinate in the fridge preferably overnight, but at least 4 hours. Agitate
   periodically to ensure that all the meat gets coated.
3. Grill the marinated beef under the broiler. This will cook quickly—maybe 3
   minutes on each side or sooner, depending on how thinly you sliced the
   meat. (You can also cook with a countertop or stove-top grill.)
4. Garnish with sesame seeds and scallions. Serve with steamed rice (see
   below) *or* wrapped in lettuce leaves.

Dwaeji Bulkogee *(Spicy Pork)*

As in the recipe above, the meat should be cut in ⅛-inch slices. Do your best.
(Again, I get mine from the Korean grocer.) You can try slicing a pork loin
roast while it's still semifrozen. This helps to get thinner slices, but the pork
may "break." That's okay. Folks eat this dish in small pieces.

Ingredients
2 tablespoons rice wine
2 tablespoons honey
1 medium yellow onion, finely diced
4 cloves garlic, pressed

3 scallions, finely sliced (Trim the roots and the top, dry portion of the green stem. You can use the rest of the scallion.)

1 tablespoon red chili powder

1-inch piece of ginger, peeled and finely diced

1 red bell pepper, finely diced

2 tablespoons sesame oil

4 tablespoons soy sauce

½ teaspoon sea salt

½ teaspoon ground *white* pepper (If you don't have it, just use black pepper.)

2 pounds thinly sliced pork loin, preferably ⅛ inch thick

For garnish:
Red pepper flakes

Let's get cooking

1. Whisk all of the seasoning ingredients together in a large ziplock bag or plastic bowl. (Pick a bag or bowl that is big enough to comfortably accommodate the pork.)
2. Add the pork and toss thoroughly to cover with the marinade. Let the meat marinate in the fridge preferably overnight, but at least 4 hours. Agitate periodically to ensure that all the meat gets coated.
3. Grill under the broiler, or on a countertop or stove-top grill. This will cook quickly—maybe 3 minutes on each side or sooner, depending on how thinly you sliced the meat.
4. Garnish with red pepper flakes and serve with steamed rice.

Jap Chai *(Sweet Potato Noodles with Beef and Vegetables)*

This will take about an hour to make.

Ingredients

4 cups water

4 tablespoons sesame oil

1 large yellow onion, coarsely chopped

½ pound thinly sliced beef, sliced for stir-fry into 4-inch strips (You could also use chicken, or even pork.)

1 carrot, julienned into 3-inch strips

¼ pound cabbage (any kind), coarsely chopped

6–8 scallions, with roots and dry portion of the green tops removed, chopped into 3-inch pieces

1 small green bell pepper, thinly sliced

1 small red bell pepper, thinly sliced

6 ounces Korean vermicelli noodles (Use the noodles that are made from sweet potatoes!)

¼ cup dried Korean tree fungus (aka *pyogo,* or "tree ears") soaked in warm water for about 30 minutes, drained, rinsed, and thinly sliced (You could substitute the more common shiitake mushroom.)

2 tablespoons soy sauce

Sea salt, if needed. (It's best to add the salt at the end as soy sauces vary in salt content.)

For garnish:
Plain 2-egg omelet cut into 3-inch slices (Whisk the 2 eggs and fry in a small skillet until cooked through, let cool, then slice.)

Let's get cooking

1. Bring the water to a boil. Add 1 tablespoon of the sesame oil to the water to help ensure that the noodles do not clump together.

2. While the water comes to a boil, heat the remaining oil in a large wok or frying pan. Fry the chopped onion for about 2 minutes, then add the meat and fry for another minute. Add the carrot, cabbage, scallions, and green and red bell peppers and continue frying until all are tender.

3. While the mixture continues to fry, add the vermicelli to the boiling water and cook for 3 minutes—no longer. Drain, rinse with cold water to stop the cooking process, and set aside. If you have timed this right, the meat/veggie mixture should finish just as your noodles finish.

4. Add the noodles to the meat/vegetable mixture, along with the tree fungus and soy sauce, and toss thoroughly. Taste and add salt if needed before garnishing and serving.

5. Garnish with the egg omelet slices and serve immediately.

Plain White Rice

Koreans tend to use medium-grain rice that is somewhat sticky. A very popular brand is actually a Japanese one, Nishiki, distributed by JFC International. You could also use the Thai jasmine rice if you want. I usually make this in a rice cooker. If you don't have a rice cooker, the standard stove-top recipe follows. (You can also use the instructions on your rice package!)

Ingredients
4 cups Japanese (preferred) or Thai (jasmine) rice
4 cups water if using a rice cooker, *or* 5½ cups water if using stove-top method
1 teaspoon sea salt

Let's get cooking
1. Look over the rice for things that don't belong (rocks, for example). Rinse the rice with cold water ONCE to remove much of the starch but not all. (Japanese rice should be sticky.) Drain the water.
2. If using a rice cooker, place the rice, water, and salt in the cooker and turn it on. The rice cooker will automatically shut off when done. Don't open the lid during cooking, and let it sit unopened for at least 5 minutes after it shuts off. (Use caution when removing the lid.)

If using the stove-top method, in a heavy-bottomed pot, bring the rice, water, and salt to a boil. Cover, reduce the heat, and simmer until the rice is finished and the water is absorbed. (This should take about 20 minutes.) Make sure the heat is low or you will scorch the rice. Try not to open the cover while cooking. Holes usually appear on the surface of the rice when it's done, so a glass lid makes this visual observation a lot easier! If you don't have one, you obviously need to remove the lid and take a look after 18 minutes or so have elapsed. Pull the rice off the stove when done, and let it sit covered until ready to serve.

DESSERT

★★★★★★★★★★★★★★★★★★★★★★★

Paesuk (Pears Poached in Rice Wine)

Ingredients
6 cups water
5 ounces fresh ginger, peeled and sliced into thin rounds
4 approximately 3-inch-long cinnamon sticks
4 tablespoons black peppercorns
1 cup light brown sugar or demerara sugar (I prefer the latter.)
2 cups rice wine
4 large firm Asian pears (or Bartlett pears)

For garnish:
2 tablespoons pine nuts, toasted until golden brown in a dry skillet
Mint sprigs

Let's get cooking
1. In a large nonreactive pot, add the water, ginger, cinnamon sticks, and peppercorns and bring to a boil. Reduce the heat and simmer for 15 minutes, skimming off any foam that forms on the surface.
2. Add the sugar and simmer for another 5 minutes.
3. Add the rice wine and simmer for another 5 minutes.
4. Strain the mixture to remove the solids, reserving the fluid.
5. Peel and core the pears and slice into 4 wedges. To prevent browning, work quickly and do not do this in advance! Place the pears in the same pot you cooked the spiced liquid in.
6. Pour the reserved spiced liquid over the pears and return to a medium-high heat to bring the mixture to a boil. Reduce the heat and simmer until the pears have softened. Depending on the variety of the pear, this may take 10–15 minutes. (They should be soft but firm when you insert a toothpick into them. They should not be limp and soggy.)
7. Remove the pears with a slotted spoon and set aside to cool.
8. Continue heating the spiced liquid (which is now looking more like a syrup) until it reduces by about a third of its volume.

Arrange the pears in individual serving dishes and pour some of the reduced syrup over them. You can serve them immediately or chilled. (I prefer the latter because I can make them in advance.) Garnish with toasted pine nuts and mint sprigs right before serving.

BEVERAGE

★★ ★★★★★★★★★★★ ★★★★★

Bori Cha *(Barley Tea)*

This unsweetened tea can be served hot, or you can ice it for a refreshing beverage. Some Korean restaurants serve water that is infused with this tea. All of these options are delicious—just pick whichever you prefer.

Ingredients
3 tablespoons barley (This can be found in many grocery stores with an ample health food or bulk section.)
8 cups water

Let's get cooking
1. Toast the barley in a dry skillet over medium heat for about 10 minutes. Agitate frequently to ensure that the barley does not burn. The grains are done when they turn a dark, toasty brown. (If you shop in Asian markets, you can buy toasted barley, in which case you can skip this step. When I can't find toasted barley, I toast large quantities and store it in a screw-top jar.)
2. Bring the water to a boil. Add the toasted grains and simmer on a low boil for 20 minutes or so. This is ample time to extract the toasted, woody flavor of the barley.

3. Strain the barley water into a teapot, removing the barley seeds.

Dossier of Iranian Perfidy

Iran is one of the charter members of the Axis of Evil, along with Iraq and North Korea. It is, irksomely, a country of both regional and international strategic significance—a point which Iranian leaders like to make repeatedly long after folks have stopped listening, much less caring. Unfortunately, Iran chooses to exercise its influence mostly by being a regional pain in the neck. Its population is estimated to be nearly seventy million, and it sits astride the intersection of Central, Southwest, and South Asia as well as the Persian Gulf, giving it large swathe for rabble-rousing and troublemaking.

In addition to these geographical and human resources, Iran is endowed with the world's second-largest gas reserve (after Russia) and the second-largest reserve of oil (right behind Saudi Arabia).[40] Iran has benefited from high oil prices spawned by the U.S. occupation of Iraq, which has given it further latitude in pursuing evermore obnoxious foreign policies while dictating increasingly oppressive policies at home—particularly with the election of hard-line president Mahmoud Ahmadinejad in 2005.[41] And Flynt Leverett has aptly noted, "Iran has used its strategic energies and resources in ways that have worked against American interests in a number of fronts."[42]

Some folks have uncharitably noted the similarities between the Iranian and American presidents: George Bush and Mahmoud Ahmadinejad both resemble Curious George, both are prone to absurd verbal outrages and preposterous claims, and both like warmongering. One big difference between the bellicose leaders is that the Iranian president actually fought when his country was at war, during which time he allegedly did some very nasty things,[43] whereas the American president dodged his military service but chose to do nasty things anyway (e.g., invading and occupying Iraq for no defensible reason, poorly planning for the occupation, and needlessly pursuing policies that put American armed forces personnel in harm's way without advancing U.S. national security).

While many countries have their episodic grouses with Iran, Tehran and Washington have remained locked in a state of persistent animosity since the Iranian revolution of 1979, the subsequent seizure of the U.S. Embassy in Tehran, and the resulting 444-day-long hostage crisis. In January 1979 Ayatollah Ruhollah Khomeini tossed out the "Shah of Iran," who was in his own right an insalubrious and repressive monarch with a fabricated royal lineage who basked in the patronage—and cash—of Uncle Sam, which considered the Shah to be an important "client."

On a Power Trip

Once in power, Khomeini, riding the waves of his Islamic revolution and a massive groundswell of popular support, did a number of unsavory things at home and abroad. His popular base began to erode when Iranians realized just what he had in store for his swooning, loyal masses. For many Iranians, the revolution was one enormous and deeply unpleasant "bait and switch." Women in particular were screwed when the ubiquitous black *hejab,* which they once donned voluntarily to support Khomeini's nationalist movement, became the oppressive writ of law with correspondingly indefatigable vice and virtue police beating and arresting women for errant locks inadequately beshrouded. Having rendered Iran into a repressive Shi'a Islamic revolutionary state and having stamped out vestiges of freedom and bare elbows in the name of Iranian nationalism, Khomeini sought to export Iran's revolution to its wary neighbors, who were nonplussed by the prospects of this plan.[44]

Khomeini, the epitome of mad mullahs, notoriously meddled in Iraq's domestic affairs and appealed to Iraq's majority Shi'a population to replace the corrupt, secular regime of Saddam with one that resembled the new Ayatollahstan of Iran. These entreaties did not go over well with Saddam, who had a penchant for torturing and killing key Shi'a leaders, often in imaginatively grisly ways. It didn't take long for Iran and Iraq to lock horns in a war of civilizations, literally. In September 1980 Iraq brazenly initiated the bloody and pointless eight-year Iran-Iraq war by seizing a chunk of desirable, oil-laden Iranian territory along the Iraqi border. Khomeini did not flinch. He saw this territorial affront as an opportunity to both defend and galvanize the newly whelped Iranian Islamic Republic and to propagate the revolution among Iraq's own downtrodden—but numerically superior—Shi'a. From Saddam's Shi'a-loathing optic, he depicted his struggle in religio-historical terms by using the moniker "Saddam's Qadısıya"—referring to the seventh-century battle wherein Arabs conquered the Persians and Islamized Iraq.[45]

In 1982, when the Iranians seemed set to win what had seemed for so long to be a pointless and sanguinary stalemate, the Americans at last stepped in. Washington saw an opportunity to both punish the Iranians for their multiplying misdeeds and wean the Iraqis off of the Soviets. When the Iraqis began using mustard gas and other chemical weapons against the Iranians—and later against Iraq's own Kurds—Washington's silence was deafening. Worse yet, Peter Galbraith claims that in 1983 the Reagan administration *ordered* the CIA to share battlefield intelligence with the Iraqis that permitted them to target Iranian troops with chemical weapons! Iran was pretty vexed that no one seemed to care that they were getting gassed, but they had themselves to blame: Their reckless and fanatical policies generated few condolences within the international community. Iraq's Kurds generated only marginally more sympathy but no interventions to prevent their genocide.[46]

The reason for U.S. apathy toward—and even *abetment* of—Iraq's gruesomely criminal activities was the belief among crazed and delusional administration strategists that the United States could replace its lost relationship with Iran's decadent Shah with Iraq's famed nutter Saddam Hussein. One could forgive grouchy cynics for pointing out the obvious: Both George Bushes opined lyrically about the savage Saddam who "gassed his own people" as they ginned up support for their respective wars. Yet, the United States did not seem terribly concerned about this at the time of the actual gassing, when additional gassing could perhaps have been prevented. On the contrary. Galbraith recounts how Reagan's special envoy to woo Saddam, the famed Iraq War II proponent and planner Don Rumsfeld, never complained about the issue when he met with Saddam in 1983. It is also worth noting that at the United Nations Human Rights Commission, the Reagan administration actually *opposed* a resolution condemning Saddam's employment of chemical weapons![47] Iran is therefore not wholly off its rocker when it whines in various fora that the United States is hypocritical and even selective in its demonstration of moral outrage.

Discontent with wrecking just *one* country, throughout the 1980s Khomeini's mullahcratic regime launched a sectarian war in Pakistan by arming elements within that country's beleaguered Shi'a population. Pakistan's Shi'a were struggling to throw off the yoke of the military dictator Zia ul-Haq, who sought to impose Sunni Islam across Pakistan and who occasionally "permitted" anti-Shi'a pogroms whenever he thought the Shi'a were getting too uppity. While Iran was busy backing Shi'a militias, Zia threw the weight of the state behind various vicious Sunni militias who hunted Shi'a for sport. To Zia's delight, the Iraqis and other Arabs—piqued at Iran's effort to export its revolutionary verve—chimed in and threw in tons of cash, Korans, Kalashnikovs, and Wahhabite madrassahs and mosques to help Zia Islamize the hapless state and support its legions of Shi'a slayers. These efforts were also motivated by the Soviet invasion of Afghanistan, when the United States and

. . . But Mahmoud Ahmadinejad Is a Monkey

Many people remark upon the similarities between Iran's current president, Mr. Ahmadinejad, and President Bush. Like his Iranian counterpart, President Bush has been likened to a monkey, and he has been rendered humorously as Curious George running and ruining the country. Mr. Ahmadinejad was born on October 28, 1956, and that makes him a Monkey. Monkeys are supposed to be clever, skillful, and flexible as well as original. Well, at least he's the latter.

its aforementioned motley crew of Arab allies (most notably Saudi Arabia) flooded Pakistan's military and intelligence services with cash and war material for the recruitment and deployment of Soviet-killing mujahideen for Afghanistan. (These madrassahs and other mujahideen-making organizations became the petri dishes for germinating the Taliban and Al-Qaeda.[48])

By the mid-1980s Iran and its Arab foes were waging a full-fledged sectarian proxy war on the back of Pakistan. The problem with Iran's calculus was the age-old problem of micronumerosity—or small numbers, if you prefer. Pakistan's Sunnis would always outnumber Pakistan's Shi'a. For every one Sunni they could senselessly slaughter, the Sunnis could massacre loads of Shi'a without even reloading their magazines. While Iran did not get much out of this failed endeavor, Pakistan was bequeathed a savage sectarian rivalry that persists to this day. In today's Pakistan, however, the Sunnis preponderantly do the killing.[49]

Shifty Behaviors

Despite all the U.S.-Iran acrimony, right in the middle of the Iran-Iraq war, the United States bizarrely shifted course in its stalwart support for the grotesque Iraqi regime. In 1985 the Reagan administration curiously began arming *Tehran*. Robert "Bud" McFarlane hauled himself to Tehran using a bogus Irish passport and bearing a Bible with an inscription to Khomeini from Reagan. Soon after McFarlane's visit, secret flights began couriering American weapons to the Iranian fanatics. This was to become the "Iran-Contra Affair," in which proceeds from these dubious weapons sales to a known U.S. enemy were funneled to help right-wing militias (aka the "Contras") fighting to topple Nicaragua's Sandinista government, which was also loathed by Washington. The one wee problem with this scheme—apart from boundless moral turpitude and rapine avarice—was that it was devised to circumvent U.S. law, which criminalized such patronage.[50] Once discovered, the gambit ended with much embarrassment, ignominy, and confusion for the American nation, which justly queried what the hell its government was doing arming its purported arch-foe Iran.

Given their history of mutual duplicity, the United States and Iran seem incapable of overcoming their past antagonisms and instead continue spewing out evermore new and vexing enmities. For Tehran's part, official government rhetoric persists in the appellation "Great Satan." As for Washington, Iran has been labeled one of the "Axis of Evil," is accused of supporting elements of the odious Al-Qaeda *prior to* both 9/11 and the U.S. invasion of Iraq, and is chastised for its unwavering opposition to the tattered remains of a Middle East peace process and for being Hezbollah's puppeteer and financier. Iran's recent escapades include arresting and detaining benign Iranian-American think-tank analysts, seizing a British naval crew and coercing them to say absurdly false things on Iranian television, and possibly arming the Taliban in Afghanistan in some measure and supporting instability and attacks against U.S. forces in Iraq.

Iran, a notorious human rights violator, is also reviled because of its repressive and totalitarian domestic policies. According to Human Rights Watch, Iran routinely tortures and mistreats dissidents whom its various security forces pick up when they feel the need arise. Iran's repertoire of abuses against detainees includes beatings, sleep deprivation, solitary confinement, and even mock executions. (Of course this list of barbarous cruelty is at least faintly reminiscent of "water-boarding" and other alleged unsavory occurrences at Abu Ghraib, Gitmo, and other "secret detention" centers.) The Judiciary, which is under the thumb of the Supreme Leader Ali Khamenei (Khomeini's far less qualified successor), is a serious human rights dasher who accepts coerced confessions for later broadcasting on Iranian television. Clandestine detention centers are operated by the Judiciary, the Ministry of Information, and the Islamic Revolutionary Guard Corps.

Iran not surprisingly has the death penalty and seems to use it with great relish. According to Amnesty International, at least 1,591 people were executed in twenty-five countries in 2006. The overwhelming majority were executed in China (1,010), Iran (177), and Pakistan (82). Amnesty reported sharp rises in execution numbers in Iran (as well as in Iraq, Sudan, and Pakistan). In fact, Iran's executions of political prisoners nearly doubled from 94 in 2005 to 177 in 2006. Iran also executes kids. According to Human Rights Watch, it has executed 13 juveniles between 2001 and 2006 and has the dubious distinction of being the "leading nation" by that metric.[51]

The Iranian regime systematically suppresses freedom of expression—except when lauding the state and its luminary leaders. This has resulted in the flight of writers and intellectuals to other countries. For those personages who have chosen to stay in Iran, they have found it prudent to just shut up. The Ministry of Culture and Guidance closed a number of reform-supporting publications, and they continue to interrogate and harass slews of journalists who dare critique the government. They have also targeted the Internet to prevent online dissemination of news and information about the regime's various evildoings.

Ahmadinejad, unlike the handsome and charming President Mohammed Khatami who preceded him and who chose *not* to sport a Members Only knockoff jacket for every interview given to the media, has no tolerance for peaceful gatherings—protests or otherwise. He even sent his goons to attack a bunch of Sufi devotees in Qom with tear gas and water cannons! The poor Sufis had gathered in front of their shrine to prevent the Iranian government from wrecking it. *Who* on earth would attack peace-mongering Sufis with tear gas and water cannons? You'd think they were a bunch of leftist, unshorn, unshowered students protesting rigged elections in Oaxaca with treatment like that![52]

An Environment of Complete Impunity

There is no organization that can monitor human rights violations in Iran, and even foreigners have perished in Iranian custody, such as the Canadian journalist Zahra Kazemi. The famed Nobel Peace Prize winner Shirin Ebadi and her associates confront persistent threats for their efforts to defend human rights and for providing pro bono legal counsel to the hundreds of journalists, students, and dissidents who have been rounded up for exercising basic freedoms. Minorities—ethnic and religious—don't fare so well in Mullahstan and suffer various forms of discrimination and persecution. Iran's Baha'i are a criminalized lot, and the regime outright prohibits them from publicly worshipping or otherwise following their faith.[53]

On top of this bedrock of variegated perfidy sits the likelihood—nay, *certitude*—that Iran will develop a nuclear weapons capability (aka "the bomb"). In fact, Iran's status as a nuclear proliferator was one of the key reasons for the Bush administration's inclusion of Iran within the Axis of Evil in the first place. Iran's nuclear program is nearly fifty years old and began in the days of Shah Reza Pahlavi with the U.S. initiative called Atoms for Peace. Under the auspices of Atoms for Peace, the United States gave loads of countries nuclear energy capabilities, and many of those grateful countries made bombs instead. In 1970 Iran signed the Nuclear Nonproliferation Treaty (NPT) as a non-nuclear weapons state. (The NPT only recognized five nuclear weapons states: the United States, Russia, China, France, and the United Kingdom.) Under this treaty, Iran was allowed to develop peaceful nuclear capabilities provided it

Remembering Khomeini

Outside Tehran—a city famous for its beautiful domes and architecture—you'll find a prefab monstrosity commemorating Ayatollah Khomeini. While the shrine was not yet completed when I was there in 2001, one has to marvel at its overall failure to impress and the rather casual manner in which folks visit the joint. In fact, one has to ask how it is that a country that has perfected shrine and mausoleum building somehow fell down on this job. Maybe it's because people didn't like the clerical geezer so much after all?

Apparently the old man wanted his memorial to be more of a public usage space rather than a shrine per se, and the architects seemed to have honored that request. The place has the feel of a Midwest indoor swap meet, with folks boisterously hanging around and picnicking, of all things, just a few feet away from the tattered remains of the revolutionary leader. While the exterior suggests some modicum of effort in building something approximating "beauty," inside the place looks like Wal-Mart meets Uzbek mosque, with its numerous cement columns adorned only with the gaudy heavy plastic that Iranians use to eat off of. The complex has numerous shops from which you can select your favorite Khomeini and Hezbollah souvenirs. (I bought Kalashnikov key chains for friends who couldn't see this heap of optical pollution for themselves.)

followed the rules and provisions of the NPT, such as submitting its nuclear facilities to international inspection. And therein lies the problem . . . or nest of problems.

Since 2003 inspectors with the United Nations nuclear watchdog, the International Atomic Energy Agency (IAEA), have produced scads of proof that Iran has been consistently hoodwinking the international community about the scope of its nuclear capabilities and ambitions for decades. Per the commonly held interpretation of Article II of the NPT, a country forgoes its right to peaceful nuclear technologies if it is found to be in noncompliance or engaging in deception about its program. Thus, given the mounting mountains of evidence of Iran's numerous acts of deceit, most non-Iranian analysts believe that Iran has proliferated away its right to an unfettered nuclear energy program—at least until global confidence is restored that Iran really is not making a bomb under the guise of civilian nuclear energy production.[54]

Obviously, the Iranians pooh-pooh this interpretation and contend that they have an absolute right to nuclear technology notwithstanding their petty infractions, which Greater and Lesser Satans alike have exaggerated and distorted without good cause, no doubt to suppress Iran's great power aspirations. The United Nations Security Council disagreed and has slapped Iran with various sanctions to no avail.[55] In Novemer of 2007, the U.S. intelligence community produced a "National Intelligence Estimate" that says that Iran stopped weapons production a few years back.[56] Many folks have taken this to mean that Iran is no longer a threat. If the Iranians did stop efforts to make a weapon, it will be difficult—but not impossible—to pick up where they left off at a time of their choosing. Given that U.S. intelligence has been so wrong about so many things in recent years and given that this assessment is at variance with everything else, I just don't know what to believe. I wish you luck sorting out the Iran mess.

> **How Many Khomeinis for That Chador?**
>
> Iranians refer to their 1,000 toman note as a "Khomeini" because that note (among others) sports his visage.

While the world says that Iran's denial and deception activities are probative of a covert weapons program, Iran insists that its peculiar behavior is just and peaceful and a nonnegotiable entitlement to the "full nuclear fuel cycle." Iran's rejection of various international proposals to have its "fuel cycle" but not the capability to produce bombs confirms what many suspected all along: Iran wants the bomb. And really, why shouldn't Iran want nukes? Israel has them, as do Pakistan and India—and neither of those two states have closed sewers and both of them have woefully lousy levels of human development. Indeed, Iran likes to make these points, or at least ask other states like Egypt to make these points on its behalf at venues such as the NPT renewal conference.

Despite various international efforts to find some means of resolving the world's desire that Iran not develop a nuclear weapon and Iran's resolve to do just that, no sensible end is in sight.[57] While many analysts think it will take Iran perhaps a decade to get the bomb, Iran's neighbors and the United States may not sit around and wait for that to happen.

Dinner in Tehran

Iran's cuisine is thousands of years old, and it remains one of my personal favorites. My affair with Persian cuisine began long before I went to Iran, where I sat atop garish cloths spread out in lovely courtyards, stuffing my mouth with pickles, cheese, and roasted meat by the handful. Rather, it was in Los Angeles where I first had my beloved *fesanjan*—a heavenly concoction of chicken, pomegranate, and walnuts. In my seven years in that town, I ate *fesanjan* at virtually every Persian restaurant in Tehrangelas—as West L.A. is appropriately called. I learned that some restaurants make a tart variant called *fesanjan-e-torsh* and others a sweet version, *fesanjan-e-shireen*. Since I'm not a fan of things *shireen* (which means "sweet"), I learned quickly which variant was cooked where and took great care to go to those establishments with the *torsh* option.

Quite apart from the food, which combines my favorite things (meat and fruit) in the same dish, I like *how* Iranians enjoy their food. They are not shy when it comes to grabbing food. They stuff themselves with basmati rice cooked with ghee and sour cherries, gulp down stews of lamb and celery, and sip overextracted tea, filtering it through sugar cubes poised between their teeth. (I *never* mastered that art!) They can consume heaps of kebab the height of the Alborz mountains above Tehran and still make room for a dessert made of fried flour and dipped in sugar water. No matter how elegantly Iranian women are dressed or how carefully they applied their lipstick, I don't get in the way of one of those perfectly manicured and bejeweled hands when it moves into position to grab a kebab—you can lose a finger that way!

Some of my fondest memories of Iran include eating simple dinners in its varied teahouses. Teahouses in Iran are often elaborately decorated with carpets, metal lamps, various kitsch items such as hats and costumes made of coins, and glass bobbles hung on every corner of every wall and suspended from the ceilings en masse. The dish I long for most is *deezii*, and I have not found it in its authentic form anywhere outside of Iran. It goes like this: At the teahouse, the server brings you a metal mortar and pestle along with a meat stew called *aab ghosht* (meat in water) and piles of the tasty Persian bread *sangak*. You mash the stew—made with chunks of lamb fat, potatoes, chickpeas, and assorted vegetables—and the *sangak* into a thick paste and eat it up. Alas, I can't even make the stuff, as I have found no Persian store that has the right equipment.

Holy Esophagus, Bat Man!

In 1989 Ayatollah Khomeini died. Millions of Iranians thronged his funeral bier, knocking his corpse out of its box. If this wasn't sufficiently ignominious for the Supreme Leader, his devotees tore at his shroud and body hoping for mystical remnants—a euphemism for body parts. Yuck!

Virtually every Persian meal begins with a plate of surprisingly simple appetizers, which usually consists of heaps of fresh herbs like mint, tarragon, basil, and chives sprinkled with feta cheese and walnuts. You can eat these herbs right off the plate, or you can take a bunch and wrap them in a Persian flatbread (*lavash*) with some cheese and walnuts. Typically a meal will also include various tart pickles, such as my absolute favorite, *badamjan torshi* (pickled eggplants). Appetizers are legion, and you can knock yourself out on these alone. Entrees can be as simple as succulent chunks of skewered meats arranged upon pillows of rice cooked with saffron and yogurt. Going up the scale in complexity—but still simple—is any number of stews (*khoresh*) of meats cooked with fresh and dried fruits or vegetables and herbs. In my view, the Queen of Iranian *khoresh* dishes, as you may have guessed, is *fesanjan,* or *khoresh-e-fesanjan.* While the most common of this glorious stew uses chicken, Persians have been making it with duck (or veal) since the fourth century—and maybe earlier.

In this chapter, I am going to hook you up with a few of my personal favorites, some of which are not available at Persian restaurants unless you happen to be lucky enough to live in California. At first blush, this menu may look daunting, but gird your cooking loins and don your apron (and believe me, you'll need that apron!)—this will be worth it. As elsewhere, I'll warn you about the tough spots in the road. Some preparation can be done the day before, and I will let you know when this is the case.

The Plan of Attack

As your guests arrive, they will be encouraged to nosh on a simple array of Persian appetizers. Don't worry: You don't have to cook all of them from scratch when reasonable store-bought substitutes are available. But I will give you a few tricks to make people *think* you made them. There is no honesty in foreign policy and there need not be at your dinner party either. While your guests are nibbling away, you will be putting the final touches on the steamed saffron rice and arranging the entrees on a buffet-style table. The appetizers remain on the table, and make sure that there are plenty of bread and herbs throughout the meal. This plan presumes that you will be cooking for eight persons; adjust accordingly.

Appetizers

- *Noon-o-Paneer-o-Sabzi* (flat bread, cheese, and fresh herbs)
- Warm *dolmeh,* or as more commonly called in the United States, *dolma* (stuffed grape leaves), with a cucumber-dill yogurt sauce
- *Torshi* (fiery pickles)

Main course

- *Khoresh-e-Fesanjan* (chicken in walnut and pomegranate stew). I recommend you try this option, but if you are a bit nervous, you can wuss out and go for the safer stew below *or,* for the culinary conservative:
- *Khoresh-e-Hulu* (chicken and peach stew)
- *Chelo Kebab Barg* (grilled meat with Persian rice). Serve this, the most standard of Iranian entrees, with either of the above stews.

Dessert

- Small, fresh, and very cold cucumbers and tangerines arranged artfully on a platter (Chill them the night before to make sure they are especially refreshing.)
- Store-bought cookies, if you live near a Persian store
- Halva (a semisweet dish made of toasted flour, butter, and saffron). Make this early the day of your bash. It's a finicky number, but with care, you'll do just fine.

Beverages and accompaniments

Alcohol is officially forbidden in the dry Islamic Republic of Iran. However, when I was there, I learned that Iranians often brew their own beverages from fruits, raisins, and anything else they can ferment with adequately small footprint to avoid detection. I didn't drink anything that required distillation, such as the arak they made from raisins. Homemade brew from such things produces methanol, which unless removed through distillation, will blind you if you are lucky or kill you through a slow and ghastly death if you are not so fortunate. Some Iranian partygoers also smoke opium, which carries something like the penalty of death in the Islamic Republic of Iran. In no way should you do those things when there are perfectly good, legal substitutes. But you can bring a bit of Iran to your own soiree, minus the threat of public execution. Here are your nonlethal and legal options:

Get a water pipe with some fragrant apple tobacco. Iranians absolutely love their water pipes, which they call *shisha*. Most urban centers in the United States and Europe have paraphernalia shops where these things can be bought. (If you are of my demographic, we called them "head shops" in our youth.) If you have college-age children, they can probably hook you up with one of these contraptions, which are also known as hookahs.[58]

> **Man of the Year**
> In 1979 Ayatollah Khomeini was chosen *Time* magazine's Man of the Year.

Buy nonalcoholic beer. I fell in love with the stuff in Iran, and even though it sounds utterly unappealing, you may also develop a taste for it. Iranians love nonalcoholic beer, and Iran has a terrific selection of the same. When I am longing for the sinless brew that seduced me in Tehran, I look for the Dutch nonalcoholic Buckler, the German nonalcoholic Clausthaler options, and Bavaria malt beverage. (The latter I drink in Pakistan with great contentment.)

The best option in countries where booze is not verboten, however, is loading up on your favorite Shiraz. After all, back in the days of the ancient Persians, this was *their* damned grape! The city of Shiraz, from which the grape takes its name, is in the heart of ancient Persia and is still considered the epicenter of Persian culture in modern Iran. Shiraz is renowned for its rose gardens, the tombs of Persia's prized poets Hafez and Sa'adi, the ruins of the ancient Zoroastrian civilization at Persepolis, and long, long ago, wine. So raise a toast to the ancient Persians and their brew and wonder if the creepy ayatollahs are quaffing some on the sly!

PREPARATION

★★★
★★★★★★★★★★★★★★★★★★★★★★★★★★★★★★★★★★★★★

APPETIZERS

A half hour before your guests arrive, assemble all appetizers on the banquet table.

Noon-o-Paneer-o-Sabzi
(Flat Bread, Cheese, and Fresh Herbs)

Buy whatever herbs are in season, and get at least three or four different varieties. Remember, this will be like a salad, so buy enough for your guests to nibble on. Purchase the herbs the day before your soiree and not a day earlier. I clean them the day I buy them and store them in ziplock storage bags with a moist paper towel to keep them fresh. Persians typically eat *lavash* bread, and many stores now carry it because it is used in the ubiquitous wrap sandwiches. I've noticed that many grocery stores catering to folks who keep kosher have this stuff. Persevere and you'll probably succeed. Failing that, any other flat bread will do in a pinch such as a nan, the Persian wonder bread *sangak,* or if you absolutely must, pita bread. I counsel against this folly because the grocery story variety simply tastes like sawdust and cardboard. What's the point?

Ingredients
Fresh herbs (*sabzi*), such as bunches of tarragon, mint, chive or scallion,
    crisp radishes, cilantro, or basil
½ pound (at least) feta cheese, either from goat's or cow's milk
¼ pound (at least) walnut halves
Lavash flat bread

Arrange your herbs in such a way that it looks artfully disorganized. Sprinkle the herbs with feta cheese, either crumbled or cubed. Finally, lavishly adorn the mound with walnuts. *Lavash* usually is found in a large sheet, so you should cut the bread into manageable sizes. I usually do 4x6-inch rectangles. Place the bread in baskets and cover with a towel to keep it fresh, as *lavash* is very thin and dries out quickly.

Dolmeh *(Stuffed Grape Leaves)*
with Cucumber-Dill Yogurt Sauce

There is no need for you to make the *dolmeh,* which are grape leaves stuffed with rice and marinated, from scratch. (You will make them in the Iraq chapter.) You can buy them virtually everywhere. I prefer the ones that are packed in olive oil. Assuming that each of your eight guests will eat three of them, get at least two cans.

Ingredients
2 cups plain yogurt (I use fat-free yogurt. You don't lose the flavor, and this small step can offset some of the less-than-healthy things in Iranian food.)
1 cup shredded cucumber (Look for the miniature ones used for making pickles; these are the closest to the Persian varietals. You'll need about 2.)
1 sprig dill
Salt and pepper to taste
2 cans *dolmeh* (aka *dolma,* grape leaves stuffed with rice). They usually come in 14-ounce cans, which contain 12 stuffed grape leaves packed in oil.

Let's get cooking
1. Prepare the sauce the day before the party. Mix the yogurt with the shredded cucumber and minced fresh dill (1 sprig or to taste), and salt and pepper to taste. Refrigerate overnight.
2. Forty minutes prior to your guests' arrival, arrange the *dolmeh* in a ceramic or Pyrex baking pan and pour some of the packing oil in the pan to prevent sticking and drying. Preferably choose a baking dish in which you can then serve the *dolmeh* to avoid more dishware to clean and to save time. (I use a ceramic dish that fits into a wicker-like shell for serving.)
3. Cover the dish with foil or a glass lid to prevent drying, and heat for 30 minutes in a 300-degree oven. Just before your guests arrive, drizzle the *dolmeh* with yogurt sauce and bring the dish out to the table. Most folks have never had warmed *dolmeh,* and this will give the illusion that you whipped these morsels up yourself.

Torshi *(Fiery Pickles)*

Nothing to do but shop for the jars, open them up, and serve on the plates you like most. Persians typically put out small bowls of spicy (sour and hot) pickles. While Persian pickles are preferred (such as eggplant and cucumber pickles, among others), you can substitute any sour Middle Eastern pickle from Lebanon or Armenia. In an absolute pinch, you can use cornichons and other pickled vegetables that are *not sweet*. Persian pickles are very vinegary and spicy, and the sweet American pickles simply will not do.

MAIN COURSE

I always use ghee for these dishes and strongly suggest you do the same, because ghee confers a traditionally buttery flavor, without the quirky cooking problems of actual butter. Because of the proteins in butter, butter has a lower smoking point than ghee and burns quite easily. Ghee does not impose this problem, because the process of clarification of butter removes these proteins, and the resultant ghee is stable and can be kept for months. If you don't have ghee, strain melted butter to remove some of the "white" proteins that form on the top. This option, while inferior to ghee, is better than using vegetable oil, which will not provide the buttery flavor or the needed texture.

Khoresh-e-Fesanjan
(Chicken in Walnut and Pomegranate Stew)

Prepare this first, beginning it about 3 hours before your guests arrive. There are several intermediate steps that take more time than may appear at first blush. You can trim some time by preparing the walnuts and vegetables the day before or the morning of the event. This entree keeps well in a covered dish in a warm oven (250 degrees). You can also make it a day in advance, then warm it up and garnish before serving.

Remember what I said: *Fesanjan* has two variants—sweet and sour. The recipe below will put you closer to the sour end of things than the sweeter. You can always adjust this according to your taste by adding a bit more sugar or a bit more pomegranate syrup. When "adjusting," do so using very small amounts of either the sugar or the syrup. You can really screw up the balance of flavors if you are not extremely careful, so do this only if absolutely necessary.

For best results, this dish requires a food processor, or at the minimum, a good blender and a small chopper.

Ingredients

1 pound shelled walnut halves

½ pound carrots

4 small yellow onions

1 cup pomegranate syrup, or more to taste (available at Middle Eastern markets)

5 cups warm water

¾ teaspoon saffron threads (While Persian or Indian saffron is preferred, Spanish or other varieties will do just fine.)

2 teaspoons rock salt (Rock salt really does make a difference.)

4 tablespoons ghee (or vegetable oil, if you must)

2 pounds skinless and boneless chicken breast

3 tablespoons demerara sugar, or more to taste (As I've mentioned, I really like this sugar, but you can use the white stuff if you must.)

1½ teaspoons cinnamon

For garnish:

½ cup fresh pomegranate seeds

Rose petals

Let's get cooking

1. Roast the walnuts. I prefer to spread them out on a thick cookie sheet and place them in the oven at 350 degrees. Watch them like a shoplifter at Wal-Mart to ensure that they do not burn. As you prepare the dish, the walnuts will continue to darken throughout the cooking process and will give a deep brown hue to the dish. I roast the walnuts the morning of the party so they can cool thoroughly before I need to use them. (Also, if I screw this up the first time, there is time to fix the problem!) The walnuts will continue to cook as long as they are warm—even if you remove them

from the oven. For this reason, I always transfer them to a cool plate to prevent them from overcooking behind my back.

2. Prepare the vegetables. Julienne the carrots; the thinner you can make the carrot strips, the better. Slicing them in a food processor works best. Set the sliced carrots aside. Next, cut the onions into very thin slices.

3. Prepare the pomegranate syrup. Dilute 1 cup of syrup into 5 cups of warm water. Agitate to make sure the syrup doesn't stick to the bottom of the vessel.

4. Prepare the saffron. With a mortar and pestle, grind the saffron threads with ⅛ teaspoon of the rock salt. The salt gives some traction on the elusive threads and helps you render it a salty powder. (Some folks prefer to use a sugar cube, which accomplishes the same thing. However, the rock salt works better for me in this dish.)

5. In a 6-quart pot, heat the ghee (or oil) over medium heat. Add the onions and fry until translucent. This will take 5–8 minutes. Next, place the chicken breasts into the pot and fry, with frequent stirring, until golden brown. This may take 15–20 minutes. Finally, add the sliced carrots to the pot and fry, with continual stirring, for another 2–4 minutes. You want the carrots to lilt and lose their "fresh" look. Cover and let sit on very low heat while you do the next step, stirring occasionally to prevent sticking and burning.

6. Grind the walnuts in a food processor or, less ideally, a small electric chopper. Stop when the walnuts look like granular sand—don't go further or you will end up with walnut butter! If using a food processor, add the remaining rock salt, sugar, cinnamon, and saffron ground with salt.*

7. Remove the chicken from step 5 and slice into strips.

8. Add the fried onions and carrots to the bowl of the food processor and blend until the sauce is creamy. (I do this because I don't want to see onion slices and carrot shreds in my *fesanjan*!) Add the sauce back to the

---

* If you do not have a food processor, blend the salt, sugar, cinnamon, and saffron ground with salt along with the diluted pomegranate syrup in a blender. Add the fried vegetables and blend until smooth. Add the creamy sauce mixture to the 6-quart pot along with the chicken strips (see step 7). Add the ground walnuts to the pot and stir well. Do not put the walnuts in the pot first! Because walnuts burn so easily, you will want to buffer their addition with the liquid. Proceed to step 9.

6-quart pot along with the diluted pomegranate syrup and stir thoroughly. Add the chicken slices to the pot.

9. Cover the pot and simmer for 40 minutes over very low heat. You will need to keep an eye on this and stir occasionally to prevent the walnuts from burning. (Walnuts burn easily in high heat, as you may have noticed in the browning phase.)

10. At first, this is *not* going to look terribly appetizing. In fact, you will no doubt wonder if this was a mistake and will consider aborting the mission. But do not despair: This unsightly phase is temporary. As the mixture continues to cook, you will see the color change from stomach-churning dull reddish brown to a sultry deep brown—almost a mahogany color. This hue is due to the continued cooking of the walnuts. By the way, the walnuts can still burn and screw up your dish, so stir thoroughly and frequently. After it has cooked for 40 minutes or so, taste the sauce and adjust to your sweet or sour preference by adding sugar or syrup accordingly. Be careful when adding the syrup as it is very, very strong. If you need to adjust, begin with 1 teaspoon increments to avoid putting too much in. If the sauce is too thin, cook with the cover off over low heat to thicken. If it is too thick, you can thin it with warm water. By this time, you should have a lovely looking sauce.

11. Once you have adjusted the thickness and sour/sweet balance, transfer the *fesanjan* to a covered baking dish and keep it in the oven at 200 degrees while you prepare the kebabs and rice.

12. When ready, you can garnish with some pomegranate seeds, walnuts, or rose petals. Serve it with the saffron rice and *teh degh* prepared in the kebab recipe.

Khoresh-e-Hulu *(Chicken and Peach Stew)*

Persians often cook meat with fruit, and while it may be counterintuitive that such a dish would be delicious, go ahead and give this a try. It's a bit like pairing prosciutto with melon, for folks who are familiar with that odd Continental treat. (Despite your reservations, I want to remind you that you have already cowered before the *fesanjan* altar, so you better rally here!) This dish can, and indeed should, sit in a warm oven once preparation is finished—just like the *fesanjan* you dismissed.

Ingredients

⅓ cup ghee (or less ideally, vegetable oil), plus an additional 2 tablespoons for the peaches

3 large white onions, sliced into thin rings

2 pounds boneless chicken breasts cut into strips (You can use chicken tenders to minimize prep time. Some folks use veal, duck, or even beef.)

1 teaspoon *advieh,* a Persian spice mixture (There are several variants; most include cinnamon, cardamom, and dried rose petals. Available through online vendors listed in the appendix.)

2½ teaspoons salt (I use either rock salt or sea salt.)

1 teaspoon freshly ground black pepper

3 cups water

12 firm peaches

¾–1 cup lime juice (I like key lime juice, either store-bought or freshly squeezed.)

1 cup demerara or raw cane sugar (Substitute the white stuff if you must.)

½ teaspoon saffron, ground with either a sugar cube or ⅛ teaspoon rock salt in a mortar and pestle and dissolved in 3 tablespoons of warm water (If it doesn't completely dissolve, don't worry. Just be sure to get all of the saffron mixture into the pot when required. You can even rinse the mortor out with another 3 tablespoons of warm water.)

For garnish:

Parsley, finely chopped

Let's get cooking

1. Heat a large skillet that has high sides and a cover. (I use a big cast-iron skillet.) When the skillet is warm, add the ghee or oil. When the ghee has melted or the oil is hot, add the onion and fry until translucent. Add the chicken strips and cook with the onions on medium heat for about 20 minutes.

2. Toss in the *advieh,* salt, and pepper. Mix thoroughly. Add 3 cups of water and bring to a boil. Cover and let simmer for about 25 minutes.

3. While this simmers, begin to prepare the peaches. Rinse off all the fuzz and remove the pits. Slice as you would for a peach pie. I usually aim for 5 or 6 wedges from each peach, depending on its size. Once the peaches are sliced, toss them with a couple tablespoons of lime juice, working fast to avoid browning. In a separate pan, heat 2 tablespoons of ghee or oil.

(Use a nonstick pan or a heavy cast-iron skillet to avoid burning.) In batches, fry the peaches until they are golden, about 3 minutes on each side. If you are good at parallel processing, you can fry up one batch of peaches while you slice up the next batch. This means you avoid browning and you obviate the step of tossing with lime juice.

4. Mix ¾ cup lime juice, the sugar, and the saffron water. Set aside.
5. Add the peaches to the same skillet as the chicken, then add the lime juice, saffron, and sugar mixture. Cover the skillet and simmer for 10 minutes or until the chicken is tender. Taste and adjust the seasoning. If it's too sweet, you can add a bit of lime juice. If it's not sweet enough, you can add a bit more sugar.
6. Keep this mixture in the oven at low heat (200 degrees) while you prepare the rest of the meal.

Chelo Kebab Barg *(Grilled Meat with Persian Rice)*

Chelo kebab means "grilled meat" (*kebab*) with cooked "white rice" (*chelo*). *Barg* refers to the kind of meat (i.e., fillet). Traditionally, this dish calls for lamb fillets, which are not terribly common in the United States. Folks living in other countries will have an easier time finding the fillets, but U.S. cooks can use a leg of lamb. If you or your guests don't like lamb, a good cut of beef (sirloin works well) will do. I'll leave the choice of animal to you. As for me and my household, we go for the lamb. As an accompaniment, this dish is always served with roasted Roma or cherry tomatoes. So let's get grilling!

Ingredients

For the meat:
(Note that you should begin marinating the meat the night before your dinner party.)

2 large yellow onions, finely chopped
¼ cup lime juice (I like key lime juice for this.)
3 tablespoons olive oil
⅓ cup plain nonfat yogurt
4 teaspoons salt (I use rock or sea salt.)
½ teaspoon saffron threads, ground with ¼ teaspoon rock salt in a mortar and pestle and dissolved in 3 tablespoons of warm water (If the saffron does

not dissolve completely, don't worry. Simply be sure to use a spoon to
scrape and push as much of the saffron as possible into the mixing bowl.)
4 pounds boneless lamb (You could also use beef sirloin.)

For garnish:
16 Roma or cherry tomatoes (2 per person)
Sumac (No, not the poison white variety! This lovely powder is made from
crushing the dried berries of the red sumac bush.)
8 small red onions, peeled
8 small red radishes, or more if desired

For the rice:
*(Persians eat a lot of rice, and it is considered impolite to have niggard quantities. You
can, however, reduce the amount below. In my experience, most folks rarely eat as much
as this recipe calls for, which is 1 cup of cooked rice, but it is the traditional thing to do.)*

4 cups basmati rice
½ cup ghee (preferable) or vegetable oil
5 cups water
1 tablespoon salt (rock or sea salt)
½ cup plain nonfat yogurt
1 teaspoon saffron dissolved in ¼ cup warm water (With a mortar and pestle, grind the saffron in ¼ teaspoon rock salt then dissolve it in the warm
water.)

For garnish:
Dried rose petals or dried rosebuds (Available at Middle Eastern markets or
through online vendors listed in the appendix.)
Zareshk, fried in ghee (If you can't find *zareshk*, which is dried barberries, you
could use red currants instead. *Zareshk* is available at Middle Eastern markets or through online vendors listed in the appendix.)

Let's get cooking

1. Marinate the meat. Do this the night before your dinner party.
   a. In the bowl of a food processor, combine the finely chopped onions
   with their juices, lime juice, olive oil, yogurt, salt, and dissolved saffron.
   Mix very well. A small electric chopper or blender will work just as well.
   Transfer all of the mixture to a large ziplock bag or bowl, large enough
   to hold all of the meat and the marinade.

b. Prepare the meat by trimming off the excess fat. You will want to cut the meat into strips, ideally about ½ inch thick, 3 inches wide, and about 5 inches long. While this set of dimensions is ideal, do what you can do with the cut of meat you have! If you don't get this right, you will lose points for style but not necessarily for taste.

c. Mix the meat thoroughly with the marinade. If using a large ziplock bag, squeeze out the air before sealing. This is a trick that more efficiently marinates the meat, and it also takes up less space in my puny fridge than the traditional "covered bowl." Sit the bag on a plate just in case it leaks, however. If using a bowl, mix the meat thoroughly with the marinade in the bowl. Cover with plastic wrap and place in the fridge.

2. Prepare the rice. Begin this about 1½ hours before your guests arrive.

a. Depending on what kind of basmati rice you bought and where it came from, you may need to clean it. Rice from South Asia, for example, may have rocks or other things you don't want to break a tooth on—much less your guests' teeth. I've seen improvement over the years, but spare yourself and your guests a trip to the dentist. Once you have gone through the rice, you will want to rinse off the starch. I do this by covering the rice in water and *gently* mixing it around with my hand for several seconds. I then pour off the water and repeat until the water becomes more or less clear. (The first round may bring up a milky white color, which is the starch from the rice.) After the last rinse, drain as much water as possible.

b. In a large *nonstick* pot, heat the ghee or oil. Fry the rice until all the water has boiled off and the rice becomes translucent. This could take 5 minutes or so, depending on how successful you were in getting the water out of the rice. (Obvioulsy, be careful throwing the water-soaked rice into the hot ghee, as it will spatter.)

c. In a bowl, whisk together the water, salt, and yogurt. (If you don't whisk the yogurt into the water, the yogurt may "clump" in your rice. While it doesn't taste bad, it looks weird.) Add the mixture to the rice and stir. Bring to a boil, then cover and reduce the heat to simmer.

d. Ordinarily, the rice would cook in about 20 minutes. However, we want this to "overcook" and actually form a crust against the side of the pot, which may take an hour or more on very low heat. I find a glass lid on the pot to be helpful, as I can watch the progress. Obviously, the goal is not to burn this stuff. The goal is make a nice, golden brown dome of rice.

When you see the rice browning along the edges and looking dry, poke at the sides with a spatula to see if the sides have firmed up and browned.

e. When you are reasonably certain that the rice is done (i.e., there are "steam holes" on the top and you can see the crust on the sides), pour the saffron water over the surface.

f. Run a spatula along the sides of the pot to loosen. Place a plate over the pot and invert. Tap on the bottom if need be. The rice should plop out, producing a beauteous golden dome of deliciousness.

g. Note that 9 out of 10 times, this process produces the desired lovely golden dome of rice. Sometimes the rice goddess is not on my side and when I invert, parts of the rice come out and much remains stuck to the bottom of the pot. Don't despair if this happens to you. That crusty stuff on the bottom is called *teh degh* (bottom of the pot), and as long as you didn't burn it, it's supposed to be there. So take a spatula (I use a wooden one) and scrape up that brown, fried, toasty *teh degh* and plop it right on the rice that came out. This is a special feature of Persian rice, and for many, it the best part of Persian rice.

Note on *teh degh*: There are complicated versions of making *teh degh* that you can find in Persian cookbooks, but this method works for me. The crunchy texture is the perfect accompaniment to most Persian stews, especially the ones made from fruit. I first had *teh degh* at an Iranian New Year's (*Noruz*) party in Los Angeles, and I can still remember ladling lamb and celery stew atop it with some trepidation, at least in part because of my two new molar crowns. But, I became a fan of this quirky item at first bite. I always ask for it at Persian restaurants, and the waiter is always so happy to find a non-Persian who is in on their secret.

h. I garnish my rice with dried rose petals and fried *zareshk*. To fry the *zareshk*, in a small skillet heat up 1 tablespoon of ghee. Add ¼ cup *zareshk* to the hot ghee and fry only long enough for the color to change to a brighter red. This will take less than a minute if the ghee is hot enough. Frying *zareshk* brings out the flavor. If you don't fry these little berries, don't bother with them. Sprinkle your fried *zareshk* over the rice along with the rose petals in a way that is visually appealing to you. (Note that if the rice finishes a little too early, you can keep it in the pot in a warm oven. It will be fine for 10–15 minutes. Turn out onto the plate and garnish right before serving.)

3. Skewer and grill the meat. While the rice is in its last 50 minutes of slow cooking, begin preparing the grill. (It is best to barbecue the meat. As a poor alternative, you can broil it.)

   a. I advise putting the meat on the skewers in the afternoon of the dinner party. *Reserve the leftover marinade for basting.* Note that Persians use wide, flat skewers that look like dull, smallish swords. If you don't have this kind, you can use any heavy-duty metal skewer. Avoid the temptation to buy the giant toothpick varieties in grocery stores. They will not do the job, because they lack the strength to hang on to the meat *and* they will burn on your grill or in your broiler. In truth, there is no useful purpose for those things other than perhaps fondue, and we are not making fondue here!

   b. Once the coals are appropriately hot, grill the Roma or cherry tomatoes first. (You can skewer them or cook them in those cute baskets that come with most barbecue sets.) Set the tomatoes aside on the upper portion of your grill. Place the skewers of meat on the grill. Cook about 3–4 minutes on each side. The meat should still be pink and juicy. Baste as needed with the marinade.

4. Arrange the meat on a platter alongside the roasted tomatoes and sprinkle with sumac. Garnish the platter with peeled and quartered red onion and red radishes. Serve with the rice and *lavash* and butter.

DESSERT

★★★ ★★★★★★★★★★ ★★★★★★

Cucumbers and Tangerines

You will want about 2 pounds of each. Be sure to buy the small cucumbers—not the huge monster ones. Chill them overnight to make sure they are as crispy and delightful as possible. This may sound like a strange combination, but the flavors of tart tangerine and cold, mellow, crunchy cucumber actually complement each other beautifully. This combination isn't so odd in some corners of the United States. My massage parlor in Los Angeles always had pitchers of cool filtered water with slices of cucumbers and oranges, and it was utterly refreshing. Tangerines and cucumbers as a dessert tend to lighten the rest of the meal, which is rather heavy.

To get ready for your guests, remove your chilled cucumbers and tangerines from the fridge, and arrange them nicely in a serving dish of your choice. I like the colors of these two items and thus put them in the same dish together, but they can be served separately.

Cookies

If you got store-bought Persian cookies, arrange them on platters as you see fit. I prefer the small raisin cookies or the little cookies made of rice flour and sprinkled with poppy seeds, *noon-barenji*.

Halva

This is the dish we are going to make. Make it the *morning of your dinner party*. If it flops, you can always go with the tangerines and cucumbers and/or the cookies. But try the halva—it's fun and it's Iranian. Note that halva has many varieties and a diverse cadre of admirers throughout the countries of the Middle East and South Asia, nearly all of which have their own halva options. (Fans of South Asian cuisine may, for example, recognize *gajjar ka halva,* a sweet concoction made of carrots.)

The traditional recipe calls for rosewater, which is made by steaming fresh rose petals and collecting the rose-infused condensate. Iranians use rosewater, as well as rose petals, for everything from "freshening" the air to making "refreshing" beverages, as well as flavoring many sweet and savory dishes. As for me, I can't stand the stuff. It is cloyingly sweet and leaves an aftertaste that reminds me of my grandmother's 1950s-era dusting powder. You can leave it out of this dish, and no one will miss it—except any Iranian that you may invite. I usually make my halva with vanilla, and while it is certainly not an authentic variant, it is delicious. But if you are a stickler for authenticity, by all means go for the rosewater option.

Ingredients

½ cup demerara or raw cane sugar (Yes, you can use the white stuff here, but I wish you wouldn't.)

2 cups warm water. (You may need more warm water than this. So keep an additional 3 cups warm and nearby.)

1 teaspoon rosewater or vanilla extract

4 teaspoons ground cardamom seeds (I grind my own cardamom using a coffee grinder reserved exclusively for grinding spices.)

1 cup whole wheat flour (Don't even think of using the bleached white stuff!)

¾ cup ghee or melted and strained butter

½ cup slivered *unsalted* pistachios or almonds

Small paper candy cups and small cookie cutters (optional)

Let's get cooking

1. Place the sugar and 1 cup of the water in a saucepan and bring to a boil. Make sure the sugar is dissolved into the water. Remove from the heat and add the vanilla or rosewater (if you insist on the traditional variant) along with the cardamom. Mix thoroughly and set aside while you do the next two steps

2. In a cast-iron skillet, or an equivalently heavy pan with good conductive properties, toast the flour over medium heat. Do this by adding the flour, all at once, when the pan is ready. (A pan is ready when you sprinkle a tiny bit of water on it and the water sizzles and evaporates.) You must stir this constantly, with a wooden or other nonmetal heat-resistant spatula, otherwise it *will* burn and you will have to start all over—or alternatively give up. You want to toast the flour until it is golden brown. This is the first step in a process that gives this dish its lovely color. It can take about 10–20 minutes, so be patient. You simply cannot rush this step.

3. Next add the ghee (or melted, strained butter) to the skillet, continuing over medium heat. Do this slowly. (This process is reminiscent of making biscuits. You fold in the fat in portions and make sure it gets worked in thoroughly.) Continue frying the flour, stirring constantly to ensure that it doesn't burn in this step either. You want the golden brown color to continue to develop, and this can take anywhere between 5 and 15 minutes depending on how you folded in the fat and the temperature you are using.

When this step is done, the mixture will look granular—not dissimilar from moist sand. Don't worry: It gets better!

4. Carefully pour the sugar water into the pan. Remember that you are pouring water into a pan of hot oil (albeit integrated into flour). Be careful because it will spatter and it will burn you. *Mix thoroughly.* Add the nuts along with another cup of warm water, and continue to mix thoroughly to incorporate. If the ingredients are not incorporated completely, add warm water in ½ cup increments, stirring to incorporate and letting the water evaporate. Repeat until you can see no unincorporated flour and all lumps disappear—except for the nuts, of course. It may take many such rounds of "add water, stir, and evaporate." For this reason, I recommend keeping 3 cups of warm water ready to use. Once you are satisfied that all of the flour has been incorporated, you should have something that is the texture of cookie dough. If it doesn't "set," keep cooking on low heat until it thickens.

5. Once the dough has set, use your spatula to shape it into something resembling a ball. Move it to a bowl, cover loosely with plastic wrap, and let it cool 10–15 minutes. This is not an exact science. You want the mixture to be just cool enough for you to handle without burning your hands on the molten ball of butter and fried flour. Moving it out of the hot pan and into a bowl hastens the cooling, because the pan retains heat and slows the cooling process. Also, the hot pan would continue to cook the dough, and without your constant attention, will burn your brown blob.

6. As the mixture cools, it will harden somewhat. For this reason, I prefer to render the halva into bite-size pieces before it hardens. As soon as it is cool enough to work with (without burning your hands), decide how you want to prepare it. I prefer to turn the dough out onto a work surface and roll it into sheets about ½ inch thick. Using small cookie cutters, you can cut the dough into shapes and place them in small candy cups (I prefer the silver and gold foil ones). They look like miniature cupcake wrappers, and you can find them in the baking section at most grocery stores or at party stores. Garnish with a tiny piece of almond or pistachio. (If using the vanilla option, use the almonds—trust me.) There is a much easier route, however: Roll out the dough into a rectangle of ½-inch thickness and using cross hatches, render the halva into several small rectangles or squares. You can put them in the candy cups and garnish, or you can arrange them on a platter as you see fit.

Serve your halva with black tea and sugar cubes. Truly Persian tea requires a samovar, an urnlike apparatus that has a large bottom vesicle for water, which is kept at sub-boiling temperatures. Modern samovars run on electricity, but in the old days, they heated these contraptions over wood-fueled flames, which also warmed the house. (Notably, they still do this in twenty-first-century Afghanistan and in parts of the Pakistani frontier, both of which share borders with Iran and once were part of ancient Persian empires.) Atop the main vesicle rests a small teapot of overextracted tea. Persians pour the preferred amount of tea into dainty glasses and dilute it to the top with the warm water from the samovar. If you have a samovar (or wish to buy one), knock yourself out with this option. Persians drink their tea with sugar cubes, sifting the tea through the cube clenched between their teeth. I can't do it, and I'm going to guess your guests won't be able to either, but it's good fun trying. For those of you without a samovar, make a pot of strong black tea. Persians do not put milk in their tea.

Dossier of Iraq's Perfidy

The Brits occupied Baghdad in 1917 as the Ottoman Empire crumbled. When Great Britain was "awarded" Iraq during the World War I peace negotiations, that chunk of land was comprised of three separate Ottoman provinces (one Kurdish and two Arab) and was hopelessly fissured by sectarian and ethnic differences. None of these folks seemed to want to live as one country then, and they still don't. They violently rose up against the Brits, who after taking a good beating, decided to install a British-backed "Hashemite Kingdom" in 1921. It became an independent and constitutional monarchy in 1932.[59]

The monarchy phase wrapped up in 1958 when General Abdul Karim Qassim led a coup. His movement was a hodgepodge of movements including Arab nationalism (Nasserist variety), the secularist Arab Ba'ath party, and the Iraqi Communist Party. Saddam Hussein established his credentials as a pain in the backside early on: He was involved in a plot to assassinate Qassim in 1959. In 1962 Qassim was removed in a coup led by the Ba'athists and other elements and replaced by a non-Ba'ath Iraqi president named Abdul

Salam Arif. More strife ensued between Arif and the Ba'athists, and he was finally ousted in 1968 by the latter, who installed one of their own, Ahmad al-Bakr, as president. Ba'athists progressively took control of the state. Saddam was a Ba'ath superstar and formally succeeded al-Bakr in 1979. Soon thereafter, Saddam went to war with Iran, whose leadership had been seized by the fanatical Khomeini. When that war ended in a stalemate, about one million folks were dead.[60]

In subsequent decades, Saddam and his regime became notorious for widespread human rights abuses and extensive utilization of capital punishment, extrajudicial killings, and torture of detainees. During his Arabization campaign, he forcibly expelled ethnic minorities (e.g., Kurds, Turkmen, and Assyrians) from Kirkuk, Khaniquin, Sinjar, and other oil-rich areas. Saddam capriciously arrested political opponents and their family members alike. While the Kurds and Shi'a received especially nasty treatment, the Kurds were not (and probably still are not) exemplars of human rights respect themselves. Human Rights Watch has detailed abuses committed by the Patriotic Union of Kurdistan and the Kurdish Democratic Party—especially against Islamists.[61]

Because of Saddam's *past* pursuit of weapons of mass destruction (WMD), Iraq was under piles of economic sanctions imposed by United Nations Security Council in 1991. Saddam—perhaps because he did not want the world to know he had no nukes—resisted weapons inspections as required by the United Nations. In October 2002 Iraq finally agreed to let the inspectors return, but it was too late. Saddam had screwed himself—and everyone else who would become involved in successfully invading but unsuccessfully occupying the hapless chunk of real estate. In the end, Saddam found it difficult to prove he didn't have nukes. In fairness to the mad nutter, it is difficult to prove a negative beyond a shadow of the doubt.

Hell on Earth As We Know It

The present phase of hell in Iraq began in January 2002 when President Bush declared in his State of the (Dis)Union Address that "the Iraqi regime has plotted to develop anthrax, and nerve gas, and nuclear weapons for over a decade."[62] It was on these very grounds that Arbusto cast Iraq as a charter member of the Axis of Evil. Alleging that Saddam was seeking nuclear weapons and other purported "weapons of mass destruction" and was allied to Al-Qaeda, the Bushies argued that Saddam posed a clear and present danger to the United States.[64]

Given the saber rattling and the explicit discussion of using "preemptive" military force that seized the airwaves by the summer of 2002, experts at the U.S. Congressional Research Service examined the U.S. historical record to determine whether the United States had *ever* taken such preemptive military action. They wrote of their recondite exercise that "the historical record indicates that the United States has never, to date, engaged in a 'preemptive' military attack against another nation. Nor has the United States ever attacked another nation militarily *prior* to its first having been attacked or *prior* to U.S. citizens or interests first having been attacked, with the singular exception of the Spanish-American War."[65]

Undeterred by precedent or the paucity of defensible evidence of Saddam's complicity in harming the United States, its citizens, or its interests—and deploying wishful thinking as a strategy—the Bush administration launched what will prove to be a devastatingly costly war when measured in dollars and lives (Iraqi, American, and anyone else involved in this "Mess-O-Potamia"[66]). As of October 14, 2007, at 6:11 p.m., the cost of the war had been *$459,953,811,462,* according to the National Priorities Project.[67] Think tanker Steven Kosiak said that when measured by congressional appropriations, by September 2007 the war had cost about $450 billion—which is pretty close to the above-cited hair-raising figure. Making various assumptions about how long we will be stuck in this quagmire and under what conditions we remain ensnared in this insurgency, Kosiak estimates that between fiscal years 2008 and 2018, the American taxpayer can be expected to fork over an additional *48 billion to 1.01 trillion* greenbacks.[68]

These measurements of direct cost dramatically underestimate the actual costs of the Iraq debacle, because they exclude what we geeks, nerds, and dweebs call "indirect costs." Indirect costs are the kind of costs that most folks never think of because they are often not obvious, often hidden, and always difficult to estimate because they may take some time to materialize. In the case of the Iraq ruination, indirect costs include the diminished lifetime earnings of injured civilian and military personnel who served in Iraq and supporting locations; second-order impacts upon dead and wounded personnel's household economic activity and earnings potential; insurance payouts related to death, injury, and treatment of the same; increased costs due to absurdly skyrocketing oil prices; and opportunity costs of spending that money on more productive things that benefit the nation and its citizenry (e.g., providing health care, education, and other "human capital" investments in the United States).

While obtuse and not terribly sexy sounding (they rarely make good headlines), these indirect costs are as important as they are ignored by most news commentators. But if you include these indirect costs, you are likely to add an order of magnitude to all of these cost estimates.[69] (Hint: That means adding a zero to those figures. So if the direct costs are $1 trillion, adding indirect costs makes that $10 trillion.) Indeed, a consensus is emerging among "über bean counters" that the war will soon cost at least a trillion dollars and maybe *two* trillion.[70]

I am not so unreasonable and silly to not concede the possibility that there are indirect and direct *benefits* of the Iraq war, especially if you are a defense contractor or other kind of purveyor of goods and services to the war machine—or a corrupt government official brokering contracts for these "vendors" and similarly well-situated beneficiaries of a war economy. The Saudis,

Saddam the Sadist Belletrist

In March 2002 the Arab press reported that Saddam was a savant as well as a savage. He reportedly completed two new novels, at least one of which was sent to "libraries and markets" by April. These two unnamed feats of literary genius complement his two previous ink-slinging endeavors titled *Zabiba* and *The King and Steadfast Edifice*, which written under the nom de plume "A novel for its writer."[71] The titles and his pen name have various English translations. The latter book, also called *The Fortified Castle*, was critically claimed as "an innovation which nobody has managed to achieve during the past century."[72]

Iranians, Russians, and other oil producers have also benefited from the obscene escalation in the price of crude oil. But, ladies and gentlemen, did you personally get rich from the war? I am going to guess that the safe answer is no. That's because these *benefits* are not as equitably distributed as the *costs*, and indeed the benefits seem to be concentrated in the hands of a few, while the costs appear to be spread all over the citizenry's pockets.

While an exact accounting of dollars and lives squandered is difficult to reckon without a supercomputer and a sea container of Prozac (or whatever serotonin uptake inhibitor your doctor prescribes for you), there is simply no question that payouts thus far dwarf the absurd estimates proffered by administration tools to mollify an American public concerned largely with tax cuts and finding ways of passing the buck on providing health care for all Americans or a decent education for kids in school districts that don't enjoy the largess of tax funding based upon rich home owners. In a September 2002 interview with the *Wall Street Journal*, White House economic adviser Lawrence Lindsey magnanimously offered what he called an "upper bound" of $100 billion to $200 billion. While thinking folks immediately detected a scent redolent of bovine leavings, Lindsey argued against all credulity that the cost was small, when one considers the "the successful prosecution of the war would be good for the economy."[73] Clearly he does not serve an infantry unit!

Lies, Myths, and Everything in Between

While there are entire aisles at your local "book megamart" solemnly devoted to demonstrating that most of the Arbusto administration's claims were and continue to be bumf, it's useful to rehearse the basic truths here once more for good measure. First, let's take the nuclear and related WMD claims. The Carnegie Endowment for International Peace (a prominent, well-respected, nonpartisan DC-based think tank) wrote, "With respect to nuclear and chemical weapons, the extent of the threat was largely knowable at the time . . . Iraq's nuclear program had been dismantled and there was no convincing evidence of reconstitution . . . Regarding chemical weapons, UNSCOM [United Nations Special Commission] discovered that Iraqi nerve agents had lost most of their lethality *as early as 1991*."[74] Note that this flies in the face of ex post facto administration claims that their mistakes were justifiable as these things were simply unknowable at the time. The Carnegie crew *did* find that there were some uncertainties when it came to Saddam's biological weapons, but "the real threat lay in what could be achieved in the future rather than in what had been produced in the past or existed in the present."[75] Only the missile program was in active development in 2002.[76]

George Bush et al alleged that Saddam was involved with 9/11 and necessarily in cahoots with Al-Qaeda too. In his 2003 State of the Union Address, the president invited Americans to envision "those 19 hijackers with other weapons and other plans—this time armed by Saddam Hussein. It would take one vial, one canister, one crate slipped into this country to bring a day of horror like none we have ever known."[77] It may surprise you to know that, strictly speaking, biological, chemical, and radiological weapons are not really capable of mass destruction, at least in part because they generally are difficult to deliver to the target without destroying the agent. If you just spray the stuff or let it evaporate, the gunk tends to dissipate and its concentration—and thus lethality—decreases with the cube of the radius (or volume, if you prefer). It's not impossible to kill several thousand people, as Saddam demonstrated, but it's not easy to kill en masse, and such effective killing with these things requires assets like helicopters dumping gunk on conurbations, which would be fairly easy to detect if our Department of Homeland Security isn't sleeping on the job—again. So, apart from the musings of Dick Cheney and associates, the sensible folks at Carnegie concluded, "There was and is no solid evidence of a cooperative relationship between Saddam's government and al Qaeda . . . In fact, however, there was no positive evidence to support the claim that Iraq would have transferred WMD or agents to terrorist groups and much evidence to counter it."[78]

Far from being unknowable and far from intel weenies making "simple mistakes," there is a growing consensus that "the dramatic shift between prior intelligence estimates and the October 2002 National Intelligence Estimate (NIE), together with the creation of an independent intelligence entity at the Pentagon and other steps, suggest that the intelligence community began to be unduly influenced by policymakers' views sometime in 2002."[79] Ouch. But that's not all: The Carnegie contingent further found that "administration officials systematically misrepresented the threat from Iraq's WMD and ballistic missile programs, beyond the intelligence failures noted above, by: Treating nuclear, chemical, and biological weapons as a single WMD threat . . . Insisting without evidence—yet treating as truth—that Saddam Hussein would give whatever WMD he possessed to terrorists. Routinely dropping caveats

Moving Heaven and Earth . . . or at Least a River

Everyone knows that Saddam had dozens of palaces littering Iraq like Soviet tanks along the Afghan countryside at a cost of over a billion bucks. To "enhance the beauty" of one of his palaces, he demanded—and received—a lake in its vicinity. To get the job done, engineers had to dig out and actually divert the Tigris River. Marble and even alabaster were brought in from historical places and tombs from the Babylonian era. So maybe we should give U.S. forces a break for letting all that looting happen: Saddam would have gotten around to those museum pieces eventually.[80]

. . . in intelligence estimates from public statements. Misrepresenting inspectors' findings in ways that turned threats from minor to dire."[81] That's a bitch slap—albeit tactfully and skillfully administered—if I ever read one! Of course, the good people at Carnegie are not alone in these judgments.

Even the U.S. Senate Select Committee on Intelligence came to somewhat similar conclusions in their comparatively banausic July 2004 report. While Carnegie took only 108 pages to cast aspersions upon the prewar efforts to manufacture national consent to a war that was not needed and a war that damaged—not advanced—U.S. national interests, the Select Committee on Intelligence took a leisurely *511 pages* to offer their critique of the "intelligence community" and its "intelligence." In that brain-bruising tome they found that "the major key judgments in the Intelligence Community's October 2002 National Intelligence Estimate (NIE), Iraq's Continuing Programs for Weapons of Mass Destruction, either overstated, or were not supported by, the underlying intelligence reporting."[82] Keep in mind that at the time, the U.S. Congress was still Republican dominated. So common sense and intellect are not partisan attributes of being a bipedal ape with opposable thumbs and a developed frontal lobe.

With these myths—in my view—decisively debunked, let's talk about what Saddam *did* do.[83] Even though he was not a clear and present danger to the United States or U.S. citizens or interests, Saddam was a terrible, nasty, gun-toting megalomaniac who killed people for sport. And it would appear that being a sadistic, egomaniacal, homicidal lunatic runs in this family. Qusay, the younger son who was likely to succeed his daddy, oversaw the Iraqi intelligence and security organizations (e.g., the Republican Guard and the Special Republican Guard). He helped his dad eliminate threats—real and imagined alike—by a variety of stomach-churning means and authorized interrogation, jailing, and execution of opponents, prisoners, and their families. Between 1988 and 1999 he ordered episodic mass prison execution of thousands of inmates (aka "prison cleansing" in Hussein parlance) and spearheaded the crackdown against the Shi'a in 1997 and other groups of folks deemed to be rabble-rousing foes of the regime.[84]

Saddam's eldest son, Uday, the president of the Iraqi National Olympic Committee, tortured athletes for losing their competitions! According to a report by ESPN, the world's sport's authority, Uday—among other crimes— imprisoned his athletes for days or months, beat them with iron bars, caned the soles of their feet, chained them to walls in contorted positions for days, and bloodied their backs by dragging them on pavement then dipped them in sewage to produce infected wounds. He was even known to urinate on detainees just to humiliate them.[85] I know ESPN is not the most reputable source on such things, but these claims have been buttressed by every human rights organization that ever glanced in Iraq's general direction.

Unnerving Ways to Get Rid of Your Own

Presidents Bush were right about Saddam's use of nerve gas: He gassed the hell out of his own citizens. In the Anfal military campaign, he tried to destroy the countryside of Iraqi Kurdistan and Kurdish residents. By the end of the summer of 1990, his regime had wiped out some 4,000 of 4,500 villages in Kurdistan. Between 1987 and 1990 the Kurdistan government believes that some 182,000 Kurds died during the Anfal. One of the means by which this genocide was perpetrated was the use of nerve gas distributed via helicopters and shells. During the gassing of Halabja, more than 5,000 persons died a truly gruesome death.

While both George Bushes decried that Saddam "gassed his own people," no one seemed to make a peep at the time of the actual gassing—far from it. Because it occurred during the Iran-Iraq war and because the Reagan administration had hoped that Saddam would become "our bastard Saddam" in the U.S. effort to squash Iran, no one squeaked about this heinous atrocity. Galbraith claims that years earlier, in 1983, the Reagan administration told the CIA to share battlefield intelligence with the Iraqis so that they could gas the *Iranians* with greater accuracy. (See the chapter on Iran.) However, even after the horrors of Halabja, the Reagan administration continued providing that information to Iraq to help them use their chemical weapons with greater lethality. Oddly, the Reagan administration removed Iraq from the State Department's list of terror-supporting states, even though there had been no substantive change in Baghdad's support of Palestinian militant groups in 1983. That year the Reagan folks began subsidizing Saddam's military needs, and by 1988 these subsidies approached *$1 billion* annually.[86] Saddam also hated the Shi'a in his country, and they too suffered horrors under his watch. This is why the Shi'a celebrated his inelegant hanging and smuggled in phones with imbedded cameras to film Saddam's "necktie party." Footage of the dangling Saddam circulated immediately throughout Iraq, generating outrage among Sunnis who feel that they are tyrannized by the Shi'a—some of whom have been dishing up plates of revenge with the same rapidity, quantity, and quality of a KBR mess hall.

In the afterglow of his victory in the six-week 1991 U.S. war on Iraq, George Bush Sr. gave a speech at Raytheon in Andover, Massachusetts, ostensibly to praise the "Patriot anti-missile missile," manufactured there. (Raytheon is a scion of the military-industry complex.) During Bush Sr.'s peroration, he glibly ad-libbed that the Iraqi military and people alike should rise up and topple Hussein. His musings were reissued and circulated widely on every squawk box in the region and beyond. Unfortunately, many Iraqis took the president at his word and rose up against the Evil Doer—and they were slaughtered for it. The Shi'a went nuts tearing apart the bodies of Ba'ath officials and looting offices and military installations. It took Saddam ten days to get control over the Shi's rebellion, but he did and his retribution was fierce. He blew up their shrines, massacred civilians, hung men en masse off the gun barrels of tanks, and, of course, raped and pillaged women and girls with rapine ferocity.[87] Similar uprisings and concomitant slaughter took place in Iraqi Kurdistan.

Bush Sr. was incredulous that his words—the words of the victorious leader of the free world—would have such an effect. In fact, he explicitly *did not want* to topple Saddam, as it would be "destabilizing." As such, U.S. troops had to stand by and watch these gruesome events, since they were not authorized to stop the killing. In the joint memoir of Bush Sr. and his national security advisor, Brent Snowcroft, the latter wrote, "While we hoped that a popular revolt or a coup would topple Saddam, neither the United States nor the countries of the region wished to see the breakup of the Iraqi state . . .

However admirable self-determination for the Kurds or Shiites might have been in principle, the practical aspects of this particular situation dictated the policy [of inaction and apathy]."[88] Thus I remain baffled and even flummoxed by the ex post facto "outrage" and "indignity" over the horrors of the Saddam regime that U.S. political entrepreneurs espouse when appropriately intemperate outbursts of moral revulsion are demanded.

There can be no doubt that Saddam was truly a horrible human being who subjected his population to violence and cruelty that is difficult to fathom. But many have questioned whether Iraqis are better off under U.S. occupation than under Saddam. The answer no doubt depends on who you are. The Shi'a are politically better off freed from Saddam's shackles and under the tutelage of Iran, which now has a free hand in the country. The Sunnis are not thrilled, because they fear that life under any government with proportionate representation would give the Shi'a free rein to exact their revenge for decades of repression—and the data suggest that this is true. The Kurds are no doubt continuing to march toward the independence that they have long craved and for which they have paid a heavy price. But throughout most of Iraq—and even increasingly in Kurdistan—various kinds of insurgency and civil war have brought a hitherto unknown insecurity. If the counterinsurgency forces are not killing folks, then suicide bombers (most of whom are not actually Iraqi) are, and sectarian militias clash with bloody consequence.

Hilarity with Hussein

Saddam once remarked of the United States, "You Americans, you treat the Third World in the way an Iraqi peasant treats his new bride. Three days of honeymoon, and then it's off to the fields."[89]

In this backdrop, it has become a morbid parlor game to offer "body counts" and to engage in silly banter over which regime was more sanguinary: U.S.-occupied Iraq or Saddam-controlled Iraq. Opponents and proponents alike have their preferred forensic arithmetic, and the estimates of the dead greatly differ. According to the Iraq Body Count project, there had been between 75,151 and 81,887 slain as of October 17, 2007.[90] The Brooking Institute, using an index based on the Iraq Body Count and incorporating figures from Iraq's Ministry of the Interior and the United Nations' Assistance Mission to Iraq, reported that between the onset of the war in May 2003 and December 2006 there were 53,000 to 76,500 deaths.[91] That's a lot of dead folks, but the true figures—like everything else involving Iraq—are likely to be higher. In fact, in October 2006 the *Lancet* reported that since the invasion in March 2003, "about 655,000 Iraqis have died above the number that would be expected in a non-conflict situation."[92]

Republicans and supporters of the Bush policy have pulled out their own wacky abacuses to come up with mortality figures that support the U.S. invasion. Writing for the arch-conservative *Renew America,* Mary Mostert claimed that "the mostly American liberation of Iraq dropped the rate of violent deaths from 50,000 a year under Saddam Hussein to 6,825 a year with the Americans in Baghdad. What [Senator Ted] Kennedy has labeled as American 'savagery' has REDUCED deaths from violence in Iraq by 87%."[93] You can be the judge of those numbers and that source.

Cooking in Mess-o-Potamia[94]

Whenever I mention Iraqi cuisine, I get a lot of quizzical queries and snide quips about the Oil for Food scam. It is true that in recent decades, layers of sanctions, Saddam's maniacal resource hogging and frequent homicidal rages, and the U.S.-led war and subsequent occupation have all made food a scarce commodity for many Iraqis. These conditions have created lucrative opportunities for personal enrichment among the Iraqi and global elite, as the defunct Oil for Food program illustrates, leaving the Iraqi people to starve.[95]

While contemporary Iraq has fallen under hard times and while there is indeed little to celebrate—the Bush administration's assertions notwithstanding—we *can* celebrate Iraq's culinary past and hope (or pray, if you are a believer) that a better future awaits the hapless country and its inhabitants who deserve much, much better. As relic-swiping archeologists, Iraqi museum looters, and curators alike remind us, Iraq was the cradle of civilization. As such, Iraqi food in its origins is biblical in, as Stephen Colbert might say, its "ancientiness." In fact, recipes from Babylon are among the first in *recorded* human history, having been imprinted on numerous cuneiform tablets that date back to *1600 B.C.* These are called the Yale Babylonian Collection, or YBC.

The past is indeed the best predictor of the future. One of those tablets (Tablet A) mapped out recipes for broths and stews—a favorite among Iraqis to this day. In the olden days, they made broths from the spleens and other organs of deer, gazelles, rams, and other critters without obvious or certain translation. Another set of tablets (Tablets Bi-Biv and Tablet C) describe—in ridiculous detail—the beheading, plucking, gutting, organ-membrane removing, and otherwise preparing various domestic and game birds for multifarious culinary demises. These small, large, and middling birds are variously roasted, cooked in milk or broth, or stuck in porridges. Tablet C even calls for some animal to be killed, chopped up, and cooked in a stew. As a penultimate step, the cook tosses in the animal's blood with some garlic—delicious![96]

For you curious wiseacres, a linguist has already translated these recipes and, in 1986, hosted a feast featuring the biblical nosh. Some French folks did the same thing, and both wrote about their messes in various arcane academic journals. The different parties wildly disagreed on the tastiness of the dishes, but the verdict is not yet in: Was it the fault of the recipes or of the cooks? The debate rages among the tiny number folks who care about such things.[97] Indeed, Iraqis still love their birds—on their plates, that is—and this dinner party will feature a popular aviary delicacy.

The Plan of Attack

This plan of attack presumes you are feeding a crowd of eight rattle-boned diners; adjust accordingly. You can make the okra in advance, as it does well in the fridge. The chicken/turkey stuffing can also be made in advance, as well as the shell and stuffing for the *kubeh*. You can't make the entire *kubeh* in advance, since it should be assembled and fried while the *dolmah* (stuffed vegetables) simmer away in their pot and the stuffed bird roasts in the oven. The dessert—date cookies—can also be made in advance and stored in an airtight container.

Main course

■ *Margat Bamya* (okra and lamb stew) with flatbread. Iraqis *love* okra, and this dish is considered an Iraqi culinary standard. Iraqis don't serve their stews over couscous like they do in North Africa; instead, they ladle it over plain boiled rice or bulgur. This dish can be served with plain rice, and you are welcome to do so, but I think this menu would then be too "ricey," given that the bird is stuffed with fruit and rice and the *dolmah* are stuffed with lamb and, yes, rice. The traditional way of eating *this* stew is to ladle it into bowls whose bottoms have been lined with a flatbread called *khubuz al-tannour*. I haven't been able to find this bread, and making it without a tandoor (aka tannour, or clay oven) seems impossible. We'll use the common pita bread instead, which is widely available.

- *Dijaj Mahshi* (chicken or turkey stuffed with rice, fruit, and nuts, then coated in yogurt and baked)
- *Dolmah* (vegetables stuffed with lamb and rice, simmered in a tomato broth)
- Iraqi *kubeh* (lamb stuffed in bulgur shells) with *tahina* sauce. *Tahina* is made from the gunk called "tahini," which is sesame paste.
- Iraqi-style salad

Dessert

- *Klaycha at-Tamr* (date cookies)

Beverages

- Beer! Beer was the beverage of choice of the Babylonians. Brewing and swigging the ancient concoction was an important Babylonian activity and has been immortalized on Sumerian cylinder seals from the third millennium B.C. We are going to drink beer with our dinner and raise our mugs to the ancient Iraqis. (Again, nondrinkers should always feel free to substitute nonalcoholic variants.) It may interest you to know that while the Hussein regime claimed to hate Israel, it seemed to enjoy Israeli beer. There are press reports (the veracity of which I cannot confirm or deny) that Saddam's sadistic sons, Qusay and Uday, spent their last hours quaffing Maccabee—a pale, simple lager of the much-loathed Zionist state. Some beer snobs would suggest that maybe Israel is loathed in the Muslim world *because* of Maccabee, trashing it as the Israeli equivalent of Miller Genuine Draft (MDG) or worse, Pabst Blue Ribbon (PBR). When my husband and I went to the Israeli Oppressor State, we actually enjoyed sipping our chilled Maccabee and couldn't figure out what the grouse was about. If you can't find Maccabee at your local Israeli supermarket, you might as well pick up Bud, PBR, or MGD. If you want to aim a bit higher, go for Pilsner Urquell or Heineken. For those who insist upon wine, I suggest a cabernet sauvignon or even a Gewürztraminer.
- Cardamom-spiced Arabic coffee to be served with dessert

PREPARATION

MAIN COURSE

Margat Bamya *(Okra and Lamb Stew)*

Be warned: Okra is a finicky flora. I loathed okra growing up because we usually ate it frozen or, worse, canned. If you use frozen okra, it will be slimy like
the innards of an aloe plant. This is not appealing, so follow these tips to minimize okra slime. If using fresh okra, which is ideal, *do not rinse* it with water.
This seems to encourage the slime. Simply wipe the okra with a damp towel
as you would a mushroom. Trim around the conical stem attached to the pod
to remove inedible parts *without cutting the pod*. This allows you to eat the entire
thing without the unpleasant glop. If you find yourself with no recourse but
frozen okra, once you thaw it, you will feel the slime all over the pods. The
gunk won't go away with cooking, so you need to get rid of it before you start.
First, trim both ends such that you can see the tiny holes in them. (Don't cut
it up—you just want to nip the ends.) Place in a bowl and coat with about ½
cup distilled white vinegar for each pound of frozen okra. Toss and let it stand
for 30 minutes. Rinse thoroughly to remove the vinegar *and,* thankfully, much
of the slime. Repeat this process if it makes you feel better. It won't remove
all the slime, but it does a good job.

Ingredients
1 pound fresh, *small* okra (Use frozen only as a last resort.)
2 tablespoons ghee (Use vegetable oil if you don't want to pick up ghee
    from the Asian section of your supermarket.)
1 yellow onion, finely sliced
3 cloves garlic, finely diced
1 pound lamb cut in 1-inch chunks (either shoulder or leg)

At least 1 cup hot water (more as needed)

2 or 3 green peppers (jalapeños or the small, slender Asian peppers), or 1 teaspoon red pepper powder (This is optional. If you want the flavor of the pepper without the heat, you can *carefully* remove the seeds and veins.)

1 cup chopped Roma tomatoes (about 2 or 3 tomatoes)

1½ teaspoons sea salt

⅛ teaspoon freshly ground black pepper

1 teaspoon ground coriander

3 tablespoons tomato paste diluted in 3 cups low-fat, low-sodium chicken broth

¼ cup lemon juice

For garnish:

Pita, torn into 2-inch pieces (Each guest should get ½ pita or more.)

Parsley sprigs

Let's get cooking

1. Prepare the okra per instructions above.
2. Heat the ghee and sauté the onions, garlic, and lamb chunks until the meat is thoroughly browned. Add 1 cup hot water or enough to cover the meat. Bring to a low boil and let the meat simmer until it is tender and the water evaporates. If the water evaporates and the meat is not yet tender, add more water and repeat. With a decent cut of lamb, this should take about 20 minutes.
3. Add the okra, green peppers or red pepper powder (if used), chopped tomatoes, salt, pepper, coriander, diluted tomato paste, and lemon juice and cook until the okra is tender and the flavors incorporated. This should take about 20 minutes.
4. Serve in bowls with pita (or plain white rice). Place pita pieces in the bottom of your guests' bowls and ladle the stew onto it. Garnish with fresh parsley sprigs.

Dijaj Mahshi *(Chicken or Turkey Stuffed with Rice, Fruit, and Nuts and Coated in Yogurt)*

The small "natural" chickens specified in this recipe most resemble the kind of birds folks eat in the greater Middle East, and, frankly, they just taste better. Feel free, however, to use a larger monster chicken or even a smallish (about 8-pound) turkey. (Arabs eat a lot of turkey, actually.) You need only adjust oven temperature and times. I prefer using 2 small chickens because they are so tasty and they cook quickly.

Ingredients

For the meat:

2 small (4-pound) organic chickens, preferably kosher, or 1 small (8-pound) turkey

Salt and pepper to season

For the stuffing:

¼ cup ghee

2 yellow onions, finely chopped

1 cup basmati rice, picked over for foreign objects, rinsed once in cold water, and soaked in 3 cups water for at least 1 hour to soften

1 cup dried fruit (I like coarsely chopped dried dates or raisins, but feel free to experiment with chopped dried apricots or prunes.)

½ cup pine nuts

½ cup coarsely chopped walnuts

1 teaspoon allspice

2 teaspoons sea salt

3 cups low-fat, low-sodium chicken stock

For the bird coating:

1 cup low-fat yogurt

1 teaspoon cinnamon

2 teaspoons dried coriander

For garnish:

Sprigs of flat parsley and cilantro

Let's get cooking

1. Prepare the bird (s).
   a. Remove the gizzards then rinse the bird(s) in cold water and pat dry. Season with salt and pepper. Set aside.
   b. Preheat the oven to 350 degrees if using 2 small chickens. If using a smallish turkey, preheat the oven to 325 degrees.
2. Prepare the stuffing.
   a. Heat the ghee and fry the onions until translucent (about 5 minutes). Add the rice and fry until translucent (about another 5 minutes).
   b. Add the dried fruit, nuts, allspice, and salt and fry for a few minutes. (The dried fruit will puff up a little.)
   c. Add the chicken stock and bring to a boil. Reduce heat and simmer until the rice is tender the fluid is soaked up and/or evaporated. This will take about 10–15 minutes. Transfer to a bowl to encourage faster cooling. Let cool until it can be safely handled.
3. While the stuffing cooks, make the yogurt coating. Whip the yogurt, cinnamon, and coriander together in a bowl. This mixture will be used to coat the bird(s) and will become a gorgeous and tasty crust.
4. Stuff the bird(s) with the cooled stuffing. (Some folks say not to overstuff birds, but I cram in as much as I can!) Sew up the bird's cavity if need be. I usually use 2 toothpicks to cinch the fat flaps together for the small birds. Be sure to unsew or remove toothpicks before serving.
5. Cook the birds.
   a. If cooking 2 chickens, place in 2 foil-lined pans. If cooking a turkey, line a large pan with foil. (The foil helps with cleanup, because the yogurt coating will blacken and is difficult to remove.) Spray the foil with nonstick cooking spray. Massage the yogurt mixture all over the front and back of the bird(s), getting the wings and legs thoroughly coated.
   b. Place the bird(s) in the pan(s) *breast down*. This helps keep them moist. The fat is on the back, and it will naturally drain down and baste the bird(s), which makes it virtually impossible to get a dry, nasty chicken.
   c. Insert a meat thermometer into the center of one of the inside thigh muscles. (Don't let the thermometer touch the bone.) Cover the bird(s) with foil. Try not to let the foil touch the bird(s) and seal carefully. This will prevent excessive browning of the yogurt "crust" that will develop. I keep the foil on the entire cooking time.

d. If you are using 2 small chickens, cook at 350 degrees until the thermometer reads about 175 degrees. Pull the birds out and let them sit covered for another 10 minutes. They will keep cooking, and the desired 180 degrees will be reached. If you are worried, keep them in the oven until the thermometer reads 180 degrees. Once the birds have sat covered for 10 minutes or so, you can begin carving. Cooking time for the chickens should be about 1½ hours or more, depending on the actual size of the birds. If using a turkey, cook at 325 degrees for about 3¼ hours (plus or minus 15 minutes, depending on actual size of bird). Using the same temperature guidelines as for the chickens, pull the turkey out of the oven when the temperature reaches 175. Let the turkey rest covered for 15 minutes before serving. (If you are afraid of nasty things in your bird, keep it in the oven until the thermometer reads 180.) For both birds, the stuffing temperature should be around 160–165 degrees. If you want to check the specs on your bird, *Better Homes and Gardens* has a roasting guide at www.bhg.com/bhg/story.jsp?storyid=/ templatedata/bhg/story/data /RoastingGuide_08242004.xml. (You have to register, but it's free to use.)

6. Carve and serve. Garnish with the stuffing and the sprigs of parsley and cilantro.

Dolmah *(Vegetables Stuffed with Lamb and Rice, Simmered in a Tomato Broth)*

Ingredients

For the stuffing:

1 pound ground lamb (I strongly recommend lamb, but you can use other ground meat if you prefer.)

1 cup basmati rice, picked over to remove nonrice objects and rinsed once to remove excess starch

1 yellow onion, finely chopped

4 cloves garlic, pressed or finely chopped

2 Roma tomatoes, finely chopped

½ cup finely chopped flat parsley leaves

½ cup finely chopped cilantro leaves

2 teaspoons sea salt, plus additional amount for salting vegetables

1 teaspoon freshly ground black pepper

1 teaspoon allspice

½ teaspoon cumin

1 tablespoon olive oil

For the vegetables:

3 bell peppers (I like red ones best, but take your pick.)

2 small zucchinis

2 small yellow squashes

2 small eggplants (Italian eggplants work well.)

2 big, beefy tomatoes

Grape leaves (These are brined and found in jars in the Middle Eastern section of grocery stores. If you can't find them, get 2 additional vegetables of your choice for stuffing.)

1 15-ounce can crushed tomatoes mixed with 2 cups low-fat, low-sodium chicken stock if using pressure cooker; if using stove-top method, double both ingredients

For garnish:

Coarsely chopped cilantro

Let's get cooking

1. By hand, mix the meat, rice, onions, garlic, chopped tomatoes, parsley, cilantro, salt, pepper, allspice, cumin, and olive oil. Make sure all ingredients are thoroughly incorporated.

2. Prepare the vegetables.

   a. For the bell peppers, slice off the tops and remove the seeds and veins. Retain the tops. Rub a small amount of salt into the peppers.

   b. For the squashes and eggplants, cut off the tops. Using an apple corer, scrape out the vegetable matter, leaving at least ¼ inch of the flesh to ensure that it retains its structure during cooking. If your squashes are long and skinny (and your apple corer can't get in far enough), you can cut the squashes and eggplants in half crosswise and scrape out the halves easily with your corer. (By the way, knifes don't work for this and it's dangerous, so don't try.) You'll lose points on style, not on taste. Put a bit of salt on your finger and rub it inside the squashes and eggplants.

There is no need to keep the tops of the squashes and eggplants.

    c. For the tomatoes, cut off the top and scrape out the jelly. Salt the inside and reserve the top.

    d. For the grape leaves (in brine), rinse off 8 leaves or so. These will be used for any leftover stuffing you may have.

3. Stuff the vegetables lightly with the lamb and rice mixture. Don't overstuff, as the stuffing will expand. Put small amounts of the remaining mixture on the grape leaves and fold like a burrito. The leaf is vaguely hand shaped. To stuff, place the leaf with the "palm" closest to you and "fingers" pointing away from you. Place the stuffing at the bottom of the "palm." Roll away from yourself while folding in the center leaves onto the mound. Set aside with the seam down. Repeat until all stuffing is used.

4. Arrange the vegetables in a pot to cook. I use a pressure cooker, but you can also use a stove-top pot. The arrangement of vegetables is the same—only the cooking time and fluid varies. Put the tops back on the peppers and arrange them on the bottom of your pressure cooker or pot. This is the base layer. Arrange the squashes, the eggplants, and the tomatoes (with their tops back on) on top of and between the peppers. Place the stuffed grape leaves between the vegetables where there is space. Prop their seams against a veggie to ensure they don't unwrap.

5. If using a pressure cooker, pour the tomato-broth mixture over all of the vegetables and cook until the rice is tender. Follow the instructions for your pressure cooker. (It takes my mine about 40 minutes to cook these things.) If using a pot on your stove, pour the tomato mixture over the veggies. (Remember that you are using twice as much tomato-broth mixture with this method.) Bring the liquid to a boil, lower the heat, cover, and simmer until the rice is cooked. This will take about 1½ hours. Serve hot.

Iraqi Kubeh *(Lamb Stuffed in Bulgur Shells)* with Tahina Sauce

Many countries in the Middle East have their own versions of *kubeh* (which some call "kibbeh" and the like). Iraqis have an array of *kubeh* variants, including one whose shell is made of saffron rice! Some variants call for the shell to be made with meat, but not this one. This one is very easy to make.

Ingredients

For the shells:

1 cup fine (e.g., #2 grain) bulgur (This can be found in the Middle Eastern or kosher section of large supermarkets or specialty shops.)

2 cups water

½ teaspoon allspice

½ teaspoon cumin

½ teaspoon sea salt

At least ¼ cup flour (more as needed)

1 quart canola oil for frying

For the meat stuffing:

4 tablespoons ghee

1 large yellow onion, finely chopped

3 cloves garlic, pressed or finely chopped

1 pound ground lamb

¼ cup pine nuts

1 teaspoon allspice

1 teaspoon cumin

½ teaspoon freshly ground black pepper

1 teaspoon sea salt

For the *tahina* sauce:

½ cup tahini paste (This can be found in the Middle Eastern or kosher section of your grocery store. It is a thick paste made of ground sesame seeds. It will likely come with a thick layer of oil on top because the oil is lighter than the paste. Be sure to stir the oil into the paste before use. Once stirred, you can keep the tahini in the refrigerator and the oil should not separate out again.)

¼ cup finely chopped parsley

2 cloves garlic, crushed

¼ cup freshly squeezed lemon juice

¼ cup warm water

1 tablespoon olive oil

½ teaspoon sea salt

Let's get cooking

1. Soak the bulgur in 2 cups water in a large bowl for 45 minutes. The bulgur will expand as it soaks up the water.

2. While the bulgur soaks, begin the stuffing. Heat the ghee and fry the onions and garlic until the onions are translucent. Add the meat and brown thoroughly. When browned, remove any excess fluid. Continue frying with the pine nuts, spices, and salt. Transfer to a bowl and let cool. The stuffing can be made in advance and kept in the refrigerator. If you do this, be sure to let it warm up to room temperature before use.

3. Make the *tahina* sauce. Using a chopper or immersion blender, mix together all the ingredients and chill until it has the consistency of a thick salad dressing (like French or ranch). If it's too thick, add more water and lemon juice in 1-teaspoon increments until desired consistency is reached. If it's too runny, add tahini paste in 1-teaspoon increments. (Every brand of tahini paste is different in its thickness.) Adjust salt to preferred taste.

4. Return to the bulgur for the shells. Squeeze out as much water as possible from the soaked bulgur and transfer to a clean bowl.

5. Add the spices, salt, and ¼ cup of the flour. Kneed to incorporate throughout. Keep adding flour and kneading until the dough holds together and can be handled without sticking to your hands. (Hint: I spray my hands often with cooking spray while handling and shaping the dough.)

6. Form the dough into 8 even-size balls. These will eventually become torpedo shaped once filled with the meat mixture, so keep this in mind as you shape the balls for stuffing. Make an indentation in the middle of each ball with your index finger. Begin working around the ball until you get a hollowed-out ovular cup, akin to an egg cup. You can stop shaping the shell when it's about ¼ inch thick and about 3 inches long or thereabouts. If you can't get it just right, do your best. Once you have the right thickness and length, gently spoon in about 1 heaping tablespoon of the filling. Add more if it will fit comfortably, but don't overstuff or it won't close. Close the end by cinching the open part until the edges meet. Gently shape the thing into the familiar torpedo shape. If it rips, you can massage it or even pinch it to close. Set aside. Repeat for the remaining 7 balls. (If it's easier, shape in whatever form you like!)

7. Fill ⅔ of a medium-size skillet with canola oil and heat. Don't fill it too much because the *kubeh,* when added, will displace the volume. When the oil is hot, add the *kubeh* gently and fry until they are golden brown. You will need to roll each *kubeh* over to ensure that the whole surface is fried evenly. This only takes about 5 minutes or so with adequately hot oil. Remove with a slotted spoon and serve with *tahina* sauce, which you can prepare before or during the frying.

Iraqi-style Salad

Ingredients
For the salad:
4 cups cleaned romaine lettuce, chopped into salad-appropriate-size pieces
4 Roma tomatoes, coarsely chopped
2 medium cucumbers (or 4 small Kirby cucumbers), cleaned and coarsely chopped
8 scallions, finely sliced crosswise
1 red bell pepper, finely chopped
1 cup finely chopped flat parsley
1 red radish, thinly sliced

For the dressing:
2 cloves garlic, pressed
1 teaspoon sea salt
½ cup lemon juice
½ cup olive oil or grape seed oil (I prefer the grape seed oil, because it has a flavor with which most folks are unfamiliar.)
⅛ teaspoon freshly ground black pepper

Let's get tossing
1. Toss all of the vegetables into a bowl.
2. Whisk the ingredients together for the dressing.
3. Dress the salad and serve immediately.

DESSERT
★★★★★★★★★★★★★★★★★★★★★★★★★

Klaycha at-Tamr *(Date Cookies)*

These cookies are a staple when folks break their fasts during Ramadan.

Ingredients

For the dough:

3 cups unbleached flour

½ cup demerara or raw cane sugar (Yes, you can substitute the white stuff if you must.)

1 teaspoon sea salt

8 ounces (1 cup) unsalted butter, softened

2 tablespoons rosewater

½ cup cold water

For the stuffing:

4 tablespoons ghee

8 ounces pitted dates, finely chopped

1 cup walnuts, finely chopped

1 teaspoon ground cardamom

Let's get cooking

1. For the dough, sift the flour, sugar, and salt together into a large mixing bowl. Cut the butter into pieces and, using a pastry cutter (or fork), cut the butter into the flour until the butter is evenly distributed and the mixture is "grainy" in texture. (This is just like making biscuits.)

2. Add the rosewater to the water and whisk together. Sprinkle the liquid onto the flour/butter mixture and knead to form a firm dough. (I find it helpful to spray my hands with cooking spray to keep the dough from clinging to them.) Let the dough rest for 30 minutes, covered in the refrigerator.

3. While the dough rests, make the stuffing. Warm the ghee in a frying pan. Add the dates, walnuts, and cardamom and stir to heat. The dates should soften. Stir often to prevent the walnuts from burning. Remove from heat and spoon into a cool bowl to stop further cooking. Let the mixture cool.

4. Before making the cookies, line at least 2 baking sheets with parchment

paper. There are a number of ways to make these cookies, and you can take your pick. I prefer the last option, because I am not a talented pastry maker.

a. Some folks use complex molds to make pyramids. They work the dough into the mold, insert the date filling, press the mold together, and gently remove the oddly shaped cookies. (You are on your own with this option.)

b. If you want a bit of elegance without the work of the option above, you can make swirl-patterned cookies. This is infinitely doable. Divide the pastry into 3 portions and roll each out into a rectangle about ½ inch thick and 4 inches wide on one side. Distribute ⅓ of the date mixture evenly along the long edge of the rectangle. Roll the pastry away from yourself, beginning with the long edge with the filling. Repeat for the remaining dough and filling. Refrigerate for 30 minutes to firm. Slice the date roll into ½-inch-thin cookies. The cookies should have a swirl pattern.

c. This is what *I* do. I remove the dough from the fridge. I make small balls, about 1½ inches in diameter. I partially flatten the balls to make the cookie. With my thumb, I make a depression across most of the cookie's surface and stuff as much of the date filling into each as possible. Each cookie ends up looking like a date pizza. Obviously, pace yourself to ensure that each cookie gets some date goo. I usually put a modest amount on *all cookies* and then, after reassessing how much date filling remains, I incorporate more filling into each cookie.

5. Bake at 350 degrees for 25–30 minutes or until the cookies are a light golden color (akin to a butter cookie). Remove and transfer to a cooling rack. Serve with cardamom-spiced Arabic coffee or regular coffee.

BEVERAGE

★★ ★★★★★★★★★★ ★★★★★★

Cardamom-Spiced Arabic Coffee

It is best to use a specialized stove-top pot for making Arabic coffee. If you don't happen to have this, you can make do with a saucepan, preferably with a lip for pouring.

IRAQ

Ingredients

8 heaping tablespoons pulverized coffee. (You may find Arabic grinds at a
  specialty market; otherwise, use a good roast of coffee bean and grind
  the heck out of it. It should be a *fine* powder.)

8 cups water

12 crushed cardamom pods

2 tablespoons sugar (optional), or serve with sugar cubes

Add the coffee, cardamom, and sugar (if used) to the water and bring to
a boil. When the froth rises up, remove from the heat for a few seconds and
stir. Repeat 2 times. Allow the coffee sludge to settle for a few minutes. Pour
into tiny glasses (if you have demitasses, go ahead and use them). I try to
avoid the sludge when pouring. Serve with sugar cubes if desired.

If all of this is a nuisance, you can make regular coffee, but do add the cardamom to the coffee basket.

PART
II

The NPT+3 States:
Israel, India, and Pakistan

THE NPT+3 STATES:
ISRAEL, INDIA, AND PAKISTAN

The Nuclear Nonproliferation Treaty (NPT) entered into force in 1970.[98] It recognized five permanent nuclear weapons states—the United States, the then Soviet Union (now Russia), China, France, and the United Kingdom—all of whom had verified bomb designs before the NPT went into effect. These states comprise the so-called Permanent Five (P5) of the United Nations Security Council (UNSC). Most countries in the world signed on to the NPT as non-nuclear weapons states. As such, the treaty—though beleaguered and beaten—still remains a global norm.

Notably, there have been other countries that sought nuclear weapons but for various reasons concluded that they were safer without them. Namely Argentina, Brazil, and South Africa abandoned their nuke programs and joined the NPT as non-nuclear weapons states. And then there is North Korea, which signed as a non-nuclear weapons state but then withdrew from the treaty and, after a decent interval, tested a device to show they had nuclear scrotal fortitude.

The three countries in this section—Israel, India, and Pakistan—are not among those states with nuclear remorse. These three, the "NPT+3," refused to sign the NPT because the nonproliferation regime did not permit any other nuclear weapons states other than the P5. Given that these states wanted nukes, it would make little sense to sign a treaty that they would abrogate—and get hammered for doing so. (So far North Korea hasn't been hammered for dumping its commitments. Far from it. Every time it throws a ballistic fit, it gets placated with all sorts of goodies such as proliferation-resistant nuclear facilities, fuel oil, and cash.) While Israel, India, and Pakistan are included in this culinary foreign policy critique because they pursued nukes outside of the scope of the NPT, they are all hideous human rights violators, a lamentable situation that merits considerable discussion herein.

Dossier of Israeli Perfidy

Israel is included in this gustatory rebuke because it, like India and Pakistan, has acquired nuclear weapons outside of the Nuclear Nonproliferation Treaty (NPT) with great stealth and deception. Israel began its quest for the bomb in its earliest years. As far back as 1948, Israeli scientists began exploring the Negev Desert for uranium. By 1950 they discovered low-grade deposits there and soon mastered extraction methods along with heavy-water production. Ernst David Bergman, a talented immigrant scientist, became the director of the Israeli Atomic Energy Commission and headed the Ministry of Defense's Research and Infrastructure Division (known by the Hebrew acronym EMET). A close friend and adviser to Israeli's first Prime Minister, David Ben-Gurion, he led the charge to get the bomb, believing that it was the best way to ensure "that we will never again be led as lambs to slaughter."[99]

France was Israel's nuclear patron, a relationship that was transformed by the fiasco that was the Suez Crisis. Israel—along with France and Great Britain—planned and staged a military operation against Egypt in October 1956, following Egypt's closure of the Suez Canal. Six weeks before the launch of that military misadventure, Israel asked France to provide a nuclear reactor. (Canada's provision of the 40-MWt CIRUS reactor to India served as the precedent.) The French agreed to provide Israel with an 18-MWt *research* reactor. However, the Suez operation was a debacle. While the Israelis fulfilled their end of the bargain and occupied the entire Sinai Peninsula by November 4, 1956, the supporting French and British invasion on November 6 was an unmitigated failure, and their effort to push south was aborted following a cease-fire brought about by American and Soviet pressure. The UK and France bailed, leaving Israel to countenance nuclear brandishments from the Soviet Union. The French were rightly humiliated by their inability to protect their ally, and French premier Guy Mollet said privately that France "owed" Israel the bomb. Chagrined, France upped their nuclear generosity and pledged to help Israel obtain a nuclear deterrent. The two countries cooperated so closely that Israel even helped France develop the nuclear-capable Mirage fighter jet.[100]

The French and Israelis beavered away in the Negev Desert to build the reactor at Dimona, and the Israelis set up an organization exclusively to maintain secrecy around the plant there (the Office of Science Liasons, or LEKEM). When construction was at a fevered pitch, there were some 1,500 individuals working in that sleepy desert town populated by Bedouins. Israel used several cover stories for the activity there, declaring it to be a manganese plant, a desalinization facility, a textile plant, a chocolate factory, a film factory, and the like. The pesky French even bought heavy water from Norway with the condition that there be no third-party transfers, but the French air force secretly flew as much as four tons of the stuff to Israel.

Under de Gaulle the French suddenly developed a conscience and fretted about the consequences should all this nuclear footsie come to light, as it surely would. (I mean, how long can you pretend a nuclear reactor in the desert is a desalinization tank destined for Latin America?[101]) Absurdly, France wanted the Israelis to demur from making bombs, come out of the closet, and submit the site to international inspections.

In hindsight, the French fussing was gratuitous. The fact is that the United States had "failed" to figure out what was going on in part because it did not want to know and in part because it was easily tricked. In fact, U.S. inspectors went to Dimona seven times during the 1960s, but the Israelis hid all of the good stuff. They even installed faux control panels and bricked over elevators and passageways to more nefarious parts of the facility.[102] We now know that Washington was not terribly interested in knowing and did nothing to stop the program. During the bomb program's critical years (1961–1973), U.S. Ambassador Walworth Barbour's mission was to insulate the president from these facts. After the 1967 war, he dispensed with military attaches' intelligence collecting in and around Dimona because they were certain to discover inconvenient truths. When Israel began mating warheads to missiles, Barbour felt obliged to cable Washington, but the information just disappeared in bureaucratic vapor. By 1968 the CIA finally concluded that Israel had begun nuclear weapons production using materials from Dimona.[103]

Nuclear Weapons or Not? That Is the Question

Unlike India or Pakistan, it is not clear whether or not Israel has ever tested nuclear weapons. However, speculation is rife that the Israelis and the South Africans conducted a joint test in the Indian Ocean in 1979. The U.S. Central Intelligence Agency believed that this was plausible at least in part because the Israelis had participated in South African nuclear research during the preceding several years.[104] It is, of course, only fitting that these two apartheid states—only one of which has since reformed, and that state is not Israel—would pair up for a nuclear fandango in the sea.

Indeed, Israel has never confirmed that it has a nuclear weapon, and was pretty peeved when its radioactive cat was let out of the bag in 1986 by Mordechai Vanunu. The "dismissed" Israeli nuclear technician photographed Israeli nukes and related underground facilities, immigrated to Australia, and published the photos along with descriptions in the London *Sunday Times*. Keeping with the long-standing and well-honed Israeli tradition of kidnapping foes, Mossad agents drugged and nabbed Vanunu in Rome, having lured him there with the charms of a deceptive, seemingly randy vixen. He was hauled back to the Land of Milk and Honey, where he was tried and imprisoned. Vanunu completed his sentence in April 2004, but the government has severely restricted his movement and speech. He can't use the Internet or a mobile phone, or approach embassies or borders because he is an active security threat.[105]

Vanunu's data indicated that Israel's program was sophisticated and advanced, with more than two hundred bombs (including boosted devices, neutron bombs, warheads for U.S.-made F-16 delivery, and Jericho warheads). As the Israeli Ministry of Defense struggled to snuff out these tidbits,

Avner Cohen let even more cats out of the Israeli nuke bag. Cohen, an Israeli researcher at the University of Maryland, published a book that further broke the code of obfuscation and opacity surrounding the program. It focuses upon the critical two decades of the program (1950–1970) when Ben-Gurion's fantasy of a nuke-wielding Israel became a "wet dream come true." (I'm referring to heavy water, of course.) He also discusses the negotiations between President Richard Nixon and Prime Minister Golda Meir that formalized the nuclear policy of "even if they ask, don't tell."[106]

Israel is in this book because of its extralegal nuclear program. It also sustains vast criticism due to its oppressive treatment of the Palestinians, whom it occupies and whom it consistently denies the right of self-determination as required by Israel's

> ## Will the Real Goliath Please Stand Up?
>
> Israeli security forces and civilians killed 4,080 Palestinians between September 29, 2000, and March 31, 2007. That's nearly 400 percent more than the 1,021 Israeli soldiers and civilians killed by Palestinians.[107]

own various multilateral and bilateral commitments.[108] If UN violations were, as the Bush administration has argued, the principle reason for invading Iraq in 2003, Israel would be in big trouble. According to a pro-Israel Christian group in the United States, Israeli Prime Minister Yitzhak Shamir commissioned Shai Ben-Tekoa to do a statistical analysis of UN voting regarding Israel in the run up to the 1991 Madrid Conference. Ben-Tekoa found that between 1946 and 1989, the United Nations Security Council passed 175 resolutions, 97 of which were against Israel.[109] There have been similar tallies by others. Former U.S. congressman Paul Findlay writes that between 1955 and 1992, Israel was targeted by at least 65 resolutions of the UNSC.[110]

Many of those sanctions and condemnations are related to key issues of refugees, borders (which Israel keeps expanding through further settlements, confiscations, and illegal wall building), and Jerusalem's disposition. Other themes in the resolutions pertain to unlawful attacks on its neighbors, consistent and incessant disregard for Palestinians' rights inclusive of illegal deportation, collective punishments (e.g., home demolition), confiscation of Palestinian lands and illegal settlements upon those lands, and refusal to abide by the UN Charter and the Geneva Convention.[111] Israel and its loonier supporters claim that this litany of UN resolutions reflects anti-Semitism in the United Nations. This is puzzling. Of course, there are anti-Semitic nut jobs (e.g., Iran's president), but to discount more than sixty years of rebukes is just silly. Don't forget there could have been many more such resolutions if the United States didn't use its veto power in the UNSC to protect its arch-espionage-committer from such sanctions.[112]

As is well-known, the United States is Israel's great benefactor, receiving more U.S. aid than any other country, even though its per capita GDP ($27,644) is on par with that of Spain ($28,140).[113] Given Israel's relative wealth, Washington astonishingly gives each Israeli 500 greenbacks every year.[114] The United States is indeed a friend with benefits. Not only does Israel get a whopping sum each year, unlike other countries that receive their dole in installments, it also gets a lump sack of cash, allowing it to earn loads of interest. Washington even pays Israel to design weapons the Pentagon neither wants nor needs and gives it access to the finest U.S. weapon systems. (Unfortunately, Israel often violates the terms of weapons acquisition, as it did in the summer of 2006 when it dumped cluster bombs on Lebanese civilians.[115])

Fairweather Friends

All of this largess would be justifiable if Israel weren't such a liability to the United States at present. The Cold War is over, baby, and so are the days of planning to launch B-52s into the Soviet Union from Israel. Now the United States and Israel claim their relationship derives from their shared threat of Islamist terrorism. But prominent American political scientists argue that this causality is backward: Israel's policies and the United States's stalwart and uncritical support for those policies animate recruitment literature of Islamist militants everywhere and make winning the war on terrorism more difficult— even if Israel is only *one* cause d'etre of Islamist militant evildoers.[116] Even the U.S. Department of State's Advisory Group on Public Diplomacy for the Arab

The Land Grab Goes On and On and On
In complete contravention of international law, the Israelis keep gobbling up Palestinian lands through policies of "establishing facts on the ground," which entails "settling" Israelis in Palestinian lands. In 1994 there were 140,684 settlers in the West Bank alone. In 2005 there were 249,573 Israelis settled on stolen land. If you include those "settlers" in East Jerusalem, the number climbs to 418,305 for 2005.[117]

and Muslim World noted, "Citizens in these countries are genuinely distressed at the plight of the Palestinians and at the role they perceive the United States to be playing."[118] Polls consistently show that folks in the Muslim world are irked by Israel's policies and U.S. support for these policies.[119] I would be derelict to not point out that Israel bites the *American* hand that feeds it. The U.S. General Accounting Office says that Israel "conducts the most aggressive espionage against the U.S. of any ally."[120]

Furthermore, Israel routinely ignores not only the international community's calls to behave like a civilized state and follow well-established norms for external and internal conduct, it frequently disregards *U.S.* requests and backtracks on promises made to U.S. leadership to cease stealing Palestinian land and building settlements on the same. The Israelis call this "establishing facts on the ground," which will make it impossible to return those lands to any future Palestine that may emerge. The United States has asked Israel to desist from targeted assassination of Palestinian leaders to no avail.

If all of this were not enough to eviscerate the sanctity of the claim advanced by the American-Israel Public Affairs Committee (AIPAC) and others that Israel is a vital partner to the United States, may I note in passing that Israel also sells U.S. weapons systems to U.S. enemies and rivals, like China.[121] Israel's credential as a democracy—often cited by its proponents in the United States—is also specious. Despite the best efforts of the Christian Taliban, who also support Israel as a part of their biblical diplomacy, the United States remains a liberal democracy where anyone (perhaps with the help of a good lawyer) can enjoy equal rights under the law, irrespective of race, creed, or gender. Not in Israel. Israel's citizenship is based upon religious identification with strong preference to those who are Jewish. In this regard, Israel—founded as an explicitly Jewish state—has more in common with Pakistan, which was founded as a state based upon the religious identity of its citizens, albeit Muslim ones. Astonishingly, Palestinians who marry Israeli citizens cannot become Israeli citizens or even live with their spouses—something decried by the Israeli human rights organization B'tselem, as well as Human Rights Watch and other groups.[122]

This policy apparently comports with the attitudes and preference of most Israelis who oppose intermarriage[123] and a healthy majority of folks who believe that "Arabs should be encouraged to emigrate."[124] In fact, the Israel Democracy Institute notes that "according to international ratings, political discrimination of minorities in Israel is among the highest in the world."[125]

All of this is catching up with Israel. In a recent poll of nearly 28,000 people across 27 countries, most people believed that *Israel* and *Iran* have a mainly negative influence in the world. (An almost equal number said the same thing about North Korea and the United States. Ouch!) Only 17 percent of respondents had a favorable view of Israel's influence. There are only two countries whose citizens have a modestly positive view of Israel's role: 45 percent of Nigerians and 42 percent of Americans, while nearly a third in both have negative views. [126]

A Cuisine Without a People for a People Without a Cuisine?

Israelis are fond of saying that falafel is their national food, and indeed postcards and T-shirts are dedicated to proclaiming this truism. A wizened cynic may state the obvious: They got their cuisine like they got their land—by snatching it from the Arabs. But this story of culinary appropriation is complex and interesting. Perhaps counteruntuitively, "Israeli food" is a subset of—not synonymous with—"Jewish food." This relationship encampsulates an important tension between the project of the Israeli state and the global peoples it claims as its potential citizenry. When most folks think of "Jewish food," it's the comforting, carbohydrate- and fat-laden, waist-expanding dishes of Eastern Europe and Germany that spring to mind (blintzes, brisket, matzo ball soup, kreplach, knish, kugle, etc.). Curiously, in Israel you don't find street stalls dedicated to those wonders. Rather, it is the Arab specialities that dominate public snack life, such as falafel, hummus, and baba ganouj and that are appropriated as authentically Israeli. Perhaps these are culinary homages to the the small numbers of Mizrahim who in fact share some culinary traditions with other Arabs. But those folks were in small number before the active colonization of the land in the late nineteenth century by the terrorized Jews fleeing horrors at home— and those folks in no way could claim the falafel as their ancestral chow. So this hardly justifies such peculiar nationalist culinary claims.

In my mind, modern Israeli eats are very much at the heart of notions of the Israeli state and its polity. Indeed to lay claim to these quintessential Arab offerings in such terms is to lay claim to something greater and to establish "culinary" facts on the ground to accompany the ever-expanding grasp over

Arab lands. Equally important is the absence of diasporic delicacies such as borscht, bagel, knish, and the like in public snacking, even if this is the stuff one may eat at home. If borscht or bagels were the Israeli national snack proclaimed on postcards, wouldn't one seriously question the maximalist claims espoused by the most extreme Zionists? (By the way: I use the word *Zionist* to reference a political ideology and identity, not to conjure up some hateful notion of a crazed global cabal!) And that's what makes the making of Israeli cuisine so interesting. It is inherently a project of colonialism, appropriation, and nation building, and these are the themes that we explore herein.

Contrary to popular belief, the colonization and appropriation of Arab land did not begin in 1947 when the Israeli state was created according to UN Resolution 181 (aka Partition Resolution), which *also* mandated an independent Palestine. Indeed, the Zionist movement dates back to the late nineteenth century and was no doubt galvanized by Europe's and Russia's pervasive and increasingly deadly anti-Semitism, which motivated many Jews to want a place where they could be secure.

By the late 1890s, Jewish commitment to "assimilation" in Europe and Russia was being questioned by prominent Jewish professionals, most notably Theodor Herzl. Herzl was a Viennese journalist who argued that the discrimination against Europe's Jews was incompatible with the otherwise secular, liberal societies emerging in Europe. He was in France during the disgraceful Dreyfus case, when a French Jewish officer was wrongly convicted of treason. This convinced Herzl that Jews must have their own state, as equality would always be denied them in Europe.

Herzl argued this position in *Der Judenstaat* (*The Jewish State*) in 1896.[127] To advance his plan of colonizing territory, he cultivated support from Europe's wealthiest Jewish citizenry. Herzl convened the first meeting of the World Zionist Organization in Basel in 1897, where participants agreed that Palestine would "host" the Jewish state. In an effort not to rile the Ottomans who controlled the area at that time, the early Zionists stopped short of calling for a autonomous state to be carved out of their territory; rather, they simply wanted a "home" to be "hosted."[128]

As with colonies everywhere, native resistance to this obviously well-intended effort to civilize them while stealing their land was seen as further evidence of the natives' own backwardness and inferiority to the colonizers. Arabs in those days were seen in terms that are distinctly racist. A famed archeologist of the era remarked that "the Arab . . . is as disgustingly incapable as most other savages, and not more worth romancing about than the Red Indians or Maoris."[130] Zionists—who were just as white and as ironically capable of racism as their non-Jewish European counterparts—applied the same rationale to Palestine. They promoted the preposterous slogan "A land without a people for a people without a land," which reflected the civilizational nonexistence of the Palestinians they sought to displace. Herzl himself sold the idea of a Jewish state as an opportunity to defend Europe's civilization against Arab barbarity. Chaim Weizmann, Herzl's successor in the Zionist movement, promoted the analogy of Arab to Jew as "desert against civilization."[131]

Ingeniously, the early Zionists pitched their colonial ambitions to Western powers on the basis that they could advance their own imperial ambitions. Moses Hess, a German socialist-Zionist, presciently understood that the construction of the Suez Canal (opened in 1869) would usher forth European settlements, which would require military protection. Hess advised the Zionists to offer their services to serve as "middlemen" between Europe and Asia. Herzl tried, but failed, to convince Bismarck (Chancellor of Germany) that a Jewish state would ensure the protection of the Berlin-Baghdad railroad. He next went to the Brits, arguing that British interests would be strengthened by a "substantial *colonization* [emphasis added] of our people at the strategic point where Egyptian and Indo-Persian interests converge."[132]

While the horrors of the Holocaust are important, to the Arabs who lived through these decades of colonization, the moral arithmetic of "giving" one people the land of another makes little sense. By 1947, there were 1.3 million Palestinians in Palestine compared to 600,000 Jews, who owned 6 to 7 percent of the total land, reflecting several waves of refugees who came to Palestine fleeing persecution elsewhere.[133] So much for "a land without a people for a people without a home" canard.

The Partition Plan of 1947 was unfavorable toward the Palestinians, as has been every other "agreement" about their fate.[134] In 1947, despite several waves of successive refugees-cum-colonizers, Palestinians were still the majority. Nonetheless, the Partition Plan awarded the largest part of the land to the Jewish settlers and in doing so included an Arab minority of 250,000 within that state. Not only were the Palestinians screwed in terms of quantity of land, they were screwed on quality too. They received little of the fertile coastal lands and were cut off from Syria and the Red Sea.[135]

The Zionists, however, were not content. They accepted the partition plan even though they wanted the whole thing. Partition legitimized the State of Israel in the comity of nations. Zionists embraced the fact that the plan set into play a number of events that made military confrontation inevitable.[136] With Palestinian rejection of the plan—for damned good reasons—Ben-Gurion and others presumed that the Palestinians would lose further territory to the Israeli state through military conquest. Ben-Gurion wrote in his diary that "we shall accept a state in the boundaries fixed today—but the boundaries of Zionist aspirations are the concerns of the Jewish people and no external factor will be able to limit them."[137] He similarly wrote in a letter, "We must expel the Arabs and take their places."[138] He got what he wanted: Between December 1947 and September 1949, some 700,000—more than half the entire Palestinian population—fled their homes.

Israel's claims that it had nothing to do with this mass exodus are no longer entertained by, among others, *Israeli* historians. In fact, the Palestinians were victims of systemic campaigns of violence and psychological operations to drive them out. Jewish underground groups such as Irgun, led by Menachim Begin (who astonishingly won a Nobel *Peace* Prize in 1978), and the Stern Gang (which claimed Yitzhak Shamir as a member) organized operations like the massacre of more than 250 villagers at Deir Yassin. (This number is debated and ranges between 100 and 700.) Following the massacre, Zionist militants drove through Arab villages with loudspeakers warning them to flee or face another Deir Yassin. The violence was also state sponsored: The entire Palestinian towns of Lydda and Ramle were run over by Yishuv's army (the Haganah) as a consequence of a direct order given by General Gurion to generals Yigal Allan and Yitshak Rabin. The Israeli state claimed—and continues to claim—

that the Palestinians fled of their own accord and as such have no right to return or repatriation as specified in UN General Assembly Resolution 194 of December 1948.[139] This would begin a long Israeli history of disregarding UN resolutions and other rulings of the international community.

And what, you ask, does any of this have to do with food? A lot, I would say. Any perusal of the foods claimed by Israel—Jaffa oranges,[140] falafel, hummus, baba ganouj, *fatoush,* the list goes on and on—suggests Israelis have busily appropriated not only the land but the cuisines of the Palestinians as well. Now this is, of course, an oversimplification, because there were Sephardic (from Spain) and Mizrahim (from Libya, Morrocco, Iraq, etc.) Jews living in the area until the massive colonization movement described above. It does merit mention that the later Ashkenazim arrivals were not terribly kind to their Sephardim and Mizrahim brothers and sisters, seeing them as rustics of sorts, although fellow scholars assure me this has improved in recent decades with intermarriage between Ashkenazim and other Jews becoming more common.

Bloggers go back and forth endlessly about whether or not there is now an "authentic Israeli cuisine" befitting the Sabra Israeli. (*Sabra* literally means "cactus" and references those who are born in Israel and stands in contrast to those who migrated to Israel.) Contemporary Israeli food is a pastiche of Arab contributions, the culinary developments of the Sephardim and Mizrahim, and the influences of the diverse immigration history of Israel's new citizens who hail from more than eighty countries, including Russia and the former "Eastern Bloc" countries, Egypt, India, the countries of the Maghreb (Morocco, Libya, Tunisia, and Algeria) and the Levant (Lebanon, Syria, and Jordan), as well as Greece, Turkey, France, Spain, Italy, and the United States. Obviously, Israeli cuisine reflects the dietary rules of Judaism.

Some cookbooks I have found go to great pains to depict ancient Israeli cuisines that stretch back thousands of years. This is, of course, little more than culinary propaganda, and even such authors concede that a truly Israeli cuisine has yet to emerge. However, Israeli chefs are busy creating a cuisine that reflects the spirit and diversity of their relatively young nation-state. Keeping with the nature of Israeli cuisine, many of the dishes to be served here draw from the indigenous Arab influences as well as quintessential Israeli and Jewish items.

The Plan of Attack

This presumes a dinner party of eight; adjust as needed. The day before your party, make the dessert (macaroons) and soak the chickpeas for the hummus. If you want, you can also prepare the vegetables (such as roasting the ones for the casserole, preparing the veggies for the salad, and roasting the eggplant for the baba ganouj). You can also make the carrot salad a day in advance. As your guests arrive, they will be greeted by hummus and baba ganouj on the table along with the carrot salad and pita. You will dress the *fatoush* when everyone is ready to eat. Finally, you will turn out your beautiful *maqlubeh* onto a serving platter, garnish, and serve to your guests. Enjoy!

Salads and snacks

- *Hummus* (ground chickpeas with tahini)
- Baba Ganouj (roasted eggplant salad with tahini)
- Pita (store-bought and warmed)
- *Salat Gezer* (Israeli carrot salad)
- *Fatush* (green salad with herbs and pita "croutons")

Main course

- *Maqlubeh* (upside-down meat and vegetable casserole)

Dessert

- Macaroons

Beverages

- Israel has an up-and-coming wine industry. One of the finest is Yarden Wines. (You can find a distributor at www.yardenwines.com/distributors .aspx.) On the red side, I recommend their cabernet sauvignon, and for the white, a Riesling. Israel also has a superb beer industry, and Maccabee and Gold Star are very popular. If you can't find these at a kosher market near you, go for the beer of your choice. Serve tea or coffee with the macaroons.

PREPARATION

★★★

SALADS AND SNACKS

Hummus *(Ground Chickpeas with Tahini)*

This "Israeli" dish is also an Arab classic.

Ingredients
1 cup dried chickpeas, soaked overnight
9 cups water, divided
¼ teaspoon baking soda
1 yellow onion, peeled
½ cup tahini (This is a sesame seed paste, available in most grocery stores
   in the Middle Eastern or kosher section.)
¼ cup fresh lemon juice
2 tablespoons finely chopped flat-leaf parsley
½ teaspoon finely chopped garlic
1 teaspoon cumin
¼ teaspoon paprika
4 tablespoons olive oil

For garnish:
1 tablespoon coarsely chopped flat-leaf parsley
1 tablespoon olive oil
10 cooked chickpeas retained before blending

Let's get cooking
1. Look over the chickpeas for things that don't belong (rocks, for example).
   Cover with 3 cups water and ¼ teaspoon baking soda and soak overnight.
2. Rinse the chickpeas. If using a pressure cooker, add the chickpeas, 6 cups
   water, and the onion. Cook until tender and the skins fall off. Follow the

instructions on your pressure cooker for timing. (This takes about 35 minutes in my cooker.) If using your stove, put the chickpeas in a medium-size pot and cover with 6 cups of water. Add the onion and cook over medium heat until the chickpeas fall apart. This could take 4 hours.

Note: You could skip this step and use a 15-ounce can of chickpeas, but it really won't be as delicious, because canned chickpeas are not as tender, have their skins, and take on the flavor of the can.

3. If using a pressure cooker, skim off the skins when the chickpeas are done. If using a pot, skim off the skins as they float to the top.

4. Remove the onion and transfer the chickpeas to a food processor or blender while they are still warm. Remove a few (about 10 chickpeas) and retain for garnish. Add the remaining ingredients and blend until smooth. *Note:* Some hummus fascists would holler at instructions to use a blender or food processor. They insist upon using a mortar and pestle. Feel free to do so if it would make you feel like a hard-living kibbutzer.

5. Transfer to a shallow bowl. Make a well in the middle and drizzle with olive oil. Sprinkle with the chopped parsley and reserved cooked chickpeas. Serve with pita bread that has been warmed for a few minutes in a 250-degree oven. (I usually cut each pita into 8 wedges.)

Odd alternative garnish suggestion. While not likely terribly "Israeli" but terribly delicious, one of our local eateries serves its hummus with a drizzling of pomegranate mollasas and a sprinkling of pomegranate seeds. If you are up for this, forget the parsley and olive oil. Garnish with the chickpeas, the molasses (go easy!), and the seeds.

Baba Ganouj *(Roasted Eggplant Salad with Tahini)*

Like much of Israeli food, this is a quintessential Arab dish that literally means "spoiled father," reflecting the luck of the man who gets to eat this lovely salad while not having to make it. It can be prepared in full or in part the day before your party. You can also roast the eggplant in advance, even if you prefer to make the dish the day of the soiree. I prefer to use the big American style, because I can roast it more easily and it peels more easily. If using the small eggplants, get about a quarter pound extra to account for the relative wastage resulting from roasting and peeling the smaller ones.

Ingredients

1 pound eggplant (1¼ pounds if small eggplants)

⅓ cup coarsely chopped flat-leaf parsley leaves (You can use some of the stem near the leaf.)

¼ cup tahini (sesame seed paste)

¼ cup freshly squeezed lemon juice

4 cloves garlic, pressed or finely chopped

1 teaspoon sea salt (or more to taste)

2 tablespoons nonfat yogurt (You can use yogurt with fat if you want.)

1 tablespoon olive oil

Freshly ground black pepper to taste

For garnish:

1 teaspoon olive oil

⅓ cup pomegranate seeds, if available

2 tablespoons finely chopped parsley sprigs

Let's get cooking

1. Lightly coat the eggplant with olive oil (the spray-on kind works well for this) and roast it on a gas burner over a flame, turning to char the whole surface. As soon as it develops a good char on the outside, put it in an oven preheated to 375 degrees for another 10 minutes to thoroughly roast. If you don't have a gas stove, skip the flame-roasting step and roast it in the oven for 20–30 minutes at 375 degrees. You can also use the broiler, taking care to turn the eggplant often to char the whole surface. The eggplant will look "deflated" and will take on a brown sheen when it's done. When finished, transfer to a cool plate and cut it open to release the heat and to help it cool. Be careful, as the steam will burn you!

2. Once the eggplant has cooled, scoop out the roasted flesh and discard the skin. If you have roasted it correctly, the flesh should easily come out.

3. Process all the ingredients *except* the eggplant in a food processor or blender until a smooth dressing results. This is necessary because the tahini is clumpy and takes a bit of blending to get it smooth. Once the dressing has the right consistency, add the eggplant and pulse until incorporated. *Do not overblend—you are not making a smoothie.*

4. Transfer to a shallow bowl. Make a well in the center and pour in about 1 teaspoon olive oil. Sprinkle with pomegranate seeds and parsley.

5. Serve with pita bread that has been warmed for a few minutes in a 250-degree oven. (I usually cut each pita into 8 wedges.)

Salat Gezer *(Israeli Carrot Salad)*

This is a savory herbed take on the ubiquitous Israeli salad. It can be made a day in advance and stored in the refrigerator.

Ingredients
1 pound fresh carrots, cleaned and peeled with tops and bottoms removed
4 cloves garlic, pressed
1 cup finely chopped parsley (leaves and soft parts of stem near leaves)
¾ teaspoon sea salt
¼ teaspoon freshly ground black pepper
¼ cup freshly squeezed lemon juice
¼ cup freshly squeezed orange juice
4 tablespoons olive oil

For garnish:
Sprigs of parsley

Let's get tossing
1. Grate the carrots or shred using a food processor.
2. Whisk all of the remaining ingredients into a serving bowl.
3. Toss in the carrots and mix well. Garnish with parsley sprigs.

Fatush *(Green Salad with Herbs and Pita "Croutons")*

This is, yep, another *Arab* salad that makes use of stale pita bread, which would be useful if you ate pita daily and had the stuff lying around. Since I'm assuming that's not generally the case in your household, we'll have to toast the pita and pretend they became stale naturally. You can chop up the vegetables, toast the pita (or leave them out, uncovered, overnight to get stale), and prepare the dressing in advance of your wingding, but this dish must be assembled right before your guests arrive or else you will have a nasty wilted mess with soggy pita.

Ingredients

For the salad:

2 pitas, either stale or toasted, broken into small pieces

8-10 leaves romaine lettuce, torn up into small, salad-appropriate pieces

5 scallions, including the tops, thinly sliced (Obviously, chop off the tip of the bulb and the hideous dry tops of the green part.)

4 radishes, thinly sliced

3 Roma tomatoes, cut into ¼-inch cubes without the jelly

1 large cucumber or 3 Kirby cucumbers, cut into ¼-inch cubes

¾ cup coarsely chopped parsley

¼ cup coarsely chopped mint

For the dressing:

⅓ cup freshly squeezed lemon juice

½ cup olive oil

1½ teaspoon sumac (If your supermarket doesn't have it, you can find it at Middle Eastern groceries or online. The salad won't flop without this spice either.)

1 clove garlic, pressed or finely chopped

½ teaspoon sea salt (or more to taste)

¼ teaspoon freshly ground black pepper (or more to taste)

1 tablespoon honey (optional)

For garnish:

¼ cup pomegranate seeds

Sprigs of mint

Let's get tossing

1. If you have stale pita, break them up into small pieces and set aside. If not, bake the pita in a 375-degree oven for 10–15 minutes, until dry and crispy. Remove and let cool on a baking rack. (You don't want these things to sweat and become soggy, which is what will happen if you put them on a plate.)

2. In a serving bowl, toss together the torn lettuce, scallions, radishes, tomatoes, cucumber, parsley, and mint.

3. Whisk together the ingredients for the dressing. Taste and adjust salt and pepper as needed. *Hint:* I like this on the sour side. You may not. If the sourness is not your thing, you can mellow it out with a tablespoon of honey.

4. Right before serving, toss the dry pita into the salad to incorporate.
5. Toss in the dressing and garnish with pomegranate seeds and mint sprigs. Serve immediately.

MAIN COURSE

★★★★★★★★★★★★★★★★★★★★★★

Maqlubeh *(Upside-Down Meat and Vegetable Casserole)*

Maqlubeh is a Palestinian dish eaten by Palestinians living under Israeli occupation and elsewhere, as well as by Israeli Arabs. In Arabic it means "upside down," which references the fact that once this layered casserole of meat and vegetables is finished, it is inverted upon a platter and garnished before serving. I think of this dish as a Palestinian version of shepherd's pie, in that it is made of whatever meat and vegetables you have left over or need to be used up. Traditionally, this dish is made by frying the vegetables. I think this is needlessly unhealthy and you actually get a better flavor by *roasting* the vegetables, and that's what I do here. I like the vegetable combos below, but I have seen versions with eggplant or with combinations of carrots, potatoes, and cauliflower. The choices are endless.

Ingredients
2 cups basmati rice
4 cups warm chicken broth
½ head cauliflower (or equivalent amount potatoes or carrots)
4 small zucchinis (or equivalent amount eggplant)
1 red bell pepper
1 green bell pepper
8 tablespoons olive oil (or more if needed)
4 teaspoons ground cumin
2 teaspoons ground allspice
1 teaspoon freshly ground black pepper
2 yellow onions, finely diced
4 cloves garlic, finely chopped

1 pound meat of your choice (I prefer shoulder or leg of lamb cut into 1-inch
   cubes, but you can use beef or even chicken if you like.)
2¾ teaspoons coarse rock salt
⅛ teaspoon saffron threads (Do not even think of buying saffron powder!)
3 cups chicken or beef broth (I use low-sodium, fat-free broth.)

For garnish:
⅓ cup toasted pine nuts
Sprigs of parsley

Let's get cooking

1. Pick through the rice and remove things that should not be there (e.g.,
   rocks, cluster bomb fragments, other foreign objects). Rinse at least 3
   times with cold water to remove any starch. Cover with 4 cups warm water
   and let the rice soak for at least an hour.
2. While the rice soaks, prepare and roast the vegetables. Break up the cauliflower into florets. If these florets are large (as is the case with genetically
   modified monster cauliflowers), cut in half. Set aside. Slice the small zucchinis lengthwise into 2 or at most 3 slices. The slices need to be thick (about
   ⅓ to ½ inch) to hold up in roasting. To prepare the peppers, chop off the tops
   and remove the seeds. Slice the peppers into about 8 pieces or so.
3. Prepare the roasting mixture for the vegetables. Carefully whisk 4 tablespoons olive oil with 2 teaspoons cumin, 1 teaspoon allspice, ½ teaspoon
   salt, and ½ teaspoon black pepper in a bowl.
4. I like to coat the vegetables either in a ziplock bag or a plastic sealable container such that I can "shake" the veggies to coat. To a ziplock bag or sealable plastic container, add the cauliflower and ⅓ of the roasting mixture.
   Shake to cover well with a thin coat. Turn onto a cookie sheet covered with
   foil and a slight coat of cooking spray. (I use the olive oil variety.)
5. Next add the zucchini to the same bag or container with another ⅓ of the
   roasting mixture and shake to toss well. Turn out onto the cookie sheet.
   (Obviously, you will need more than one cookie sheet! These veggies
   should not be crowded.)
6. Into the same bag or container, add the peppers and the remaining roasting
   mixture. Shake and turn out onto a cookie sheet. Do try to the keep the same
   vegetables grouped together, as the vegetables will cook at different speeds.

7. Roast the vegetables at 375 degrees for about 15–20 minutes, depending on your cookie sheet's thickness and composition. The peppers and the zucchini will take on a char, and the cauliflower will brown. Watch the veggies closely: This isn't an exact science, and you don't want to ruin them. The zucchini will finish first and the cauliflower last. Remove the various vegetables as soon as they are done, and set aside on a plate.

8. While the veggies are in the oven, in a large pot, brown the onions and garlic in 4 tablespoons olive oil.

9. While the onions are browning, season the meat with about 1 teaspoon salt and ½ teaspoon black pepper.

10. Add the meat to the pot and sear on all sides. Add the remaining 2 teaspoons cumin and 1 teaspoon allspice and fry together for 2 minutes. Add just enough water or broth to cover the meat. Bring to a boil. Reduce the heat and let simmer until all of the liquid is absorbed by the meat and/or boiled away. You should have a beautiful brown glaze of meat, onions, and spices.

11. While the meat cooks, with a mortar and pestle, grind the saffron threads with ¼ teaspoon coarse rock salt. (The rock salt gives you some friction to help grind up the saffron threads.)

12. Add the saffron/salt mixture to about 4 cups broth in a small saucepan along with 1 teaspoon salt. Heat to warm and to dissolve the saffron and salt. (Heat in a covered pot to prevent evaporation. You want 4 cups of liquid to cook the rice.)

13. In the same pot in which you cooked the meat, arrange the vegetables in layers on top of the meat. Spoon the rice onto the vegetable layer.

14. Pour the warm saffron/broth mixture over the casserole and bring to a boil. If the water does not cover the rice (which it may not depending upon how you layered your pot!), try to push the rice into the water later. Resist the temptation to add more fluid. Otherwise you will get runny, unpalatable rice. The idea here is really to cook the rice by steaming.

15. Reduce the heat and let simmer, slightly covered, for about 30 minutes or until the rice is tender.

16. When the casserole is nearly done cooking, toast the pine nuts by heating them over medium heat in a small, dry skillet. Turn frequently to brown while avoiding burning them.

17. Invert the casserole onto a large serving platter. Garnish with the toasted pine nuts and parsley sprigs.

DESSERT

Macaroons

Because macaroons do not use flour, they are always kosher for Passover. Macaroons are absurdly easy to make, and they can be made a day or two ahead. They store nicely in the fridge. Serve them with tea or coffee.

Ingredients
3 large egg whites, at room temperature

1 14-ounce package sweetened shredded coconut

1 14-ounce can sweetened condensed milk

1 pinch sea salt

1 teaspoon real vanilla extract

2 teaspoons finely grated fresh lemon zest

Let's get cooking
1. Preheat the oven to 350 degrees. Line 2 cookie sheets with parchment paper. (If you don't have parchment paper, apply a nonstick cooking spray.)
2. Whip the egg whites until they form stiff peaks.
3. In a separate bowl, mix the coconut, condensed milk, salt, vanilla extract, and lemon zest.
4. Fold in the egg whites to incorporate. Do not overmix to avoid "deflating" the egg whites.
5. Drop heaping tablespoons of the mixture onto the baking sheets, with about 2 inches between each. (You can also use a small ice-cream scoop for uniform size.)
6. Bake about 20 minutes, until they turn a golden brown.
7. When cool, store in an airtight container or resealable plastic bag. If you seal them up while they are still hot, they will sweat and become much less appealing.

Dossier of Indian Perfidy

India refused to enjoin the Nuclear Nonproliferation Treaty (NPT), which entered into force in 1970.[141] The NPT recognized five permanent nuclear weapons states—the United States, the then Soviet Union (now Russia), China, France, and the United Kingdom—all of whom had verified bomb designs before the NPT went into effect. These states comprise the so-called Permanent Five (P5) of the United Nations Security Council (UNSC). India hectored the P5—especially the United States—that nuclear weapons are immoral, and whined in various international fora that the NPT legitimizes nuclear weapons among the P5 and establishes a permanent nuclear apartheid.[142]

Despite its moralizing, in fact India was in a perpetual swivet because it was excluded from the nuclear club: Had India been allowed to join as a "one-day-bomb-possessing" member, it surely would have signed onto the NPT. Instead India complained bitterly that the NPT "enshrined the denial of great power status to India,"[143] reflecting India's—largely accurate—understanding that nuclear weapons are a currency of power, thus vitiating the purported moral claims New Delhi advanced.

Playing in the Radioactive Sandpile

After the 1998 nuclear tests, a Hindu nationalist outfit, the Sangh Parivar, wanted to distribute the radioactive sands of the Thar Desert as the symbolic prasad of India's atomic goddess, Shakti. To some folks, prasad is an odd concept. In some varieties of Hindu worship, food items are presented to the gods (in idol form), who are believed to nibble away at the offering. The god's "leavings" are distributed as prasad. Since caste-conscious Indians believe it is defiling to eat another's leftovers, consumption of prasad reflects the lowliness of man before god, for whom it is an honor to eat the crumbs from a god's (or goddess's) plate. Fortunately, sensible scientists alerted the Hindu fanatics to the dangers involved in the exercise, and the plan was abandoned.

Other crazies sought to gather up the radioactive grains, cocoon them in a suitably appointed and pious-looking vessel, and schlep them around the country so that India's citizenry could venerate the stuff. The Hindu nationalists next tried to build a temple at the epicenter of the nuclear blast. Again, better sense prevailed. Ultimately, they settled upon the open-air memorial that exists today as an important tourist destination. Indialine Expeditions' "Rajasthan Treasure Trail" parades proud Indians to the site, to visit "where India conducted its Nuclear programmes and showed to the world that She will not tolerate any interference from outside."[144] You can't make this stuff up.

To blast its way into the bomb club, India tested its first nuclear "device" at Pokhran in Rajastan's Thar Desert in 1974, under Prime Minister Indira Gandhi's direction. Risibly, India called this a "Peaceful Nuclear Explosion" (PNE). The PNE would pave the way for bombs that would grace India's various peaceful nuclear-capable delivery vehicles, such as planes, ships, and missiles—if and when India would finally manage to make such things. This test irked the Canadians and the Americans in particular because the "peaceful device" was made from both plutonium that was separated from the Canadian-supplied CANDU reactor and from U.S.-supplied "holy water" (that's heavy water, or D^2O for chemistry nerds). This misappropriation violated treaties with both countries and roiled both Washington and Ottawa. In the wake of the PNE and associated American and Canadian disgrace, the United States and the international community promulgated several nonproliferation regimes to retard India's ability to develop nuclear weapons and to limit further horizontal proliferation.

It is perplexing that India had such "great power" pretensions in those days, given that it was unable to feed teeming masses who largely lived in poverty, wallowed in illiteracy, had little access to potable water, and suffered from numerous health ailments that are not terribly appetizing and thus will not be explicated further in this *cookbook*. While India has made great strides in improving the lot of its peoples and has had various booms such as the "IT boom," the "call center boom," and the "back office boom," there is *much* progress to be made.

With nearly 1.1 *billion* people, only 59.5 percent of the adult population (over fifteen years of age) can read and only 48.3 percent of India's adult females can make sense of a book. This is not exactly impressive: The comparable literacy rates in *Sudan* are 61.5 percent and 50.5 percent respectively.[145] When India's human development is measured against that of 176 other countries using a composite measure called the Human Development Indictor, it ranks toward the bottom at 126. While India may trail Tajikistan, Uzbekistan, and Kazakhstan, with the exception of Sri Lanka, it still outranks *most* of its neighbors, which it seeks to dominate politically, militarily, and, alas, economically.[146]

Despite the popular euphoria surrounding those 1974 nuclear tests and the scientists' exaggerated claims of success, they were ultimately a technical disaster. Unable to confer India with the bomb her scientists and leaders lusted after, the scientific enclave would have to test again. And with one pusillanimous exception, *every* prime minister after Mrs. Gandhi tried to test. Each was ultimately dissuaded from doing so by, inter alia, the mean United States, which sought to deny India her rightful place at the world's table of hegemons.

Weapons of Mass Deception

Indian leadership finally girded its loins under the Hindu nationalist party, the Bharatiya Janata Party (BJP). Atal Bihari Vajpayee of the BJP gave the go-ahead, and the mad scientists of the Thar Desert conducted the "Pokhran II" tests in May of 1998. To avoid preemption, they used various means of subterfuge and deception with great mastery. In fact, the CIA was taken utterly by surprise. To the horror of CIA analysts, they had to learn about the tests from the most wretched of sources, the U.S. State Department, who in turn learned about them ignominiously from—gasp—CNN.[147] Like the 1974 tests, mushroom clouds of uncertainty linger over the yields of the 1998 tests, with

Western scientists doubting their veracity. U.S. analysts believe that if the Indians really want a thermonuclear wad, they'll have to explode their device . . . yet again.[148]

While there are still some nonproliferation devotees who bemoan India's extralegal nuke stockpile and prognosticate that recognition of India as a nuclear power will encourage other nuclear-minded nut jobs to follow suit, a number of U.S. analysts and political leaders want to encourage India's nuclear weapons program to prevent the godless Chinese communists (aka "Chicoms") from establishing unfettered hegemony over Asia. In an effort to enable India to undermine China—or at least frustrate Chicom expansion—the United States has launched a strategic partnership with India that includes opening up the pantry of the Pentagon as well as a bomb-friendly "civilian" nuclear cooperation program.[149] Thus it seems that India will join the ranks of Israel and get a free—or even encouraged and subsidized—pass for its extralegal nuclear weapons. It sucks to be Pakistan.

Even the most Indian-nuke-happy Bush official is episodically concerned that some kind of nuclear confrontation could develop between India and Pakistan—and rightly so, as these nuclear-armed states have not yet reconciled their enmity over the disposition of Kashmir. Kashmir precipitated limited wars in 1947–1948, 1965, and 1999 and has been the battleground for a protracted sub-conventional conflict since 1989. Of course, Pakistan—the revisionist power—started all of those conflicts. But India's recalcitrance and mismanagement of the Kashmiri populations under Delhi's prickly thumb has only exacerbated the human rights plight of the embattled Kashmiris and

Where Rats Are Gods

In Bikaner, an otherwise sleepy town in India's state of Rajasthan, one finds the rat temple (Temple to Karnimata, the Mother Goddess), where the humble rodent is fed, adored, and worshipped. In fact, devotees present the thousands of rats with milk and sweets, and once the rats have nibbled away, temple priests distribute the remaining offerings as prasad. It is considered to be a good omen if a rat scampers over your bare foot, and sightings of white rats are most auspicious. The rats are revered because they are believed to have been the army of the Mother Goddess.

For testimonials about miracles that have taken place at the rat temple, see www.karnimata.com/frame_intro.html.

encouraged Pakistani misadventures, including the comprehensive backing of vicious militants who fight "on behalf" of the Kashmiris. Analysts of nuclear deterrence in South Asia fear that any war that would eventually escalate to nuclear use would likely be started by some conflict in or over Kashmir.[151]

I would be remiss if I failed to mention that while India is formally included in this gustatory castigation because it is part of the NPT+3, it has an appalling human rights record in Kashmir and elsewhere. Pakistan is also surely culpable for the sanguineous violence perpetrated in Indian-administered Kashmir and is responsible for numerous breaches of human security in the chunk of Kashmir it oversees.[152] Indeed, both countries will likely fight until the last Kashmiri gets blown up by a Pakistan-based militant or dies in the custody of some Indian paramilitary organization.

Dinner in Srinagar

India is a vast country. Its landmass is about 1.15 million square miles—roughly equivalent to one-third of the United States. So while folks often talk about "Indian food," there are, in fact, several Indian cuisines. Most Indian food aficionados are aware of the differences between "North Indian" food (such as the Punjabi buffets that are ubiquitous in "Indian" enclaves in major cities) and the harder to find "South Indian" variety, the *sina qua non* of which is *masala dosa, idli* with coconut chutney, and spicy *upma*.

Rather than providing you with a road map to make the predictable food you find shriveling away in the steam trays of the buffet of your choice, we are going to pay culinary homage to the poor peoples of India's Kashmir Valley

Where Can I Get My Cheating Coach?

It is true you can find anything in India. Indeed, in India's busy cities, one can apparently find coaches who will help you cheat on important exams and even help you manage the situation should you get busted. One coach cautioned that if you are going to sneak in notes (called "chits" in India), you should be able to swallow them quickly.[153]

and its main city, Srinagar. The majority of the valley has always been Muslim. However, prior to the onset of the insurgency, there were about 130,000 Hindus living there in relative harmony with their Muslim majority neighbors. In fact, religious practice of both Hindus and Muslims in the valley has been influenced by the other. Unlike the high-caste Brahmins in India's south, Kashmiri Brahmins even eat meat. Following a number of heinous attacks on the Hindu minorities by Islamic militants, most of the Hindus fled the valley for safer places such as Jammu or Delhi. Thus Kashmir has had two interrelated cuisines specific to its Muslim and Hindu populations.

The "spice system" of Kashmiri food differs from that of other Indian cuisines. The flavor of Kashmiri food draws from powdered fennel seeds (*saunf*), mint (*pudina*), dried ginger powder (*sonth*), saffron (*kesar*), black cardamom (*moti illaichi*), green cardamom (*choti illaichi*), asafetida (*hing*), and a specialized Kashmiri *garam masala* known as *vasi masala,* as well as the ubiquitous cloves (*laung*), cinnamon (*dalchini*), and bay leaf (*tej patta*) that pervade Indian foods generally.

Kashmiris tend not to offer appetizers; however, they always place yogurt on the table. Incidentally, like Iranians, Kashmiris tend to eat dinner seated on the floor with the various plates and serving dishes arrayed upon a large plastic sheet, which often resembles the plastic tablecloths of my youth. Keeping with these traditions, our dinner party will feature homemade yogurt (or storebought, if you prefer). The main dishes will be lamb meatballs in yogurt sauce (*gushtaba*) served "Muslim style" accompanied by a spinach and lamb dish called *palak maaz* and a dish that is served in nearly every Kashmiri home I have ever visited, *dum aloo*. (The latter two dishes are shared in Kashmiri Hindu and Muslim culinary traditions.) These will be served with plain basmati rice.

Kashmiris are not really dessert buffs. In fact, I have never been offered a specific dessert while dining with friends and contacts in Kashmir. Reminiscent of Iran, folks sometimes bring out a plate of fruits with tea, but I have never been given a dessert at a casual dinner. At weddings and at restaurants, however, *firnee*—a delightful rice pudding flavored with nuts, dried fruit, and saffron—is often available. Thus our dinner party will wrap up with the delicate saffron *firnee* and saffron-spiced Kashmiri green tea (*kahwa*).

The Plan of Attack

This plan presumes that you will be cooking for eight ravenous folks; adjust accordingly. Indian food is time-intensive—this is why Indian women have daughters-in-law or at least a bunch of servants. Where appropriate, I have indicated what can and indeed should be made ahead of dinner night. All of these ingredients can be purchased at any South Asian market or on the Internet. The appendix provides some online vendors if you don't have a South Asian market in your neighborhood, but even Fort Wayne, Indiana, now boasts several. I'm sure you can find something within a few zip codes of your locality. Folks living in countries with strong colonial legacies will have an easier time getting this stuff.

Main course

- Homemade yogurt. This should be made preferably the morning the day before your dinner party or the evening before, if you must. If the yogurt flops, you can always put out store-bought plain yogurt that you whisk up before serving.
- *Gushtaba* (lamb meatballs in yogurt sauce). I recommend you make the meatballs the day before your party and keep them in the refrigerator. This will allow the flavors to distribute and will also make the remaining preparation less frenetic.

I'll Have a Tummy Tuck and a Hammock, Please
India has become a preferred destination of choice for "medical tourists." Entrepreneurial Indian companies such as Global Surgical Inc. will help design a surgical and tourism package in India for folks who want an exotic vacation while securing infertility treatments, knee replacements, nose jobs, boob jobs, cardiac procedures, and virtually any other thing that your insurance won't cover and that you can't afford at home.

- *Dum aloo* (potatoes in spicy gravy). This Kashmiri specialty uses a unique breed of potato that is not available beyond Kashmir, so we will have to make do with Yukon Golds. This dish is almost always served to guests in Kashmir, and we would really be remiss to not make it here.
- *Palak maaz* (spinach with lamb). You can also use chicken if you prefer.
- *Sada caval* (plain rice)

Dessert

- *Firnee* (rice pudding with nuts, dried fruit, and saffron). This should be made the day before your party and stored in the fridge. It will be served with Kashmiri tea.

Beverages

- I have never been served alcohol while dining in Kashmiri homes, but I have observed Kashmiri *men* sipping various brews at high-end restaurants and the occasional dive. So feel free to serve up the happy elixirs at your wingding. Personally, I suggest Indian pale ale, which can be found at many grocery stores. For those who prefer wine, a Syrah or a Rioja (including the lovely Temperanillo) works nicely. For those hostesses and hosts who want to stay "old school," various juices with ice can be served—especially pomegranate or mango. We will serve Kashmir green tea (*kahwa*), flavored with saffron, with our delicious *firnee*.

PREPARATION

★★ ★ ★★★★★★★★★★★★★★★★★★★★★★★★★★★★★★★
★ ★ ★ ★ ★★★★★★★★★★★★★★★★★★★★★★★★★★★

MAIN COURSE

Homemade Yogurt

Yogurt is delightfully simple to make. You will need some milk and some plain "starter yogurt," available at your grocery store. Be careful what you buy: It must contain "active live cultures." This just means that the bacteria in the yogurt are alive, and it is these living bacteria that are going to do the job of making milk into yogurt. The savvy host is right to ask: Why I am I buying yogurt to make yogurt? My not-so-savvy answer is simply to say you made it. Actually, I prefer the flavor of homemade yogurt, but the choice is yours. In the subcontinent, yogurt is made of buffalo milk, which is fantastically delicious, but we will likely have to suffice with quotidian cow milk. This recipe calls for whole milk, but you can obviously use skim milk or reduced fat should you choose.

Because you are cooking with live bugs, the temperature of the milk-cum-yogurt has to be warm enough to let them do their job efficiently but not so hot that they will die. Many recipes will fuss over a thermometer and the need to keep within the 90- to 120-degree range. However, I have eaten yogurt all over India and Pakistan, where most folks don't have ovens, and since the climate there does not reach the "culture killing" temperature limit, this stuff is mostly made in ambient conditions. When temperatures decline, the critters work less effectively and the yogurt takes on a sour flavor—which I love! But if you are finicky, use the thermometer.

One final note: South Asians make yogurt in clay dishes. These vessels impart the best "earthly" flavor, and I actually bring them back from the subcontinent when I can. They don't last long and are meant to be thrown away, but being made of clay, they are infinitely environment friendly. Absent a local

South Asian (or possibly Hispanic) market stocking these wonders, you will have to make do with a ceramic dish.

Ingredients
½ gallon whole milk
1 cup yogurt with live cultures

Let's get cooking
1. Bring the milk to a boil in a heavy-bottomed pan. Stir constantly with a wooden spoon to prevent a skin from developing on the milk's surface and to avoid burning the milk. (If a skin does develop, remove it with a spoon.)
2. Let the milk cool to around 120 degrees, continuing to remove any skin that develops. Stir in the starter yogurt using the same spoon you used to stir the milk.
3. Transfer to 2 1-quart bowls. Cover with cheesecloth and set in a place between 90 and 115 degrees. You can put the bowls in an oven with a pilot light or, if it's summer and you live in Chicago, your porch will suffice! You can also put them in an insulated cooler to maintain the temperature, which is what I do.
4. The yogurt will completely set in about 10–16 hours, so give yourself lots of time. If it flops, you can always serve up the store-bought stuff! Prior to serving, whisk it up to make it creamy. (If you do the store-bought option, be sure to whip it up as well.)

Gushtaba (Lamb Meatballs in Yogurt Sauce)

Prepare the meatballs the night before or the morning of the party. You can finish this dish a couple hours before your guests arrive. It keeps well in the oven, allowing you to prepare the other dishes, which do *not* hold up so well in the oven. You will get raves for months after you serve this up to your friends.

Ingredients
For the *kofta* (meatballs):
1 pound minced lamb if available; otherwise, 1 pound cubed lamb shoulder
1 teaspoon dried ginger powder (*sonth*)

2 teaspoons ground fennel (*saunf*), made by grinding fennel seeds in a coffee grinder (You will need a lot of it for this dinner party, so grind up around 5 tablespoons of the seeds for use throughout the dishes.)

1 teaspoon cumin powder (*jeera*)

1½ teaspoons sea salt

Seeds from 2 black cardamom pods (*moti illaichi*), powdered (With a small mortar and pestle, grind the seeds with some of the sea salt. The seeds are oily, and if you try to grind them alone, they will clump into a gooey mass.)

For boiling the *kofta*:
3 cups water

4 cloves (*laung*)

2 *tej patta* bay leaves (I prefer the *tej patta* found at Indian markets, but any bay leaf will do in a pinch.)

2 *desi* cinnamon sticks (*Desi* cinnamon is different from that commonly found in conventional U.S. grocery stores, which is mostly the Mexican variety, *canella*. You can use *canella,* but I prefer the authentic *desi* kind.)

1 teaspoon sea salt

For the yogurt sauce:
4 tablespoons canola oil

4 tablespoons ghee

2 medium yellow onions, finely chopped

½ teaspoon dried ginger powder (*sonth*)

1 teaspoon ground fennel (*saunf*)

1½ teaspoons dried mint (*pudina*)

½ teaspoon *garam masala* (You can find this at any Indian store. Ask for *vasi masala* and use if available.)

Seeds of 2 black cardamom pods and 4 green cardamom pods, powdered (Prepare as directed above.)

2 cups yogurt (store-bought or homemade)

For garnish:
¼ cup toasted pumpkinseeds (Available at most Hispanic markets, but usually not Indian ones since the use of pumpkinseeds is somewhat unique to Kashmir.)

Fresh mint leaves

Let's get cooking

1. Prepare the *kofta* the night before or the morning of your party and store them in your refrigerator. Kashmiri women traditionally spend hours beating various extremely fatty meats with enormous mortars and pestles. Fortunately, there is no need for that labor with the modern-day food processor.

    a. Whether you are using minced lamb or lamb cubes, grind the meat in a food processor until it is a fine paste. Be patient: The meat will clump around the spindle of your food processor a few times before the final desired consistency is achieved. Transfer the meat paste into a large bowl.

    b. Add all of the dry ingredients to the meat paste and incorporate thoroughly with your hands. (Spray your hands with canola oil cooking spray before mixing, or just rub them with some oil to keep the meat paste from sticking.) *Resist the temptation to add the spices to the meat mixture in the food processor.* While it sounds logical, the spices don't incorporate because of the tendency of the meat to cluster around the spindle, leaving your hard-ground spices all over the processor bowl. Just do it the old-fashioned way: by hand.

    c. Spray (or rub) your hands with additional canola oil. Shape the meat mixture into balls about the size of a golf ball and place them on a tray. This recipe will make about 12–16 balls. (Traditionally, Kashmiris form enormous grapefruit-size meatballs, but they have the texture of a dog toy when cooked. I find that the small *kofta* always taste better.)

    d. Cover the meatballs with plastic wrap and put them in the fridge.

2. Begin preparing the remainder of the *gushtaba* about 2 hours before your guests arrive. It will keep very nicely in a warm oven while you prepare the other dishes.

    a. About 20 minutes prior to cooking the *gushtaba*, take the meatballs out of the refrigerator and let them begin warming up to room temperature. Because they will be added to boiling water, letting them warm up will diminish the temperature drop of the water once they are dropped into the pot.

    b. Bring 3 cups water to a boil in a medium-size pot. Add the cloves, bay leaves, cinnamon sticks, and salt. Gently add the *kofta* to the boiling water. Place a lid on the pot, slightly askew to retain most of the moisture while still letting some steam escape. Make sure that all the meatballs are cooked evenly, turning them occasionally if needed. They can cook for 30 minutes or more as long as the water does not evaporate. If the water does evaporate, just add more warm water and bring it back to the gentle boil. (I usually keep the meatballs in the boiling water until I finish the yogurt sauce.)

3. Prepare the yogurt sauce.

   a. Heat the oil and ghee in a heavy skillet. Add the onions and fry until golden brown. Don't skimp on this step, as the caramelized onions give the dish its signature hue.

   b. Add the ginger powder, fennel, mint, *garam masala,* and powdered cardamom seeds to the onions and fry for a few minutes. Whisk in the yogurt and bring the mixture to a boil for about 1 or 2 minutes, stirring constantly. Add about 1 cup of the water used to boil the *kofta,* being sure to leave the solid spices behind.

   c. If you have an immersion blender, blend the mixture in the skillet until it has a smooth consistency. There should be no clumps. (A regular blender will suffice, but this means more things to clean.)

4. Remove the meatballs from the pot and place them in a casserole dish with an appropriate lid. (I also make sure the casserole is one I can use to serve my guests.) Cover the meatballs with the yogurt sauce. This dish can be kept in a warm oven for up to an hour before your guests arrive, or it can be kept at room temperature for longer and warmed in the oven before serving.

5. Right before serving, lightly toast the pumpkinseeds in a small skillet, turning frequently to avoid burning. Tear off a number of lovely mint leaves. Sprinkle the *gushtaba* with the pumpkinseeds and mint leaves.

Dum Aloo *(Potatoes in Spicy Gravy)*

The small, round Kashmiri variety of potato for which this dish is suited is unavailable outside of Kashmir. In fact, you cannot even get this potato in the Indian hinterland. I've tried many different potatoes, and I suggest using Yukon Golds. They hold up well, and while the visual of quartered Yukon Golds is not the same as the charming round Kashmiri potato nuggets, that's just life. (To paraphrase the former U.S. Secretary of Defense, you make dinner with the potato you have, not the potato you want.) However, at some specialty markets you can find "baby" Yukon Gold potatoes, which are perfect. If using these, you need not quarter them.

Ingredients

1 pound firm Yukon Gold potatoes, peeled and cut into pieces that are roughly 1½ inches thick (Alternatively, with the baby Yukon Golds, you just peel and go.)

¼ cup canola oil for frying the potatoes

¼ cup ghee and ¼ cup canola oil for making the spicy sauce

2 bay leaves (See note on *tej patta* bay leaves in *gushtaba* recipe.)

2 cinnamon sticks (See note on *desi* cinnamon in *gushtaba* recipe.)

8 cloves (*laung*)

¼ teaspoon asafetida (compounded powder) mixed with ¼ cup water to make a slurry (Asafetida won't dissolve entirely in the water. Just mix into a slurry—a suspension of the powder into the water. If it dissociates with a black gum at the bottom, just mix before use.)

2–4 teaspoons red chili powder (I use 4 because I like the heat. You can use less, but I don't recommend fewer than 2.)

½ cup nonfat, plain yogurt whisked into 1 cup water

4 teaspoons ground fennel (*saunf*)

2 teaspoons dried ginger powder (*sonth*)

Seeds of 2 black cardamom pods, ground into a powder (With a small mortar and pestle, grind the seeds with some coarse salt.)

For garnish:

1 teaspoon cumin powder (*jeera*)

1 teaspoon *garam masala* (or *vasi masala*)

Chopped cilantro leaves

Toasted pumpkinseeds

Let's get cooking

1. Prick the chopped potatoes with a fork or a toothpick in places to facilitate the permeation of the spices into the flesh. Briefly boil the potato pieces in salted water for about 5 minutes. Remove them from the water, transfer to a cool bowl, and cover with cold water and some ice. This will stop the cooking process. Keep them in cold water until ready to use.

2. Heat ¼ cup canola oil in a heavy-bottomed pan. Dry the potato pieces and carefully place them in the pan. Any water that lands in the hot oil will cause the oil to spatter and potentially burn you. Fry them until they develop a rich golden brown color, which may take about 12–15 minutes. Add more oil if needed. Set aside the potatoes and discard the oil.

3. Heat the ghee and another ¼ cup canola oil in a medium-size pot and fry the bay leaves, cinnamon sticks, and cloves for about 1 minute. The cloves and cinnamon sticks will puff up. Don't let these burn!

4. Carefully add the asafetida water to the oil and spice mixture. Remember to *be careful*: The oil will spatter when the water hits it. Stir for about 30 seconds to fry.

5. Add the chili powder and fry for another 30 seconds.

6. Add the yogurt water to the hot oil *carefully* to minimize spattering. Next add the fennel, ginger powder, and powdered cardamom seeds and mix thoroughly to incorporate. Add the fried potatoes. Cook until oil floats on top and the potatoes are cooked throughout. The potatoes should not be white inside; instead, the color of the pepper should penetrate the potatoes, imparting a reddish color. If the red does not penetrate throughout, prick the potatoes a few more times, add a bit more water (began with ¼ cup), and let the mixture simmer longer until done.

7. When the cooking is finished, transfer to a serving dish. (Some folks prefer to remove the cinnamon sticks, cloves, and bay leaves. I leave them in as do most Indian cooks I know. But you can certainly remove them if you prefer to do so.) Toast the cumin and *garam masala* in a small pan and sprinkling the spices over the potatoes. Sprinkle the dish with chopped cilantro leaves and toasted pumpkinseeds.

Palak Maaz *(Spinach with Lamb)*

Kashmiris eat a lot of lamb, so I am going to use lamb in this dish. If you prefer, you can substitute chicken thighs. I also use frozen spinach, as fresh spinach has a lot of water and is a pain to work with because you have to add it in portions, waiting for it to wilt down before adding more. If you do use the fresh stuff, be sure to buy the kind in bags that has been washed multiple times and is therefore "ready to eat." Otherwise, you will have the added step of laboriously cleaning your spinach.

Ingredients

½ cup canola oil

4 cloves (*laung*)

1 cinnamon stick (See note on *desi* cinnamon in *gushtaba* recipe.)

1 bay leaf (See note on *tej patta* bay leaves in *gushtaba* recipe.)

½ teaspoon asafetida (compounded powder)

2 medium yellow onions, finely chopped

4 cloves garlic, minced

1 pound lamb shoulder cut into roughly 1½-inch cubes

1 pound frozen spinach, thawed with the water squeezed out, or 10 cups
 fresh, cleaned spinach

3 ripe Roma tomatoes, finely chopped

2 green chiles, finely chopped (Use the small, slender Asian green chiles, or
 jalapeños in a pinch. Remove the seeds and white "ribs" of the peppers
 to minimize heat, if you wish, but use caution and wear gloves, as the
 pepper oil will burn. The oil is not water soluble, so washing your hands
 will not remove it.)

½ teaspoon dried ginger powder (*sonth*)

1 teaspoon ground fennel (*saunf*)

½ teaspoon *garam masala* or *vasi masala*

1 teaspoon coarse salt

½ cup water (or more as needed)

For garnish:

Chopped cilantro leaves

Let's get cooking

1. In a large, high-walled pot, heat the oil and fry the cloves, cinnamon stick, and bay leaf for 1–2 minutes.
2. Add the asafetida and fry for another minute. (When you add this to the oil, sprinkle it all over the surface. Otherwise, it will clump in the pan and will not distribute evenly.)
3. Add the onions and garlic and fry until slightly browned. This should take about 3 minutes.
4. Add the lamb to the pan and fry, turning as needed to ensure that each side gets a good sear.
5. Add the spinach, tomatoes, chiles, and the remaining spices. If using thawed frozen spinach, you can do this in one step. If using fresh, you will have to do this in several portions, filling up your pot with the leaves and waiting for them to wilt down to make room for the next bunch. Once the spinach is incorporated, add the tomatoes, chiles, and the spices.
6. Stir this mixture until all of the water is absorbed and/or evaporated. Spinach, especially the fresh stuff, has a lot of water that will be released in the cooking process. Continue stirring until the spinach is well "fried," though given the amount of water in the pot, it is no longer technically frying.
7. Add about ½ cup water and let the mixture cook until the lamb is tender. Add more water if needed during the cooking process.
8. Transfer to a serving dish. (Again you can remove the cinnamon sticks, bay leaf, and cloves if you prefer.) Garnish with chopped cilantro.

Sada Caval *(Plain Rice)*

Kashmiris tend to eat nan *or* rice with their food, but basmati rice is most appropriate for the dishes served at *this* dinner party. Proper preparation of fluffy, delicious rice requires a thorough cleaning of the starchy particles. Failure to do so will result in clumpy, heavy rice. To remove the starch, place the rice in a bowl, cover with cold water, and *gently* agitate the mixture. Too vigorous washing will cause the rice grains to break, resulting in rice that is less visually appealing. The water will become cloudy as the starch comes off of the rice. Drain this water and repeat until the cloudiness of the water stops *changing*. Because rice *is* starch, there will always be some cloudiness, as each wash will result in starch releasing into the water. The first wash will be very cloudy, but by the third or fourth, there will be a stable minimum amount of cloudiness. This is when I stop washing.

Ingredients

2 cups long-grain basmati rice
3 tablespoons ghee or canola oil
4 cups cold water
1 teaspoon coarse salt

For garnish:
Chopped cilantro leaves
¼ cup toasted pumpkin seeds

Let's get cooking

1. Per note above, gently rinse the rice about 3 or 4 times with cold water to remove the starch.
2. Heat the ghee or oil in a medium-size pot. Fry the rice until it becomes translucent. This step is important because it coats the rice grains with oil and further prevents the grains from clumping. Be careful while agitating the rice in this step to minimize breakage.
3. Add 4 cups water along with the salt and bring to a boil. Once the water boils, cover the pot, lower the heat, and simmer until the rice is tender. For 2 cups of rice, it will take between 15 and 20 minutes. Try not to open the lid of the pot, as it is the steam that cooks the rice. The rice is done when holes appear on the surface.
4. Fold the fluffy rice onto a platter and garnish with chopped cilantro and toasted pumpkin seeds.

DESSERT

★★ ★★★★★★★★★★★★ ★★★★★★

Firnee *(Rice Pudding with Nuts, Dried Fruit, and Saffron)*

This dish is composed of gently boiled milk and soaked rice. It is of utmost importance that you do not rush the boiling process and risk scalding—or worse, burning—the milk. For this reason, I suggest you make it the day before your party, which also gives the pudding time to set. The *firnee* will be served with Kashmiri green tea (*kahwa*).

Ingredients

½ cup plus 1 tablespoon basmati rice, soaked in water for about 4 hours

1 quart 1 percent milk (You can use a higher percentage of milk fat, but you don't need to.)

½ cup sugar (I use demerara or cane sugar rather than the white stuff, but suit yourself.)

½ teaspoon saffron, powdered (With a mortar and pestle, grind the saffron into a fine powder with a cube of sugar.)

¼ cup golden raisins

For garnish:

⅛ cup chopped pistachios or almonds

Let's get cooking

1. Clean the rice to remove any nonrice fragments and wash it thoroughly. Cover with water and let soak for 4 hours.
2. Grind the soaked rice into a grainy paste in your blender or with an immersion blender.
3. Bring the milk to a gentle, rumbling boil in a heavy-bottomed pot. Stir constantly to avoid milk solids from sticking to the bottom and burning. Be careful that the milk does not boil over the sides of your pot, and sustain this level of loving attention for about 5 minutes or so.
4. Transfer the boiled milk to a clean pot and add the rice paste. *Do not scrape the solids into the clean pot.* In fact, I change pots because no matter how diligent and doting you are, milk solids do form on the bottom and they are the enemy. Not only do these solids burn, they also attract the rice solids, which also burn.

5. Return to a medium flame and stir continuously until the mixture begins to thicken.
6. Add the sugar, powdered saffron, and raisins. Let the mixture come to a boil, all the while stirring constantly.
7. Remove from the flame and pour into 8 ramekins.
8. Decorate with chopped pistachios or almonds.
9. Cover with plastic wrap, place in the refrigerator, and chill overnight.

Kahwa *(Kashmiri Spiced Green Tea)*

Traditionally this tea is brewed in a samovar, similar to the Iranian style. You don't need a samovar, but you do need to take care to avoid overextracting the tea, which will make your beverage bitter. The secret is to steep the tea leaves between 30 seconds and 1 minute. This can be done with a tea ball or an infusion teapot, which I use.

Ingredients
4 cups water
2 cinnamon sticks
4 cloves
4 green cardamom pods, pounded lightly with a mortar and pestle (The objective is not to pulverize the pods, only to open them to release the fragrant seeds. Do not discard the pods.)
Pinch of saffron, powdered (With a mortar and pestle, grind the saffron into a fine powder with a cube of sugar.)
1½ teaspoons green tea leaves

For garnish:
Almond or pistachio slivers
Sugar cubes

Let's get brewing
1. Warm your teapot by adding boiled water until it is full. This step properly prepares your teapot such that you will not be pouring freshly brewed tea into a cool pot. Keep the hot water in the pot until ready for use.

2. Bring 4 cups of water to a vigorous boil along with the cinnamon, cloves, and cardamom pods and seeds. Boil for 5 minutes. This step is needed to extract the flavors from the spices. Add the powdered saffron and dissolve. (If you don't grind it into a fine powder, the saffron will not completely dissolve.)

3. If you are using an infusion teapot, put the leaves in the center of the pot and pour the spiced water over the leaves. Let the tea infuse for about 1 minute, agitating as needed. If you are not using an infuser, you can add the tea leaves directly to the spiced water and turn off the heat. This will require a tea strainer. *Have the strainer on hand so it is available when the 1-minute steeping time ends.* You can also use a tea ball, which can be easily removed after 1 minute. If using a tea ball, be sure to agitate in the water to ensure proper brewing. While the tea steeps, empty the water from your teapot. Transfer the tea mixture to the teapot.

4. Sprinkle almond or pistachios slivers into the bottom of your guests' tea cups and pour the hot tea over the nuts. Serve with sugar cubes and enjoy!

Dossier of Pakistani Perfidy

I am going on record to say that, with respect to its nuclear program, Pakistan had no options! Had India not plunged headlong into the pursuit of nukes, Pakistan probably would not have gone there. Had India signed the Nuclear Nonproliferation Treaty (NPT) as a non–nuclear weapons state, Pakistan probably would have too. However, since India refused, so did Pakistan. Pakistan also claims that had India signed the Comprehensive Test Ban Treaty, it would have done so as well, and Pakistan says the same thing about a fissile material cutoff treaty too. Pakistan also claims that it would give up its nukes if India would. But all of this is cheap talk, because Islamabad well understands that India will not do any of these things in any policy-relevant future—if ever. So Pakistan can offer up any well-sounding declaration in full confidence that India would never be compelled to call Islamabad's bluff.

Pakistan understands that India seeks to prepare itself for the threat from China even while Delhi pursues accommodation of and better relations with the godless Chicoms (see chapter on those jokers in this volume). Pakistan knows this full well because China has been its only enduring friend, and Pakistan is no doubt up in a swivet over the India-China hanky-panky going on in its own backyard.

As with many contemporary problems that are intractable and sanguinary, the British can be blamed. In 1947, when the Brits finally hauled tail out of the subcontinent, they divided the detritus of their fiefdom—aka "the Raj"—into two states called India and Pakistan. The British did a criminally crappy job delineating the borders of these two successor states and provided no security as the states were hacked out of the bygone empire—and while their newly emergent citizenry hacked each other to death. The partition of the subcontinent was the world's largest and most violent transfer of people and needlessly killed or grievously injured millions in the heinous violence that broke out as Muslims sought to drive out Hindus and Sikhs from the nascent Pakistan and as Hindus sought to drive Muslims out of the newly born India.[154]

The Short End of the Stick

Pakistan inherited very little of the military, political, and civic infrastructure—the bulk of which went to the larger successor state, India. India predictably reneged on providing Pakistan the most rudimentary military equipment as obligated under the terms of partition. Pakistanis continue to see partition as an unfair process that privileged India and adversely positioned Pakistan and, most important, one that deprived Pakistan of Kashmir. Oddly, sex may have had something to do with Pakistan's inequitable transfer of assets. Lord Mountbatten was the last viceroy of India, and he was selected to hand a united India over to Indians. That was not to be, in part, due to Mohammad Ali Jinnah and the mounting demand of the Muslim League for an independent Muslim state to be carved out of the Raj. This demand was based upon the "two nation" theory, which argued that Muslims and Hindus comprise distinct nations and that, by extension, without such a Muslim state, Muslims would suffer under the tyranny of a Hindu majority.

Mountbatten, according to at least one Pakistan-origin historian, Akbar S. Ahmed, was *very fond* of the Indian political leader, Jawaharlal Nehru, who would become the first prime minister of independent India. Ahmed alleges that Mountbatten looked out for Nehru's interests, and by extension that of India, and had a healthy spite for Jinnah. Not only did Lord Mountbatten like Nehru, but so it seems did his wife, Lady Edwina. Edwina and Nehru graced archives with loads of flirtatious notes. Ahmed recalls one day when "Edwina lay on her back, raised her lovely lissome legs high above her head on the surrounding lawn and, grinning, said [to Nehru] in her inimitable sweet frank way, 'Not bad for fifty, is it?'"[155] Mountbatten's purported predilection to fish in both ponds and Edwina's reputation for being on the tarty side have tantalized historians about the connections between prurience, national boundaries, and communal politics ever since.

Pakistanis still provide evidence of India's enduring perfidy by reminding us that there were two "princely states" within the borders of new India: Junagad in present-day Gujarat and Hyderabad in south India. While the subjects of both were predominantly Hindu, they were governed by Muslim princes who refused to join India and sought to join Pakistan. India forcibly annexed these two, arguing the infeasibility of Pakistani pockets within India. To Pakistan's eternal vexation, Kashmir was a Muslim majority state but governed by a Hindu king. Pakistan believed that based upon the majority Muslim population, geographic proximity to Pakistan, and the precedent of Junagad and Hyderabad, Kashmir should have become a part of Pakistan.[156]

But the maharaja (king) of Kashmir dithered as to where he would cast his lot, and by extension the lot of his mostly—but not all—Muslim subjects. Impatient with the irresolute Hindu maharaja, Pakistan dispatched Muslim tribesmen with the help of the army to seize Kashmir by force. This gave rise to the first Indo-Pakistan war of 1947–1948. Had the tribesmen not bogged themselves down in raping and pillaging innocents, they may have succeeded in taking the Kashmiri capital of Srinagar. Alas, these crimes of moral turpitude afforded the maharaja the opportunity to beg India for help. India's price was succession. The king of Kashmir signed the instrument of accession, India dispatched troops to repel the Pakistanis, and the fate of Kashmir was thus forever doomed. The cease-fire that was negotiated resulted in about one-third of Kashmir falling under the auspices of Pakistan and the rest under India's control.

To be clear, the Kashmir region is composed of several different areas, including the Northern Areas of Pakistan, Baltistan, Leh, Ladakh, Jammu, the Valley of Kashmir, and so forth. So one needs to be careful and remember that "Kashmir" is merely a shorthand for a more complex pastiche of ethnic, linguistic, and religious communities. Anyone who talks about Kashmiris as if they are one folk should be seriously discounted because, while it is politic to say so, it's just not true. But, back to our story of how Pakistan got the bomb and why.

If this historical bequeathal wasn't bad enough, until circa 1998 India's leadership rejected the very principle upon which Pakistan was founded, the "two nation" theory, which argued that Muslims and Hindus comprise distinct nations and that, by extension, without a Muslim state, Muslims would suffer under the tyranny of a Hindu majority. Rightly or wrongly, for most of Pakistan's sixty-year existence, it has feared that India seeks to destroy it, conquer it, or disable it.

The 1971 war with India provided ample proof of India's malevolent intentions. That year India stepped in to help Bengali Muslim insurgents (the Mukti Bahini) in what was then East Pakistan. Of course, the insurgency in East Pakistan emerged due to successive and deliberate mismanagement by the predominantly Punjabi political elites in West Pakistan, who viewed their Bengali citizens with derision. After more than two decades of extracting East Pakistan's resources with little or no return and systematically suppressing Bengali ethnic, political, and cultural aspirations, the Bengalis were simply fed up and launched an insurgent campaign for their freedom. West Pakistan responded with decisive force and began a genocidal pogrom.

With refugees streaming into India, Prime Minister Indira Gandhi began an international diplomatic campaign to justify Indian military intervention. While the United States formally sided with Pakistan and sent the USS

Enterprise to the Bay of Bengal to signal its support, the U.S. Consul General, Archer Blood, sent a "dissent" cable noting that the United States was on the wrong side.[158] The war ended with Pakistan's dismemberment and the emergence of an independent Bangladesh. The war proved to Pakistanis that India was intent upon its destruction. Since 1971 Pakistan has exacted—or has sought to exact—revenge by supporting insurgency, separatism, and good old-fashioned criminal nut jobs throughout India.

Pakistan Jumps Onboard

After the humiliating defeat in the 1971 war, Prime Minister Zulfiqar Ali Bhutto committed Pakistan to the development of nuclear weapons. By then Pakistan was already convinced that India was fast developing a capability, and these fears were confirmed by India's "peaceful nuclear explosion" in 1974. Bhutto employed the now notorious A. Q. Khan—a German-trained metallurgist who worked at URENCO, a Netherlands-based nuclear-enrichment plant. Khan essentially stole enrichment technologies (e.g., centrifuge designs) from URENCO. Upon launching Pakistan's program through theft, Khan pioneered a global network to obtain nuclear technology by every legal and illegal means possible. By 1986 Pakistan likely produced enough weapons-grade fissile materials for at least one weapon, and by 1987 it was capable of testing a device.[159]

By the late 1980s, it was clear to the United States that Pakistan was acquiring a nuclear weapon that would trigger U.S. sanctions. To accommodate the White House's interest in continuing military assistance, despite concerns in Congress and the intelligence community about nuclear proliferation, the Pressler Ammendment was drafted. It permitted military aid to continue flowing to Pakistan, provided that the president could certify its ally to be "nuke-free." In 1990, vexed with Pakistan's nuclear accomplishments and no longer requiring its services to toss the Ruskies out of Afghanistan, President Bush declined to certify Pakistan's nuke-free status. This resulted in a complete cessation of military assistance to Pakistan, including delivery of a batch of F-16s that Pakistan had paid for despite the warnings of sanctions and full knowledge it was micturating on U.S. law.

This galled—and continues to gall—Pakistanis, who were and are blissfully unaware of the numerous and systematic warnings (aka "demarches" in diplomatese) given to General Zia. This has led many Pakistanis to hold a belief that was colorfully explained to me by one lieutenant general a few years back that

"Pakistan is the condom the U.S. uses to screw [he used a different word] Afghanistan. When you are done, you toss us away." Rickshaw drivers throughout Pakistan know of Mr. Pressler and his presumed sanctions, and F-16s continue to be painted on trucks, cars, and oxen carts, attesting to their symbolic importance. In the end, Pakistan correctly chose nukes over a bunch of planes.

When India tested in 1998, Pakistan found itself in an impossible situation. Indian leaders taunted the Pakistanis, claiming that they were incapable of testing a device and intimating that perhaps Pakistan didn't even have one. This had to tick off Pakistan because, unlike India, it actually acquired verified designs from its Chinese friends. Pakistan probably didn't need to test, but while it knew that it would be immediately hit with yet more sanctions that would further devastate its economy, to not test would be tantamount to conceding India's domination and living as a nuclear eunuch in the subcontinent. A few weeks later, the Pakistanis tested, knowing full well that a fresh layer of sanctions were waiting. Predictably, they claim to have tested one more device than did the Indians—the nuclear version of two plumbers arguing over whose snake is bigger. Like the Indians, they exaggerated "how big"

Zia and the Boob Brigade

Everyone knows that Zia ul-Haq was an Islamic obscurantist who sought to Islamize his country even though no one seemed to welcome those initiatives. What many don't know, however, is that Zia's critical supporter in the United States was congressman Charlie Wilson, who was arguably the most important person in securing loads of cash and weapons to kill Russians in Afghanistan—almost all of which was laundered through Pakistan.

Wilson was a renowned rake who constantly surrounded himself with hot, busty women. He vowed that he would never go to Pakistan without a dame in tow, and he honored that promise. Wilson paraded a number of women through Pakistan, including a belly dancer who became a guest of Zia's. Not only did Zia amicably endure this particular vixen, he chaperoned "Sweetums," another Charlie consort. When the Defense Intelligence Agency (DIA) refused to let Sweetums fly with Wilson to the frontier on a DIA airplane (which pissed Wilson off enough to use his massive influence on the defense appropriation committee to remove funding for the plane), Zia generously offered his own personal aircraft to get her there. Zia, ever the sport, also entertained another Wilson hottie named "Snowflake." When she met him, she was sporting a flight-suit-inspired jumpsuit. Apparently, she had an odd sense of modesty.[160]

their devices were, as none of the professed yields have been independently verified.[161] The always-helpful Saudis relieved some of the pinch by providing cash and subsidized oil.

It should be noted that while Pakistan is included in this book because of its extralegal acquisition of nuclear weapons, it gets a lot of grief for a multitude of other things. Its government has been controlled by the army for the majority of its existence. While Pakistan is a critical partner in the U.S.-led global war on terrorism and has captured and detained more terrorists than any other partner, that is largely due to the fact that there are more terrorists that need catching in Pakistan than in any other partner country. Pakistan has a long and sadly well-documented history of supporting a slew of militants that operate in Indian-administered Kashmir, India, and Afghanistan. Pakistan was one of only three countries that recognized the odious Taliban. Moreover, it provided every kind of assistance to that repugnant regime because they hoped that a Taliban-controlled Afghanistan would be friendlier to Pakistan than to India.

Born an insecure and weak state, Pakistan has only become more insecure as its neighbor to the east has grown stronger along all dimensions of national power. It has courted international opprobrium, started wars doomed to failure, and supported an array of Islamic militant nut jobs in the pursuit of maximizing its security. It sucks to be Pakistan—and any of its neighbors who have prefigured in this political folly.

Dinner with the Taliban: A Night in Hyatabad . . . or Maybe University Town

While it is unlikely that Pakistan had any strategic ties with Al-Qaeda, its militant groups benefited from the largess of Osama bin Laden, who funded the network of training camps in Afghanistan. It is now well documented that Taliban and Al-Qaeda operatives alike, including bin Laden, made their homes in the lovely mansions (or *kotis*) of Hyatabad, a "bourgeois" well-landscaped suburb of Peshawar, the notorious city in Pakistan's frontier. The locality offered everything: the amenities of a city, proximity to the Khyber Pass and other routes to Afghanistan, a well-structured militant community, and access to ISI (Pakistan's notorious intelligence agency) headquarters only two hours away in Rawalpindi.[162]

Perhaps the most notorious of all frontier edibles is the *chapli* kebab. It is so named because when executed appropriately, it is very thin and fried to a crisp. In Urdu (and other languages in the region), *chapal* references a simple, flat sandal traditionally made of leather. Thus these kebabs are called *chapli* because they are supposed to be reminiscent of the heel of a *chapal*. These flat patties are traditionally fried in enormous flat, round pans filled with thick black oil or filthy beef tallow sitting atop a wood fire. Whenever I go to Peshawar—one of my favorite cities anywhere—I like to hunt out tiny *chapli* kebab stalls where the patties are bursting with coriander and pomegranate seeds and green chiles and fried to a blackened crisp. They are often served with mint chutney or other divine sauces. While the *chapli* kebab is hands-down the culinary *sina-qua-non* of the frontier, as a general rule Pakistanis and Pashtuns (who inhabit the frontier) do a good job grilling up a wide array of critters. It is a paradise for folks doing low-carb diets.

Another speciality of the frontier is various forms of tea (*kehva* or *sabz chai*) brewing in a samovar. *Kehva* is often infused with cardamom and other spices and is very light on tea content. I have been served some variant of *kehva* that is made only of the herbal infusion of cardamom, cinnamon with dried mint leaves en lieu of the green tea leaves.

To remind ourselves of those days gone by, our dinner party will feature the foods of the frontier in what I'd like to imagine as a feast of the Taliban.

The Plan of Attack

This chapter aims to feed eight Tora Bora cave dwellers; adjust as you see fit. The night before the party, I suggest you mix the ingredients for the *chapli* kebab, begin marinating the kebab *qabergha,* and make the dessert (*sheer seemiyan*). In addition, you need to soak the dried chickpeas for the *peshawari chana.* You *could* use canned chickpeas, but I advise against this. In my humble opinion, the canned chickpeas take on the flavor of the metal in which they are preserved. Moreover, in this dish, the chickpeas acquire their distinctive hue from boiling them raw with a teabag, and the canned chickpeas do not pick up the color in the same way. Plus, I soak the dried chickpeas overnight with sodium bicarbonate, which makes them infinitely more tender—and therefore more delicious—than the canned kind.

If you are grilling the kebab *qabergha* outside on your barbecue, you won't need your oven for anything other than the nan. However, if the weather is not conducive to a barbecue, you'll have to use your broiler. In that case, when the nan are nearly done, you will turn on your broiler to cook the *qabergha* and the nan will finish baking from the retained heat in the oven. I put the kebabs under the broiler just as guests begin to arrive, because they cook quickly and I want them served up quickly.

Four hours before your guests arrive, make the dough for the nan. Two hours before arrival, make the chickpeas if you are using a pressure cooker. Otherwise begin this *three hours* before arrival time. One hour before your guests arrive, make the *chapli* kebab, and about 30 minutes before arrival, begin forming and baking the nan. Right before they arrive, cook the kebab *qabergha*. Round off your meal with a vermicelli pudding and green tea.

Main course

- *Chapli* Kebab (spiced lamb patties, flattened and fried) with *pudine ki* chutney (mint chutney). You can buy or make the chutney.
- *Peshawari Chana* (mildly spiced chickpeas)
- Kebab *Qabergha* (mildly spiced lamb ribs)
- *Nan* (nan with sesame seeds)
- *Pullow* (rice cooked with spices and onions)

Dessert

- *Sheer Seemiyan* (vermicelli in milk pudding)

Beverages

■ Pakistan is technically a dry country, and I really can't see the Taliban quaffing illegal brew. The occasional neo-Taliban may partake of a derivative of his associated goons' poppy crop, but he probably doesn't get liquored up and lacquered down. In keeping with etiquette of the frontier, this dinner party will feature *kehva* (aka *sabz chai* or green tea), a frontier specialty. However, as a proud daughter of the Great Satan (or *Shetan-e-Bozurg* or *bara shetan,* as they would say in Peshawar), I will recommend a pleasant Shiraz (or Sirah) or perhaps an Indian pale ale. The latter may seem a strange choice, but in 1947 the folks of Peshawar actually wanted to stay with India—not Pakistan. So if you serve up some Indian pale ale, raise a toast to the secular Pashtun nationalists who wanted to stick with Gandhi and Nehru.

PREPARATION

MAIN COURSE

Chapli Kebab *(Spiced Lamb Patties)*

When making these, I try to remove all excess water from the vegetables. As I chop them, I squeeze out any extra water and then place the veggies in a strainer, where they sit until I'm ready to use them. I prefer to mix the meat ingredients the day before and refrigerate overnight to allow the spices to mingle. (Do the same for the mint chutney if you make it yourself.)

Ingredients
2 pounds ground lamb (substitute beef or buffalo if you wish)
3 tablespoons coriander seeds
3 tablespoons dried pomegranate seeds

1 tablespoon red pepper flakes

2 bunches scallions, sliced very thin (Use only the bulb and the pale portion of the stalk, and dry thoroughly before slicing.)

4 ounces (about ½ bunch) fresh cilantro, finely chopped (Use only the leaves and the parts of stem nearest the leaves. Dry thoroughly before chopping.)

1 medium yellow onion, finely diced and squeezed

2 Roma tomatoes, finely diced and jelly removed

2 green chiles, finely chopped (If you want less heat, remove the seeds and veins. Use gloves, as this is where the heat-producing, non-water-soluble oils are most concentrated, and be careful not to touch your eyes or other sensitive places.)

5 cloves garlic, pressed or ground into a paste

1 teaspoon coarsely ground black pepper

1 tablespoon coriander powder

1½ teaspoons sea salt

½ cup gram flour, or *besan* (This flour is derived from ground chickpeas and is available at most South Asian groceries. Use bread flour if you must as a workable substitute.)

2 eggs, slightly beaten

Several thin tomato slices (for garnish while frying)

Oil for frying (For best flavor, use beef tallow. Otherwise, use canola oil or some combination of both.)

For garnish:

Pudine ki chutney (mint chutney). You can buy this or easily make it. Blend 1 cup fresh coriander leaves (no stems), ½ cup fresh mint leaves (no stems), 1 green chile, 2 cloves garlic, juice of 1 lemon, 3 tablespoons water, ½ teaspoon sea salt, and ½ teaspoon sugar into a thick liquid. Add water in 1-teaspoon increments to get desired texture and consistency. Make this well in advance of your party and keep it in the fridge.

Sprigs of cilantro

Fresh pomegranate seeds (optional)

Let's get cooking

1. Put all ingredients (except the garnish and oil) in a large bowl and mix thoroughly. Let sit in the refrigerator until ready to use. (It's best if the mixture can sit for several hours or even overnight before use.)

2. About 1 hour before your guests arrive, begin cooking the kebabs. Form the meat mixture into several thin patties about ¼ inch thick and 4–5 inches in diameter. Press one slice of tomato into the top of each kebab before frying.

3. Prepare a large, heavy-bottomed frying pan by heating the oil and/or tallow. Be sure that the oil is at least ¾ inch high in the pan. (Traditionally, the patties are submerged in oil, which seems a bit excessive.)

4. When the oil/tallow is hot, carefully slide the kebabs into it. Don't crowd the pan. Let the kebabs sit in the hot oil until they have a nice crispy surface. Flip and cook the other side. (This could take 5 minutes or more on each side, depending on your pan and thickness of the kebab). When finished, remove the kebabs and put them on a paper towel to drain the excess oil. Transfer to a covered dish to keep warm. Continue cooking in batches until done.

5. Place on a platter and sprinkle with chopped cilantro and pomegranate seeds. Serve with mint chutney as a condiment.

Peshawari Chana (Mildly Spiced Chickpeas)

The night before the party, pick through the dried chickpeas and remove anything that should not be there, such as rocks, dirt, etc. Cover with about 6 cups of water and add 1 teaspoon sodium bicarbonate (aka baking soda). This will produce very tender chickpeas. This dish takes its unusual color from the teabag with which the chickpeas are cooked.

Ingredients

8 ounces dried chickpeas, soaked overnight in 6 cups water and 1 teaspoon baking soda
1 black tea teabag (Lipton will work.)
5 tablespoons canola oil
2 cups diced yellow onions

2 slender green chiles, finely chopped

2 tablespoons finely chopped ginger

2 tablespoons finely chopped garlic

1½ teaspoons red chili powder (I actually use much more than this, up to 2 *tablespoons*. But, unless you like things fiery, stick to the lower amount.)

2 teaspoons cumin powder

4 tablespoons (No, that's not a typo!) coriander powder

2 bay leaves (I prefer to use the *tej patta* variety found in South Asian markets.)

1 cup finely chopped tomato

1 cup warm water

3 tablespoons pomegranate seed powder (Also known as *anardana* powder, it's available at South Asian markets.)

Sea salt to taste (I usually use about 2 teaspoons.)

1½ tablespoons *garam masala*

For garnish:

¼ cup finely chopped cilantro

¼ cup finely chopped yellow onion

Let's get cooking

1. Cook the soaked chickpeas in 6 cups water with the teabag. If you are using a pressure cooker, follow the manufacturer's instructions. (In my cooker, it takes about 10–15 minutes.) If you are not using a pressure cooker, this could take 40 minutes or longer to complete. Strain the chickpeas, remove the teabag, and set aside.

2. While the chickpeas are cooking, begin making the spicy sauce. In a big pot, heat 3 tablespoons of the oil. Fry the onions, chiles, ginger, and garlic until the onions are golden brown.

3. Add the other 2 tablespoons of oil and heat. Add the chili, cumin, and coriander powders along with the bay leaves. Fry the mixture for about 2 minutes.

4. Add the tomatoes and fry for another 10 minutes.

5. Add the cooked chickpeas, 1 cup warm water, pomegranate seed powder, and sea salt to taste. Let simmer on low heat until the spices are incorporated. Remove from the heat until your guests arrive.

6. Warm up the chickpeas to serve. Right before serving, add the *garam masala*. *Garam masala* can be destroyed by heat, and for this reason, I add it right before serving, in addition to more salt if needed. Transfer to a serving bowl

and garnish with chopped cilantro and finely chopped yellow onions. You could remove the bay leaves if you prefer. (Most folks I know do not bother.)

Kebab Qabergha *(Mildly Spiced Lamb Ribs)*

Qabergha literally means "rib." This dish is very easy to make and quite mild. The longer the meat marinates, of course, the better it will taste. At a minimum, let the ribs marinate for an hour, but I recommend you get this going the night before or the morning of the party and keep them in the fridge until you are ready to cook them. I cook this dish last. If I have to use my broiler, I begin broiling the ribs when my nan are nearly finished baking. (The nan bakes in a 500-degree oven. When I switch over to the broiler, the oven retains the heat *as long as the oven door doesn't remain open for long.* So be quick with placing those ribs in the oven!) You can also use a stove-top grill, but the best option is grilling over charcoal on the barbecue.

Ingredients
5 cloves garlic, crushed
1 tablespoon coriander powder
1 teaspoon freshly ground black pepper
1 teaspoon sea salt
½ cup water
8 small lamb chops

For garnish:
Sprigs of cilantro
1 teaspoon red pepper flakes

Let's get cooking
1. Whisk together all of the ingredients, except the lamb and garnish, in a medium-size bowl. Dunk each lamb chop in the mixture, ensuring that all sides are coated, and transfer to a ziplock bag large enough to accommodate all of them. When all of the ribs have been dunked and transferred to the bag, pour the remaining marinade into the bag and seal, squeezing out as much air as possible. Let sit for at least an hour (preferably overnight), turning often to ensure that the meat is coated well. Store in the refrigerator until ready to use.

2. When ready to cook, skewer the meat and grill. It's best to do this on a barbecue over coals, but a broiler or stove-top grill will suffice. Cook until done with a nice charred surface.
3. Serve the ribs on a platter with red pepper flakes sprinkled over them along with sprigs of cilantro.

Nan *(Nan with Sesame Seeds)*

The nan of Pakistan's frontier and Afghanistan are not the soft, fluffy loaves you typically get in Indian restaurants. These are thick, hearty, crusty breads often baked with sesame or poppy seeds. (Well, there is a lot of poppy in the area, after all!) Nan is traditionally made in a tandoor, which I certainly don't have in my kitchen and assume you don't have in yours either. Fortunately, I have found that a pizza stone heated in a 500-degree oven comes pretty close to the real thing. They are cheap (between $10 and $15) and can be used for many things other than nan, so it's a good investment. If you are not convinced of the need, you can put aluminum foil over your broiler pan. (If using the foil, be sure to lightly grease it with oil, preferably a spray-on one such as canola.) The heated air between the two pans of the broiler tends to produce a crispier nan. You can also use a heavy cookie sheet (greased or sprayed with oil) as a third-ranked alternative.

Ingredients
½ teaspoon sugar and ½ teaspoon flour for proofing the yeast
2 cups warm water
1 package dry yeast
5 cups bread flour
1 teaspoon baking powder
1 teaspoon sea salt
2 tablespoons canola oil or warmed ghee
1 egg beaten with 4 tablespoons water (egg wash)

For garnish:
Sesame seeds or poppy seeds

Let's get cooking

1. Proof the yeast by mixing the sugar and flour into the warm water and adding the yeast. Stir gently to incorporate the yeast into the sugar/flour water. The sugar and flour will help the yeast grow. Proceed with the recipe *only* if the yeast mixture begins to bubble on the surface of the water, providing evidence that the yeast is alive. This should take no more than 10 minutes. *Do not proceed if the mixture does not bubble,* which means you bought bad yeast. (It's rare but it does happen.) If needed, start all over with a new package of yeast.
2. While the yeast is proofing, sift the dry ingredients together into a large mixing bowl.
3. Incorporate the oil or ghee into the flour mixture with your hands.
4. Pour the *proofed* yeast water mixture over the dry ingredients mixed with the oil. Knead until a smooth dough is produced. This will take about 10 minutes of good hard kneading.
5. Form the dough into a ball. Cover with a damp cloth and let it rise. The dough is ready to use when it doubles in size.
6. Once the dough is ready, heat the oven to 500 degrees, along with the pizza stone (or foil-covered broiler pan or cookie sheet). On the bottom of the oven, place a pan of water to keep the oven air moist.
7. Once the dough has doubled, divide into 4 parts and form into loaves that are about ⅛ inch thick. In the frontier, nan are thick and round with some sort of design. In Afghanistan, nan are typically oblong with parallel grooves in the surface. This can be done by wetting your fingers, placing them at one end of the nan, and slowly pressing up and down across the surface to create a groove, repeating at regular intervals. (I skip this altogether and just make a pretty design with a fork.)
8. Once the nan is shaped as you like, brush on a thin coat of egg wash and sprinkle with sesame or poppy seeds.
9. If using a pizza stone, sprinkle it with a bit of cornmeal to ensure that the nan does not stick. (If using a cookie sheet or broiler pan with foil, grease or spray with oil.) Place the nan on the stone and bake until golden brown. Don't let it overcook or you will have dry and crusty nan. This should take about 8–10 minutes or less on a stone. When one nan finishes, wrap it in a towel and put it in a plastic bag to keep warm and moist. Repeat until all are cooked. (Obviously, if you have more than one stone or pan, you can cook them simultaneously.)

Pullow *(Rice Cooked with Spices and Onions)*

This light and fragrant dish is the perfect accompaniment to chickpeas and kebabs.

Ingredients

3 cups basmati rice

3 tablespoons ghee or canola oil

1 3-inch cinnamon stick

5 cloves

5 black peppercorns

2 black and 5 green cardamom pods (slightly crushed with a mortar and pestle to expose seeds)

1 medium yellow onion, finely chopped

5 cloves garlic, finely chopped

4½ cups water

2 teaspoons sea salt

Let's get cooking

1. Wash and rinse the basmati rice thoroughly. It is important to rinse the starch off the rice to ensure that the grains do not clump together. (I typically rinse 3 times.) While rinsing the rice, agitate carefully to avoid breaking it. Drain as much water as possible from the rice and set aside.

2. In a large pot, heat the oil. Add the cinnamon stick, cloves, peppercorns, and green and black cardamom pods and fry until the spices have "puffed up." This will only take a minute. Be sure to not let them burn.

3. Add the onions and garlic and fry until the onions are golden brown. (Add a wee bit of oil if needed.)

4. Add the rice and stir gently until it is translucent. This should take 2–4 minutes. Along with removing the starch, this important step will ensure that the rice is light and fluffy and less inclined to clump.

5. Add the water and salt to the pot with the rice and spices. Once the water boils, lower the heat, cover the pot, and let simmer until done. This should cook in about 15 minutes. (Holes will appear on the surface of the rice when done.) Serve on a platter. (As elsewhere, feel free to remove the cinnamon stick, cloves, and peppercorns before serving. I don't both and nor do most folks I know cooking this stuff.)

DESSERT

★★★★★★★★★★★★★★★★★★★★★★

Sheer Seemiyan *(Vermicelli in Milk Pudding)*

Ingredients

6 ounces vermicelli (durum semolina variety, not the rice variety)

3 tablespoons ghee or canola oil (Try to get the ghee—it tastes better.)

4 cups boiling water

2 tablespoons cornstarch

2½ cups skim milk (You use higher fat milk if you prefer, but there is no reason to do so to achieve desired flavor or consistency.)

1 cup sugar (Demerara or raw cane sugar is best, but white granulated sugar will suffice.)

½ teaspoon rosewater (If you loathe rosewater as much as I do, feel free to substitute ½ teaspoon of the essence of your choice, like vanilla, almond extract, etc.)

¼ cup golden raisins

Seeds of 4 green cardamom pods (You can easily remove the seeds by lightly crushing the pods with a mortar and pestle. Remove the green husks and pulverize the seeds.)

For garnish:

¼ cup sliced pistachios or almonds

Let's get cooking

1. Most vermicelli comes in tightly wound spindles, which you need to break up into a bowl. Aim to produce 2-inch fragments, but don't beat yourself up if you get smaller pieces. This is inevitable, and it doesn't matter as long your vermicelli doesn't become dust! Do this in the sink, because they will fly into the air as you break them up.

2. Heat the ghee in a tall-sided frying pan. When it's hot, add the vermicelli fragments to the pan and fry on medium heat until the pieces are golden brown. Depending upon your pan, this could take about 5 minutes. Stir constantly to ensure that it doesn't burn. While the vermicelli is browning, boil 4 cups of water. (I do this in the microwave or an electric tea kettle.)

3. When the vermicelli pieces are a lovely golden brown, *carefully* and *slowly* pour the boiling water into the pan. Turn the heat up to high and boil the fried fragments until they are soft. This will take 5 minutes or fewer.

4. While the fragments boil, prepare a small-holed strainer by placing a few ice cubes in it. These will be used to stop the cooking process.

5. When the fragments have finished cooking, strain them into the colander with the ice cubes. Run cold water over the noodles. Remove the ice cubes and set the chilled vermicelli aside until ready to use.

6. Dissolve the cornstarch in ¼ cup of the milk. Set aside.

7. Bring the remaining milk to a boil in a heavy-bottomed saucepan. Stir constantly to avoid burning, scorching, or other outcomes that will ruin this delicate dessert.

8. Slowly add the dissolved cornstarch to the milk and stir until it thickens. (It's good to go when you pull out your spoon and the mixture clings to it.)

9. Once the milk has thickened, add the sugar, rosewater (or more personally palatable substitute), and raisins. Stir continuously to dissolve and to ensure even thickening of the mixture. Let cook for another 2–3 minutes after adding the ingredients.

10. Add the browned, cooked vermicelli to the warm, thickened milk mixture. Stir well to incorporate. Pour into 8 ramekins and place in the fridge to set, preferably overnight (at a minimum, 2 hours). Sprinkle with the nuts of your choice to garnish and serve with ginger tea.

Kehva *(Sabz Chai, Spiced Green Tea)*

Some Pashtuns drink this stuff with loads of sugar, while others drink it without the sweet stuff. I like to serve it in small glasses with saucers and a few sugar cubes placed on the saucer. As far as teas go, this is very light on the tea. However, its hallmark is the infusion of the spices.

Ingredients
8 cups water
24 green cardamom seeds, lightly crushed in a mortar and pestle to open the pods
2 cinnamon sticks

1½ teaspoon green tea or two teabags
Optional. Pinch of saffron ground with a sugar cube in a mortar and pestle

Let's get brewing

1. Bring the water to a boil (1 cup for each of your diners).
2. Add the crushed cardamom seeds along with the cinnamon sticks to the boiling water. If using the saffron, add the saffron/sugar powder to the water.
3. Cover the pot, reduce the heat, and bring to a low boil. Let the spices infuse in the boiling water for 10–15 minutes.
4. While the spices infuse, warm your teapot by adding very hot water. This is to prevent the temperature of your tea from precipitously dropping when it hits a cool teapot.
5. Add the tea leaves or bags and brew for about 2 minutes. (If using loose-leaf tea, have your strainer ready to avoid overextraction.) When the tea is nearly done brewing, dump the warm water from your teapot. Pour the brewed tea, straining the teabags (or leaves) and spices, into the pot and keep warm with a tea cozy.
6. Serve in small glasses with sugar cubes.

PART

III

The Dashers of Democracy: Cuba, Burma, and China

THE DASHERS OF DEMOCRACY: CUBA, BURMA, AND CHINA

T his section takes a solid gander at three notorious Dashers of Democracy: Cuba, Burma (or Myanmar if you despise freedom), and China. Cuba has been a particular itch in the armpit of the United States since Fidel Castro took over the place in 1959. Decades of sanctions, designation as a sponsor of terrorism, and other tough measures did not do a darned thing to weaken Castro's grip over hapless Cuba. After languishing in his tracksuit from some unknown illness, Fidel bequeathed the island to his wacky fraternal heir apparent, Raúl, whose hygiene and sartorial flare offer little improvement over his brother.

Folks who say Buddhists are peaceful have never met the crazy Buddhist generals of the Burmese junta, whose oppressive ways were televised in the summer of 2007. That junta really dislikes democracy, and they have kept Burma's duly elected leader, Daw Aung San Suu Kyi, under house arrest since 1989 with little respite.

China is a mixed bag. It has an authoritarian political system hegemonized by the Communist Party, and the party formulates all major state policies before the government rubber-stamps them. Americans nearly universally decry the Chicom (or "Chinese commie," if you prefer) threat while running to invest in the Chinese economy and hoping that the Chinese keep gobbling up U.S. debt, which renders China a huge stakeholder in the U.S. economy. One can hardly forget the hundreds of democracy proponents who were killed in confrontations with infantry and tanks in Tiananmen Square in 1989.

China does seem more tyrannical than the other democracy dashers included here. But Condoleeza Rice excluded China from the list of countries comprising the "Outposts of Tyranny," which included Burma, Cuba, Iran, North Korea, Zimbabwe, and Belarus.[165] Obviously, Iran and North Korea were double counted, already having been corralled in the Axis of Evil.

In short, Cuba, Burma, and China remain a perpetual focus of U.S. democracy ayatollahs and by any measure are irritating—at least to the U.S. Congress and the various lobbies that support the demise of these regimes. These countries don't have freedom, but they have great food!

Dossier of Cuban Perfidy

Cuba has been a stye in the eye of the United States since Fidel Castro (né Fidel Alejandro Castro Ruz) seized the reins of power from the "U.S. dictator of choice," Fulgencio Batista, in 1959. Arthur Gardner, former U.S. Ambassador to Cuba, liked Batista so much that he described the thuggish leader as "doing an amazing job."[166]

Despite this fondness for Batista, Washington ended arms sales to his government as the Castro-led rebels battled on, ensuring that Castro's faction would prevail. This decision was vociferously denounced by U.S. Ambassador Earl T. Smith and prompted U.S. State Department adviser William Wieland to opine famously, "I know Batista is considered by many as a son of a bitch . . . but American interests come first . . . at least he was our son of a bitch.[167] And, alas, Washington has a long history of patronizing such SOBs in the pursuit of preeminent U.S. interests.

Upon prevailing, Castro promised that his government would be free of corruption and would remain honest to the people. He actually retained much of Cuba's 1940 constitution—for what that was worth. Despite promises to the contrary, he executed thousands of Batista Party members over the years.

While that certainly may make Castro an "evildoer," the Batistas murdered thousands of their political opponents and used every means at their disposal to oppress the masses.

Despite lounging in athletic wear and bathrobes following a 2006 "intestinal surgery" for an illness that is a closely guarded state secret, former President Castro at eighty-one years of age was the world's longest-serving "national leader" (excluding monarchs), with forty-eight years of bearded domination prior to stepping down. And to the vexation of the CIA, Castro saw ten sitting U.S. presidents come and go, each of whom despised the loquacious and hispid "El Commandante."

These various administrations loathed him so much that the U.S. government purportedly tried *638* times to kill him, says Fabian Escalante, the man who was for many years responsible for keeping the hirsute despot alive. Indeed, various declassified CIA documents suggest that these claims are not entirely unfounded. Ruefully, many of those stratagems seemed more worthy of a *Beavis and Butthead* episode than actual plans executed by the world's most powerful spy agency, and many were as puerile as their names suggested. "Operation Mongoose," approved by President John F. Kennedy in the wake

Singh-ing Castro's Praises

The United States has bent over backward to woo India, its "New Strategic Partner," with the promise of nuclear know-how and Pentagon goodies. In the midst of the U.S. Congress pondering changes to its laws to accommodate a nuclear-armed India, the prime minister of India, Manmohan Singh, traveled to Cuba in September 2006 for the meeting of the ever-so-pointless "Non-Aligned Movement." (With the Soviets dead and buried, it's time to update the name and the concept and get on with it.) Singh said of Castro, the human rights abuser, "I felt I was in the presence of one of the greatest men of all time." He further opined that his personal forty-minute meeting with the ailing Cuban tyrant was the most satisfying meeting he had ever had. At the end of their chat, Castro and Singh posed for a photo. For his part, Castro gushed, "I want this photo to be seen by one billion people," presumably referencing India's billion-plus population.[168]

of the flopped Bay of Pigs invasion, aimed to topple Castro by infiltrating hundreds of fighters into Cuba. Victory was snatched from the tiny, toothy rodent mouth of "Op Mongoose" when the Soviet Union's Nikita Khrushchev dispatched some 40,000 soldiers, 1,300 field pieces, 700 antiaircraft guns, 350 tanks, and 150 jets *and* nuclear-tipped ballistic missiles to Cuba to deny Op Mongoose's success. The operation devolved into the Cuban Missile Crisis, which kept the world on pins and needles waiting to see if the two superpowers were going to battle it out with nukes over the obscure little Caribbean island. Krushchev withdrew the missiles when President Kennedy agreed not to invade Cuba.[169]

Castro and the Spooks

Many of the CIA's operations never got out of the planning stages—likely because those ideas were imbecilic. Knowing Castro was fond of scuba diving, the CIA sought to poison his wet suit with a nasty skin infection. Keeping with the aquatic theme and seeking to exploit his enthusiasm for diving, they also planned a silly death by a mollusk-born improvised explosive device (MBIED). To create the MBIED, the CIA's spymasters-cum-bomb-makers tried to develop a monster conch shell that they hoped to cram with explosives. Painted with garish hues and planted conspicuously on the seabed, the CIA hoped the MBIED would lure the curious Castro to his ignominious marine death. Other preposterous ruminations included putting thallium salts (a potent depilatory) in his shoes to ensure that all of his hair would fall out, including his beard, eyebrows, and, yes, pubic hair.[170] (While I am not a fan of Shaggy Castro's sartorial flare, I am not sure how rendering him as hairless as a newt advances U.S. national security interests.)

Predictably, the CIA also sought to exploit Castro's youthful lust for a good cigar—preferably the Cohiba Esplendido. Perhaps inspired by a Daffy Duck episode, the CIA whiz kids considered "smoking" him with a booby-trapped cigar, which would blow up in his face. Another plan involved lacing a cigar with hallucinogens to give the illusion—without a trace of irony—that Castro had gone insane. The spooks also tried to give him cigars laced with the lethal botulinum toxin.[171] (He reportedly gave up smoking in 1985, ostensibly to encourage Cubans to "live healthy."[172] But I have my doubts: I think he just tired of suspecting his smokes.)

In 2007 declassified CIA internal reports confirmed a plot reported by Jack Anderson in 1971 whereby the CIA tried to hire a "mob hit" on Castro. In August 1960 the CIA hired Robert Maheu, a former FBI agent turned top aid to Howard Hughes in Las Vegas, to approach mobster Johnny Roselli under the pretext of being a representative of unnamed international corporations who wanted to whack Castro, ostensibly in retaliation for all the gambling revenues lost in Cuba. This was plausible: In the 1930s Batista forged business as well as personal ties with U.S.-based mafioso Meyer Lansky, who paid him millions of greenbacks in exchange for control over Cuba's sprawling casinos.[173] The mafiosi loved to leisure in Havana's hotels and casinos until Castro Killjoy came to power, outlawed gambling, and closed Lansky's infamous establishments.

With this plausible ruse, Roselli introduced Maheu to Momo "Sam Gold" Giancana (Al Capone's successor in Chicago) and Santos "Joe" Trafficante (one of the most powerful crime bosses in Batista's Cuba). Both were on the U.S. government's list of ten most wanted fugitives, but rather than capturing these notorious threats to public safety and remanding them to the FBI or the police, the CIA gave them six poison pills with which to eliminate Castro. They tried, with no success, to plant them in his food for six months. The CIA was happy to report, however, that they were successful in retrieving all six pills.[174]

While dodging harebrained U.S. efforts to whack him, Castro consolidated his reputation as an impressive tyrant. The Cuban government represses nearly every form of political dissent, and Castro has shown no inclination to consider even a modicum of democratic reforms. Castro is a wise man: Democracy is rarely good for revolutions. The Cuban government uses a host of coercive measures to ensure compliance, including various forms of detention, criminal prosecution, harassment, intimidation by the police, travel restrictions, and dismissals from jobs when folks get too uppity. For example, it's a criminal offense to spread "unauthorized news" and to insult patriotic symbols, whatever those may be. The government also imprisons or harasses folks who are considered to be "dangerous." These abuses of criminal proceedings are effectively used to deny Cubans free speech in the name of ensuring state security.[175]

Destination: Nowhere

To ensure that Cubans don't escape and defame the island paradise, they can't leave the country without getting permission from the government, which, of course, is frequently denied. For those who are granted permission to leave, they are often not allowed to take their children, ensuring that the poor bastards will return. Journalists seeking to report these less-than-idyllic Caribbean conditions find themselves in the world of nasty Cuban prisons. Reporters without Borders claims that there are currently twenty-three journalists stuck in a Cuban pokey, and most have been prosecuted for the absurd charges of threatening "the national independence of Cuba." Only China has more journalists behind bars. The end result, in the words of Human Rights Watch, is that "Cubans are systematically denied basic rights to free expression, association, assembly, privacy, movement and due process of law."[177]

Needless to say, conditions in Cuba's prisons are suboptimal. Prisoners have insufficient food and receive inadequate health care, and many have to suffer through physical and sexual abuse at the hands of other inmates, often with the acquiescence of the prison guards. Cuba has the death penalty for an expansive set of crimes, but human rights aficionados can't ascertain how often it's used. (Cuba, unlike China, doesn't go around advertising when they kill purported criminals.) Human rights organizations don't believe that Cuba has executed anyone since April 2003, however—which is a heck of a lot better than the United States, a country that frequently resorts to capital punishment. In fact, Amnesty International claims that the United States is the only country in the entire Americas that has used capital punishment since 2003.[178]

Ironically, Cuba was elected to the new United Nations Human Rights Council in June 2006.[179] This was, of course, inconsonant with the council's requirement that its members "uphold the highest standards of human rights promotion and protection."[180] This council was supposed to replace the widely discredited Human Rights Commission, whose members also committed outrageous human rights abuses. Cuba had the audacity to declare the mandate of the Human Rights Commission "spurious" and pronounced that it had no intention of cooperating with it. Critics of the new body contend that "election of Cuba and other countries with poor human rights records confirmed that the Council has not risen above" the past follies of the defunct Human Rights Commission.[181]

Apart from systematically and efficaciously stamping out all forms of opposition, the United States had its own bones to pick with Castro. On April 30, 2007, Secretary of State Condoleeza Rice certified that Cuba remained a "State Sponsor of Terrorism."[182] This view is not widely shared beyond Washington, and the empirical basis for this claim strikes me as weak. Reasons for declaring Cuba a state sponsor of terrorism include its continued and public opposition to the U.S.-led Global War on Terrorism (GWOT). Moreover, to "US knowledge, Cuba did not attempt to track, block or seize terrorist assets . . . [And, no] new counterterrorism laws were enacted . . . in this regard."[183] The last time I checked, the only Al-Qaeda and Taliban operatives in Cuba were, in fact, wearing orange jumpsuits and hoods and hoping their Qurans don't get flushed down the toilet at the U.S. gulag Gitmo. The State Department also claims that Cuba has provided safe haven to members of U.S.-recognized terrorist groups and has close relations with other state sponsors of terrorism like Iran. This is odd since the U.S.'s newest strategic partner, India, has cosied up to Iran in loads of ways.[184]

In what can only be called the "Fugitive Follies," the State Department whines that Cuba continues to allow U.S. fugitives to live there and is not inclined to satisfy U.S. extradition requests, while Cuba has made reciprocal demands of its own, including the return of five agents convicted of espionage in the United States. The State Department does concede that Cuba has stated that it won't provide safe haven to *new* American fugitives trying to sneak onto the island.[185]

While all of this demonstrates that Cuba continues to relish foisting its middle finger in the face of its northern neighbor, Washington has not been

Cuban Doctors Without Borders?

While the United States casts many aspersions upon Castro's island fiefdom, Cuba has been dispatching doctors throughout the world. Some 14,000 Cuban doctors provide free medical care to Venezuela's poor, and around 3,000 Cuban medical staff hauled up the Himalayan heights to provide earthquake-affected Kashmiris in Pakistan with much-needed medical services. Cuba founded its first international medical brigade in 1963 and soon thereafter dispatched 58 medical professionals to newly independent Algeria. In 1998 the Cuban government began developing the capability to deploy large-scale medical missions to poor folks affected by natural disasters throughout its region and beyond. In the wake of hurricanes George and Mitch, Cuba provided integrated health-care services to the Dominican Republic, Honduras, Guatemala, Nicaragua, Haiti, and Belize. While Havana may be a tyrannical government at home, between 1963 and 2005 it sent more than 100,000 doctors and health workers to 97 countries across Africa and Latin America. By March 2006 Havana boasted that it had 25,000 Cuban health professionals in 68 nations. The most seriously ill are even brought to Cuba for treatment. Maybe Cuba is the solution to the United States' crippled health-care system.[186]

above employing inane gestures of its own. The Cuban government insists that the United States hand over an aging terrorist named Luis Posada, a Venezuelan who was involved in bombing a Cubana Airlines plane in 1976, which killed seventy-three people.[187] Havana also claims Posada tried to kill Castro at a summit in Panama. Venezuela considers him a fugitive too, since he escaped jail in 1985 while awaiting trial. Posada was jailed in New Mexico because he lied about how he returned to the United States in 2005, and his April 2007 release on bond riled Havana and prompted others to accuse Washington of inconsistency in its global war on terror. Cubans suspect that the U.S. Department of Justice will never hand over their senescent asset. In any event, he's an old geezer, and he's unlikely to enjoy the fruits of freedom for long.[188]

In a final twist of irony, while the United States rails against Cuba for its human rights abuses, international human rights organization decry U.S. policies targeting Cuba on the same grounds. In an effort to deny the commie Cuban regime funding for its perfidy, the U.S. government has sustained an economic blockade for more than four decades. This has imposed indiscriminate hardship on the Cuban people and has made legal travel to Cuba nearly impossible, with stiff penalties imposed for illegal travel. (This author has *not* visited Cuba!) In a further effort to deny cash-strapped Cuba greenbacks, the "family-friendly" Bush government imposed yet new restrictions on family-related travel to Cuba in 2004. Under this new law, persons can visit their relatives only once in three years and only if the relatives fit the U.S.'s narrow notion of family, which excludes aunts, uncles, cousins, and other next of kin—all of whom are integral to Cuban family structure. Human Rights Watch alleges that these policies "undermines the freedom of movement of hundreds of thousands of Cubans and Cuban Americans, and inflict profound harm on Cuban families."[189] Cuban authorities insist that the embargo is illegal and calls for its repeal, and, indeed, the United Nations General Assembly (UNGA) routinely calls for the same.[190] In November 2007 the UNGA made this demand for the fifteenth consecutive year to no avail.[191]

Decades of sanctions, designation as a sponsor of terrorism, and other tough measures did not do a darned thing to weaken Castro's grip over hapless Cuba. In the end, it wasn't a MBIED, a booby-trapped cigar, or funny toxins in his wet suit that brought about the end of his rule. Instead, it was good old-fashioned, age-related bodily decline—and his brother is no spring chicken either. So while the Castros are likely to remain a pest for at least a little while longer, we can all be relieved that Cuban cuisine is absolutely fabulous.

Cuba: Culinary Colonialism and Its Contents[192]

Like many islands in the Caribbean, the food of contemporary Cuba derives from a many-layered interaction between outside and "native" influences. Prior to the Spaniards showing up to loot and plunder, Cuba was populated by the Carib and Arawak populations. Reflecting the fact that they lived on an island, they ate a lot of fish as well as game animals, yucca (in the agave family of plants), and corn. The Spaniards arrived in the late fifteenth century, building the first permanent settlement in 1512 at Baracoa, and then they just kept coming for hundreds of years. As is often the case with colonizers, they were bewildered by the plants that locals ate, such as squash and corn and the like, and busied themselves with adapting their cooking techniques from the motherland to these strange and wondrous eats.

The conquistadors—in Cuba as elsewhere—decimated the local population with their germs, steel, and guns. Undaunted, their expansion continued. Having killed off every last local and faced with the prospect of doing their own work, they needed to import labor to subsidize their land grab and associated enterprises. So they did what every imperial power did at that time: They brought in slaves from Africa. These unfortunate souls brought with them their culinary customs, and they too adapted the local flora and fauna to their customary methods of food preparation. Thanks to these slaves' toil, by the mid-sixteenth century, Cuba was booming and turning out cacao, sugarcane, coffee, and, of course, tobacco. As the island began to specialize in sugarcane, another hundred thousand slaves were forcibly brought in to support that industry.

As Cuba became a primary hub for Spanish commercial, political, and military interests in the Caribbean, people from the varied regions of Spain flocked to the island and added their regional influences to the culinary mélange. But wait—that's not all. In the late eighteenth century, French (!) plantation owners were on the run from their Haitian estates, where their slaves revolted against them. Undeterred by standards of civility, morality, or humanity, they set up a French enclave on the eastern side of the Cuban island. Nestled in their re-creation of their slave-driven paradisiacal empire back in Haiti, they cultivated coffee—or, more aptly put, they made their slaves cultivate coffee. This gave a nice kick start to the Cuban coffee trade, for which it would eventually become world famous. You can still observe the French culinary impact on Cuban cuisine, as evidenced in the use of pepper and various meats that are stuffed and rolled before cooking.

But wait again—there is still more of these outside influences upon Cuban comestibles! As any frequenter of Cuban eateries in New York, Los Angeles, or Miami knows, even the Chinese made their way to Cuba. They arrived in the mid-nineteenth century as indentured servants, most likely because globally slavery was becoming a decisively despicable thing and many countries even outlawed it. But what was a poor plantation owner to do with all those crops and no slaves to tend them? In slavery's stead arose a system of equally loathsome indentured servitude. This had the moral palliative of wages that permitted the "master" to sustain the illusion that these poor folks are working of their own accord. The Chinese heaped their soy sauce and other spices upon the island, sowing the seeds for what has developed into an awkward genre of eats: Cuban Chinese.

And this wraps up my tale explaining why Cuban food, like a lot of cuisines from the Caribbean, is so downright odd—yet, nonetheless, so delicious.

However, like many countries in this volume, Cuba suffers from food insecurity. The eastern provinces of Guantánamo, Granma, Santiago de Cuba, Las Tunas, Holguín, and Camagüey have countenanced the worst drought in ten years, and despite the government's best efforts—such as they are—food availability is well below needs in those areas. Despite the best efforts of the World Food Program, this food shortage has hard hit the most vulnerable, such as children, pregnant and lactating women, and the elderly.[193]

The Plan of Attack

The day before the soiree (or the morning of if you are procrastinator), prepare the *pescado en escabeche* (marinated fish with cilantro, aka ceviche). The longer the fish hangs out in the pond with the spices, lemon juice, and vegetables, the better your ceviche will turn out. This can sit in your fridge and marinate for days and it just gets better. Also the night before, begin marinating the pork roast. Finally, be sure to soak the black beans overnight. The next morning, I make the beans and let them marinate all day long. The longer the beans can mingle with the spices, the tastier they will be.

I give you two dessert options, depending upon your preference. If you have a sweet tooth and like it when things are so sweet your tongue gets fuzzy, I offer you a flan option. However, if you want something more flavorful and decidedly more *uniquely* Cuban than the ubiquitous Hispanic flan, I suggest a delightful squash custard. Irrespective of the selection, I make the dessert the morning of the soiree, after I get the beans simmering.

Main course

- *Pescado en Escabeche,* aka ceviche (pickled fish), served with fried green plantain chips
- *Lechón Asado* (pork roast marinated in citrus juice and spices)
- Cuban-spiced *Frijoles Negros* (black beans)
- Parboiled Rice Fried with Garlic

Dessert

■ Flan (baked custard), or *Budin de Calabaza* (baked squash custard)

Beverages

■ Mojitos
■ Cuban coffee

PREPARATION

MAIN COURSE

Pescado en Escabeche, aka Ceviche *(Pickled Fish)*

Ceviche is made of raw fish and is "cooked" by pickling it in a delicious marinade of lime juice, wine, and other good stuff. You can use any hearty, fleshy fish. I prefer a combination of salmon and swordfish, but you can also use red snapper or any other robust fish. Don't be afraid to use high-quality frozen fish. I almost always use frozen, because it is easier to chop and clean and I don't have time to go to a fishmonger. Whatever fish you use, be sure to remove the skin and bones. (Yet another reason why I like to use frozen fish: This is generally already done.) Definitely make this dish one day ahead of the dinner party.

Ingredients

1¾ cups fresh-squeezed lime juice (This could be up to 10 limes, depending on their size and juice content. Microwave the limes for about 10 seconds each and roll them around on a countertop for a few seconds to loosen up the flesh and permit easier juice extraction.)

½ cup dry white wine

⅓ cup olive oil

1½ cups chopped red onion
½ cup finely diced red bell peppers
½ cup finely diced green bell peppers
6 cloves garlic, finely minced
1 bay leaf
1 teaspoon dried basil
1½ teaspoons sea salt
12 ounces salmon and 12 ounces swordfish, peeled and cut into ½-inch
cubes

For garnish:
Finely chopped cilantro
Hot, salted, and freshly fried green plantain chips (see recipe below)

Let's get cooking

1. Put the lime juice, white wine, and olive oil in a large ziplock bag and whisk gently, being careful not to puncture the bag. Add the onions, peppers, garlic, bay leaf, basil, and salt. Mix thoroughly into the liquids.
2. Add the fish and toss well with your hands.
3. Store the bag with the fish in the fridge, agitating every few hours to make sure all of the fish chunks are pickled effectively.
4. Before serving, taste and adjust seasoning if need be. Feel free to add more lime juice.
5. When ready to serve, spoon into cocktail glasses, garnish with finely chopped cilantro, and serve with warm, salted, fried green plantain chips.

Green Plantain Chips

Ingredients
3 *green* plantains
½ cup olive oil (more as needed)
Fine sea salt

Let's get cooking

1. Prepare the plantains. Do not attempt to peel them like a banana! It will not work, and the plantain will simply break. Instead, slice ¾ inch off from

each end of the plantain. Cut the rest in half and trim off the peel with a paring knife. Slice the peeled plantains into dime-width slices.

2. In a heavy-bottomed pan, heat the oil over a medium-high flame. (Be careful to keep the oil below its smoking point). Add the plantains in batches, ensuring they are covered in oil, and fry to a brown crisp.

3. Remove the plantain chips with a slotted spoon and place in a large shallow bowl with a paper towel to absorb the excess oil. Salt to taste. Serve warm or at room temperature. (I like to serve them warm with the ceviche.)

Lechón Asado *(Pork Roast Marinated in Citrus Juice and Spices)*

When I lived in Los Angeles, I *always* got this dish at the Cuban dive near my home. I have tried to reproduce that delicacy now that I live in DC, and here is my best effort—enjoy! Be sure to get the pork into the marinade the night before the shindig.

Ingredients
10 cloves garlic
1 teaspoon coarse rock salt
½ teaspoon black peppercorns
1 bay leaf
1 teaspoon cumin
1 teaspoon oregano
2 tablespoons olive oil
1 cup sour orange juice (If sour oranges are not available, use ½ cup fresh orange juice and ½ cup fresh lime juice.)
3 pounds pork roast

Let's get cooking
1. Prepare the marinade by grinding the garlic, rock salt, and peppercorns into a fine paste with a mortar and pestle. The rock salt works well here because it gives you traction for smashing the garlic. Take care to ensure that the peppercorns don't leap out of the mortar when you start grinding.

2. Put the garlic paste and all the other ingredients except the pork in a large

ziplock bag (use one large enough to hold the roast) and whisk carefully. (Be careful to not puncture the bag.)

3. Remove any excess fat and skin from the roast. Pierce the meat all over and add the roast to the bag with the marinade. Let sit overnight in the refrigerator, agitating it every once in a while to ensure that the marinade gets all over the roast.

4. About 3 hours before your guests arrive, preheat the oven to 350 degrees. Remove the roast and place it (fat side up) into a roasting pan. Keep the marinade for basting as needed. Roast the pork for about 2½ hours or until the temperature of the meat reaches 165 degrees. Baste the pork frequently with the reserved marinade. If the drippings and herbs begin to smoke, add a little bit of water. (Don't add a lot of water: We want to roast this thing, not steam it.)

5. Let the meat rest for several minutes, during which time it will continue to cook. Once it has cooled, cut the roast into thin slices to serve.

Cuban-Spiced Frijoles Negros *(Black Beans)*

The night before the party, pick through the black beans to remove anything that should not be there (such as rocks, debris, etc.) and soak as described below. I finish this dish a few hours before my guests arrive because I like the beans to marinate in their spices.

Ingredients

16 ounces dried black beans (cleaned and soaked per instructions below)

6 cups water

3 tablespoons olive oil

4 cloves garlic

1 teaspoon rock salt

¾ teaspoon black peppercorns

1 cup chopped yellow onions

¾ cup diced red bell pepper

¾ cup diced green bell pepper

1 serrano pepper, finely chopped (This is optional and not terribly Cuban, but I'm a pepperphile and have difficulty eating beans when they don't have any punch.)

2 bay leaves

1½ teaspoons ground cumin

1½ teaspoons dried oregano

¼ cup cider vinegar

¾ cup white Spanish wine (I use a white Rioja.)

1½ teaspoons sea salt (or more to taste)

1–2 teaspoons demerara sugar, per taste

For garnish:

¼ cup finely chopped cilantro

¼ cup finely chopped red or yellow onion

Let's get cooking

1. The night before, soak the beans in about 6 cups water with ½ teaspoon baking soda.
2. The next day, drain the beans and rinse well to remove most of the baking soda. Cook the beans with 6 cups water and 1 tablespoon olive oil. If using a pressure cooker, follow your machine's instructions. (It takes 15 minutes or so in my wretched cooker.) Alternatively, bring the beans, water, and oil to a boil a large pot. Cover, lower the heat to a simmer, and cook until the beans are tender. This can take about 1 hour. Check frequently and add water if needed. (Some people add salt while cooking, but I've been advised that doing so at this point will produce tougher beans.)
3. While the beans are cooking, prepare the spice mixture. Begin by mashing the garlic, rock salt, and black peppercorns with a mortar and pestle. (Use rock salt or coarse sea salt to help grind the ingredients.)
4. Heat 2 tablespoons olive oil in a sauté pan and fry the onions, bell peppers, and serrano until the onions are translucent. Add the garlic mash and fry for another minute.
5. Add this mixture to the pot of beans. This means that you do *not* drain the water in which the beans were cooked. (I usually remove a cup of the cooked beans around in my frying pan to make sure I get all of the flavor out, then return them to the pot.)
6. Add the bay leaves, cumin, oregano, vinegar, wine, 1 teaspoon sugar, and sea salt. Simmer, covered, for about 20 minutes. Taste and adjust the salt and black pepper if desired. Add 1 teaspoon more sugar if sweeter beans are preferred.

CUBA

7. Remove from heat and let the beans sit until time to serve. They can be easily reheated. (If your beans are runny and you'd like to thicken them, mash a cup and add back to the mixture or simmer until some of the moisture has evaporated.)

8. Right before serving in bowls, garnish with chopped cilantro and onions. Feel free to remove the bay leaves and pepper corns if you want to and if you can find them. I don't bother.

Parboiled Rice Fried with Garlic

Ingredients

3 cups long-grain white rice (e.g. jasmine)
1 tablespoon olive oil
2 cloves garlic, minced
4½ cups water
1 teaspoon salt

Let's get cooking

1. Look over the rice for things that don't belong (rocks, for example). Rinse with cold water a few times to remove the starch. Drain the water thoroughly.

2. In a heavy-bottomed pot, heat the oil and fry the garlic for a minute.

3. Add the rice and fry until translucent.

4. Add the water and salt and bring to a boil. Reduce the heat, cover, and let simmer until the rice is done (about 15 minutes). Fluff the rice with a fork before serving.

DESSERT

★★★★★★★★★★★★★★★★★★★★★★

Here are two dessert options. The first is the quotidian flan that has made its way throughout the miscellaneous lands raped and pillaged by the Spaniards. From Mexico to the Philippines, you find a variant of this artery clogger. Honestly, in my view, flan is *okay*—it's not worth a coronary. But others violently disagree with my insouciance toward what they view as the wonders of the flan. My preferred option is a squash custard (*budin de calabaza*), which is more uniquely Cuban, less sweet, and equally dangerous for the ole ticker. (You could even make both if you like!)

Flan *(Baked Custard)*

Ingredients
1 cup granulated sugar dissolved in 4 tablespoons water (for the caramel)
1 14-ounce can sweetened condensed milk
½ cup milk
½ cup water
¼ teaspoon ground cinnamon
Pinch of nutmeg
4 egg yolks, well beaten
1 teaspoon vanilla extract (Use the real kind, not that artificial stuff found in your mother's cupboard.)

For garnish (optional):
Finely diced tropical fruit of your choice (e.g., mango or, better yet, papaya sprinkled with fresh lime)
Mint sprigs

Let's get cooking
1. Preheat the oven to 350 degrees.
2. Make the caramel by dissolving the sugar into the water over medium heat, stirring until it comes to a boil. Leave uncovered and undisturbed until it turns golden, then begin swirling the pan to turn the syrup a deep amber

hue. Watch this like a hawk to prevent it from burning, and don't even think of multitasking. If you burn it (you'll smell this), dump it out and start over. Pour the mixture into 8 ramekins, working quickly. (The caramel will harden almost as soon as it gets into the ramekins.) Caution: It is extremely hot.

3. Mix all of the remaining ingredients and pour the mixture into the caramel-bottomed ramekins.

4. Place the ramekins in a large pan (a roasting pan works well). Add water to the pan up to about ⅓ or ½ of the ramekins' height. (Obviously, the water level should not be higher than the height of the ramekins!) Bake at 350 degrees for 40–50 minutes or until the custard is softly set. Remove the ramekins and allow the custard to cool. Refrigerate, covered in foil, until ready to serve.

5. When you are ready to serve, add some warm water to a pan and place the ramekins in it for a couple minutes. This is intended to melt and loosen the caramel at the bottom of the ramekins. Run a knife around the edge and invert onto serving plates.

6. If you desire, garnish by spreading some finely diced tropical fruit beside the flan, along with some mint sprigs, to cut the sweetness of the flan. You can use mango or my favorite: finely diced papaya dressed with a small amount of fresh lime.

Budin de Calabaza *(Baked Squash Custard)*

Ingredients

1 cup granulated sugar dissolved in 4 tablespoons water (for the caramel)

1¼ pounds butternut squash or pumpkin, peeled and chopped into 2-inch cubes

1 cup water, or more as needed (for boiling the squash)

4 tablespoons unsalted butter

⅛ teaspoon sea salt

1½ cups skim milk (I try to keep food on the nonlethal side since I eat this stuff all the time. But you can use a higher fat percentage if you want.)

½ cup sugar (I prefer demerara or raw cane sugar, but any will do.)

2 tablespoons cornstarch dissolved in ½ cup warm water

1 teaspoon *real* vanilla extract (See snooty note in the flan recipe on the artificial stuff.)

¼ teaspoon freshly ground nutmeg (You can grind it in a spice grinder or grate it using a rasp.)

1 teaspoon ground cinnamon (I like to grind my own for this recipe, but you need not.)

¼ teaspoon allspice (Again, I grind my own from the allspice pods, but you don't have to.)

3 eggs

For garnish:
Mint sprigs

Let's get cooking

1. Preheat the oven to 350 degrees.
2. Make the caramel by dissolving the sugar into the water over medium heat, stirring until it comes to a boil. Leave uncovered and undisturbed until it turns golden, then begin swirling the pan to turn the syrup a deep amber hue. Watch this like a hawk to prevent it from burning, and don't even think of multitasking. If you burn it (you'll smell this), dump it out and start over. Pour the mixture into 8 ramekins, working quickly. It's hot—be careful.
3. Bring the squash chunks, water, butter, and salt to a boil. Lower the heat to a simmer and cook *uncovered* for about 25 minutes, checking on it every once in a while. This is done cooking when the water is nearly gone (evaporated and/or sucked up by the squash) *and* when the squash is absolutely tender. The squash should be a little brown as well from sitting in a hot pan with butter. Just be sure it doesn't burn! If the water has evaporated and the squash is still not tender, add another ½ cup hot water and keep cooking it, repeating if necessary until tender.
4. Remove the squash chunks to a plate, ensuring that they are separated from each other, and smash them up a bit so that they cool faster. (The objective in cooling the squash is simple: You don't want to add magma-hot squash to the egg mixture, otherwise you will get squash and scrambled eggs, which is not the desired result.) You can also do this the night before and stick your squash chunks in the fridge.
5. Put the cooled squash and the all ingredients except the eggs in a blender

and blend. The cool milk should further cool the squash. Add the eggs and blend until smooth.

6. Pour the mixture into the 8 caramel-bottomed ramekins. Place the ramekins in a large pan (e.g., a roasting pan) and add water to the pan up to ⅓ or ½ of the ramekins' height. The water should not be so high that it can get into the ramekins! Place the pan with the custards in the 350-degreee oven and bake for about 40 minutes. (Test for doneness by inserting a toothpick in the custard. It's done when the toothpick comes out clean.) If you have leftover batter, you can store it in the fridge for a few days and make a second batch later.

7. When I serve this, I don't bother inverting: I just put a mint spring on top of each ramekin and serve as is.

Mojitos

Ingredients

For the "base":

1 cup mint leaves, with parts of the stalks near the leaves (Discard the tough, woody bottoms of the stalk. Retain a few sprigs for garnish.)

1 cup demerara or raw cane sugar (You can use other sugar, but I *really* like the intense flavor of these.)

1 cup freshly squeezed lime juice (I usually squeeze the limes into a strainer to make sure that the pulp and seeds stay out.)

1 bottle (750 milliliters or 25 ounces) light or white rum of your choice

For the mixed drink:

1 bottle of chilled, sparkling water (or more if desired)

Ice (of course!)

For garnish:

Strips of sugarcane (Optional and hard to find unless you have a Hispanic market or specialty store like Whole Foods in your 'hood.)

Mint sprigs (cleaned and with discolored leaves discarded)

Let's get mixing

1. Shred the mint leaves and finely chop the stalk. With a mortar and pestle, grind the mint with the sugar. (Depending on the size of your mortar and pestle, you may have to do this in batches.) The objective is not to smash the mint into a paste; rather, you just want to release the aromatics of the mint from the plant material. It's good to do this with the sugar, because the sugar provides some friction for the mashing and it absorbs the oils of the mint.

2. In a pitcher (that can fit in your fridge and is big enough to hold the lime mixture plus the rum!), mix the mint/sugar combo with the lime juice and stir briskly. Add the rum. This is your base, and you can keep it in your fridge for a few weeks. (We don't have it lying around for long, but I am told that it will keep for up to a month.)

3. To mix, fill a tall (12-ounce) glass with ice and add about 2 ounces of the prepared liquid (or more if you want a bunch of drunk folks at your house). Top off the glass with fizzy water and stir. Garnish with mint sprigs and serve with sugarcane strips as stirrers if you have them.

Dossier of Burmese Perfidy

For liberty lovers, Burma is in bad shape. Wracked by a presumably Buddhist military junta, Burma is rife with narcotics trafficking, human trafficking, forced labor, and oppression of ethnic minorities, which has spawned an enduring problem with refugees and internally displaced persons seeking respite from the state's lethal harassment. Suppression of the voices of democracy persists, with a sustained brutality that has spanned decades.[194] Given that about one in one hundred persons in Burma is a monk, monks carry a lot of weight there. For decades, the 500,000-member Buddhist clergy and General Than Shwe's 450,000-strong military has shaped the lives of Burmese with the former offering moral authority and the latter oppression and intimidation.[195]

In August 2007 the uneasy coexistence between the men in robes and the men in uniform was shattered when demonstrations broke out to protest the junta's decision to ratchet up fuel prices. Thousands of monks flooded the streets to protest the junta's economic mismanagement of the country and its long-standing policies of severe political repression. The khaki-clad goons responded with beatings and shootings. Until a media blackout was imposed, the world saw poor monks and others getting the snot kicked out them and shot by thugs directed by General Than Shwe, Burma's de facto ruler and military leader. Throughout the country, the general's men arrested and beat monks and nuns, many of whom have been killed and thousands of whom have "disappeared." Monasteries, a cultural backbone of the battered Burmese, have been looted and pummeled, and under the cover of darkness, "intelligence units" round up political and religious leaders alike.[196] So far, "the guns have prevailed over mantras."[197]

After various fleeting monarchical reigns and waves of Asian invaders, the British began their ingress into Burma in 1824, waging three devastating wars with the Kongbaung and expanding British hold successively after each victory. By 1885 the Brits owned the whole darned thing. The Burmese finally extricated themselves from the British in 1948, under the leadership of General Aung San, the father of Daw Aung San Suu Kyi. The Burmese had a brief constitutional period that lasted less than two decades. In 1958, after widespread political and social discord, Prime Minister U Nu asked the military to come in on a *temporary* basis. Surprisingly, the men in khaki actually did step down eighteen months later, but, alas, in 1962 General Ne Win led a coup, ditched the constitution, and established a military government with socialist economic policies, which ruined the country's economy—or whatever there was to ruin.

In 1988 students rampaged in Rangoon to demand regime change. Despite oppressive and repeated resort to force, the demonstrations expanded. During massive protests in August 1988, the military slaughtered more than a thousand protestors. Following that melee, Aung San Suu Kyi made her political debut and assumed the helm of the opposition.

The following September, the military kicked out Ne Win's socialist-military government, again threw out the constitution, and established the ominous-sounding State Law and Order Restoration Council (SLORC). SLORC dispatched the army to quell the wellspring of public protest, killing at least three thousand students and chasing another ten thousand into the hills and borderlands. SLORC ran the show under a vicious martial law regime until they held parliamentary elections in 1990—apparently for no good reason. Why they held these elections is anyone's guess, because they clearly had no intention of honoring the results of the futile exercise of constrained democracy.

Aung San Suu Kyi's National League for Democracy (NLD) won by a landslide despite the fact that she was confined to house arrest. SLORC never convened the parliament and tossed the political activists into the slammer, where many of them reside to date. Aung San Suu Kyi, who has since picked up a Nobel Peace Prize, continues to languish under house arrest with little respite.

Introducing the State Peace and Development Council

In 1997, after contracting the services of a Washington, DC–based image consultant, SLORC changed its name to the less ominous-sounding State Peace and Development Council (SPDC). This may have been done with the hope folks would seriously think SLORC turned over a new leaf, luring tourists and investors alike with their kinder, softer militarism and suppression of democracy.[198] It was surely also done to appease regional critics who were prodding Burma to consider democratic reforms. While SPDC sounds less like an evil empire than SLORC, the fundaments of state tyranny did not change. In fact, few were fooled. As one activist group based in lovely Bangkok quipped, "A junta by any other name would stink as bad."[199]

The SPDC junta is indeed a committed foe of democracy and freedom and everything that is good, right, and reasonable. The majority of Burma's forty-seven million people endures persistent brutal dictatorship by a regime that the United Nations and Amnesty International have condemned for a wide array of human rights violations, including systematic rape, torture, imprisonment, summary executions, and forced labor, which in 1998 accounted for 3 percent of Myanmar's GDP.[200] In addition to these egregious concerns, the SPDC engages in more quotidian oppression. For example, it hand picks the prime minister of its choice. Perhaps in an effort to cultivate an image of the "warmer, fuzzier" tyrannical state, SPDC purported to set up a "National Convention," whose members were ostensibly tasked with developing a new constitution and providing a road map for new elections. But, as one would expect, SPDC restricted public input and cherry-picked the delegates, assiduously assuring that its critics were excluded.[201] Only the foolish expected a road map to democracy to come out of this citadel of totalitarianism, which convened for the last time in July 2007.

The junta is notorious for its repression of ethnic minorities who are not Burmans. As you may have guessed, that's where Burma got its name. While SLORC changed the name to Myanmar, supposedly to mitigate the association of the fatherland with one ethnic group, the duly elected parliamentarians of 1990 reject the appellation and have persuaded freedom lovers everywhere to spurn the new moniker. The U.S. government has taken up this banner, and as such Burma is the official nomenclature for the place.

To the dismay of Christian evangelicals everywhere, there has been no constitutional support for religious freedom since the junta dumped the constitution in 1988. That being said, the government does allow people to practice "registered religions," and these folks are generally permitted to do what they want subject to the whim of the junta. The junta privileges Buddhism over other faiths even though Myanmar does not have a "state religion." The government does what it can to promote Buddhism, such as publicly funding pagodas. In Arakan, which is home to the beleaguered Rohingyan Muslims, Muslims are not allowed to repair extant mosques or build new ones—and they are conscripted into forced labor to build pagodas in Muslim areas without pay and without even being fed while working. Rohingyas have it so bad that they are fleeing to *Bangladesh*.[202]

At one time the "Rice Bowl of Asia" and well on its way to prosperity, Burma has been driven into poverty and penury under the military junta. In fact, the United Nations Human Development Program, using its Human Development Indicator, ranks Myanmar at 130 out of 177 countries.[203] While the generals eat well, as do the urban sophisticates of Rangoon (or Yangon, if you want to flaunt your support for the Buddhist junta), the rest of the folks eek out their caloric intake in whatever way they can, including mountains of rice, which is ubiquitous in Burma—that is, unless you happen to be a Muslim Rohingya in Burma's Arakan state.

Mike Thompson of the BBC suggests that the Rohingyas are probably the most persecuted—and most forgotten—persons *in the world*.[204] I would

The Capital Escape . . . to Nowhere

On November 6, 2005, at 6:30 in the morning, government workers were ordered to move immediately to Burma's new capital, Pyinmana, two hundred miles north of Rangoon. They were not allowed to bring their families or even to resign—they just did it. The place had inadequate housing and, yes, inadequate food for the workers. This flummoxed foreign missions ensconced in Rangoon. They were told by the Foreign Ministry, "If you need to communicate on urgent matters, you can send a fax to Pyinmana."[205]

quibble only on this point: To say that they are forgotten means that someone actually gave a rat's anatomy at some point in the past. These people
would be lucky to get a plate of leftover rice dug out of a Dumpster. The
hunted, sequestered, and culturally devastated Rohingyas are utterly depend-
ent upon the World Food Program, who fights the junta for the right to keep
them alive. The Burmese junta has penned the Rohingyas into two townships
in areas that a high-ranking U.S. official interviewed by this author called
"concentration camps."[206] Denied the right to marry or move beyond the hell
that is their lives, the junta seems to prefer that they just disappear, and starvation and forced labor appear to be key means to achieving that objective.

There are other ethnic groups that are also persecuted in Burma, but they
all have colorful ethnic apparel, have sought refuge in tourist-attracting places
like Thailand, and have developed well-spoken lobbies in Thailand, the United
States, and elsewhere who publicize their miseries. Consequently, everyone
knows about problems facing the Karen and the Shan, but no one knows
about the Rohingyas. Suffice it to say, the world isn't terribly mindful of state
oppression of Muslims these days anyway. As with North Korean chow, when
pondering Burmese food, one has to always keep in mind who has access to
it and who doesn't.

Something's Fishy in Rangoon[207]

If you take a look at Burma on the map, you'll see it's sandwiched between the
South Asian countries of India and Bangladesh and the Southeast Asian countries of Thailand and Laos, as well as China. Its cuisine reflects its geography.
South Asia's influence is evidenced in the system of spices used in Burmese
curries (e.g., garlic, turmeric, ginger, chile, onion, and even shrimp paste),

which is similar to that used by Bengalis in India and Bangladesh. Notably, Burmese food tends not to use cumin, which is ubiquitous in many kinds of Indian food, and it is not nearly as spicy as Indian food. Its Southeast Asian imprint is seen in the use of coconut milk, condensed and sweetened milk, fruits, and, of course, fish paste and fish sauce. The pungent odor and flavor of these fish products distinguish Burmese curries from their Indian cousins. China's influence is manifest in the use of noodles and soy sauce. Burmese culinary offerings also include dals and vegetable preparations, which are also reminiscent of Indian edibles nearby. Rice is a staple, usually boiled and plain.

While Burma is overwhelmingly Buddhist, meat is eaten in large quantities, and you can find virtually any animal swimming in a pool of lukewarm curry, including frogs, deer, pork, and anything else that moves and can be caught. Pork curry is one of my favorites, because you just don't find that in too many places where curries are served. The Burmese often eat their food at room temperature, which is something I cannot get accustomed to. However, soup and rice are important exceptions: Soup is always magma hot, and rice is always freshly steamed.

One of the odder delicacies in Burma is fried rat. The Burmese apparently quite enjoy it. One Burmese prisoner wrote of the rodent delicacy:

> Believe me, there are not enough words to describe the taste of rat meat. It was fried with red pepper and ginger. The ribs were the best—very crispy. To be honest, it was the most delicious meat I have eaten in my life. To the best of my knowledge, we successfully captured more than three hundred "Underground Fighters" [rats] in Insein prison. In this way, the rats supported us. We got our energy and courage back again. I might not be here today if I hadn't eaten those rats during my prison term. Some of our

Of Tourists and Slaves

Burma has a long, well-established, and reprehensible history of using forced labor to build everything in the country without compensation and often without food. Human rights abuses and tourism are tightly linked in Burma. To prepare for the junta's tourism offensive under the banner of "Visit Myanmar Year 1996," the government uprooted tens of thousands of forced laborers to build tourist infrastructure, gild thrones in garish gold paint, renovate the Mandalay palace, build and re-pave roads, and even construct airports.[208]

inmates died of malnutrition. Thank you, Mr. Rat. Twenty-five years have passed, but I still remember them, especially when I have barbecue ribs. So the next time you eat barbecue ribs, please remember this: someone is chewing on a rat's ribs in a part of this wonderful world. Then, you'll be sympathetic to the political prisoners in Burma. Oh, how I can still smell those ribs with red pepper and ginger.[210]

I demurred from feasting upon the critter when the opportunity presented itself along a roadside outside of Rangoon. However, I regret that closed-minded decision, particularly after reading the eulogy to the crispy rat rib. The Burmese are by no means alone in this peculiar taste for varmints. The Thais also eat rat, as well as moles and squirrels and other members of the order Rodentia. And to be fair, the Peruvians love their guinea pig, and I hear that Americans in the Bayou eat nutria, which is (I think) a re-branded river rat of sorts. Like their Thai and Chinese neighbors, the Burmese also grill just about any animal or any part thereof. Pig snouts, pig tails, and other such things grace the barbecues along the sidewalks.

Another characteristic feature of Burmese cuisine is fish condiments. The Burmese use shrimp paste and fish paste, which are often frozen fish solids that are fried in preparation. Another common ingredient is fish sauce. This stuff can be overpowering, and it is certainly an acquired taste. For those of you with finicky snouts, it will get you with its funk. This is not surprising when you ponder what it is: a brown liquid condiment derived from *fermented* fish. In the below recipes, I suggest that you move slowly on the fish sauce. Buying fish sauce should be easy, as most supermarkets sell it in the "Asian Specialties" section. In any event, Dynasty has a reliable brand that will suffice for these recipes, but if you want to go native and if you have a Burmese, Thai, Laotian, or Cambodian store in your neck of the woods, be prepared to be overwhelmed. The varietals of fish sauce are legion, and they are often packaged in scripts that I certainly can't read and are usually not transliterated, plus they have odd and even disturbing pictures of corpulent children playing with fishy-looking monsters. Ask your proprietor for his or her suggestion—then be prepared to follow it.

The Plan of Attack

There are a few things you can make in the days or day before your wingding for eight folks. First, you can and *should* make all of the necessary condiments (i.e., the fried onion, garlic, and beans and concomitant flavored oils) days in advance. You can also slice all of the vegetables the day before and store them in airtight containers with a moist paper towel to keep them from going limp. You can even make the *ohn-no kaukswe* broth days in advance and store in the refrigerator. (It gets better after one or two days.) This dish requires hard-boiled eggs, so be sure to boil them before preparing the soup. Similarly, the pork curry can be made the day before, as can the dessert. As elsewhere, this menu serves eight folks, so adjust as needed.

Main course

- *Lephet Thote* (fermented green tea salad). You can substitute ginger if you prefer to not use the funky tea or if you can't find it.
- *Ohn-no Kaukswe* (chicken-coconut soup served with egg noodles)
- *Wata Majeedi* (pork curry with tamarind)
- *Phazun Hin Asa* (spicy shrimp curry)
- Plain jasmine rice

Dessert

- *Sanwinmakin* (semolina cake)

Beverages

- Beer! Burma has a delightful award-winning, eponymous brew called Myanmar Beer. If you live *outside* the United States, you might be able to obtain it.[211] If you are in the U.S. of A., forget about it. Beer bloggers laud it as a good accompaniment to Burmese food and the oppressive heat. Myanmar Beer is a well-carbonated dry lager that lies somewhere between the Asian rice lagers and the Indian Euro-style lagers—which makes sense given its geography. If you can't find this elixir where you live—and fellow Americans, we can't—I suggest these alternatives: Kirin Ichiban Maribana, Sapporo, or Asahi draft. Otherwise, pick the beer you like.

■ Iced coffee or tea with sweetened condensed milk, served with dessert

PREPARATION

★★
★★

MAIN COURSE

Condiments

The day before your festivities (or earlier), you should prepare these needed condiments. You will have to make them yourself, unless you live near an Asian store that sells this stuff. However, even if you buy the fried onions, garlic, and beans, you still need to make the onion oil. If you absolutely don't want to do this and are happy with your store-bought fried goods, substitute a flavorful oil (such as garlic oil or sesame oil) whenever onion oil is called for. Chances are your guests have never been to Burma or eaten Burmese food, so they'll never know.

Fried, Crispy Onions and Onion Oil

Ingredients
3 medium yellow onions
1½ cups peanut oil
1 teaspoon turmeric

Let's get cooking

Slice the onions into very thin strips. The thinner and more consistently they are cut, the more evenly they will cook. Heat the peanut oil in a medium-size skillet. When hot, add the sliced onions and turmeric. All of the onions should be covered with oil. Stir frequently to make sure that all of the pieces brown nicely without burning. When they are on the verge of blossoming into a dark golden brown, turn off the heat and begin removing them with a slotted spoon, letting as much oil as possible remain behind. Spoon the onions in a colander lined with a paper towel to remove excess oil. You can store these in the fridge. Pour the onion oil into a jar with appropriate labeling and also keep in your fridge as a condiment. This whole affair should take you about 10–15 minutes, depending on how evenly and thinly you sliced the onions.

Fried, Crispy Garlic Chips and Garlic Oil

Ingredients

¾ cup peanut oil

½ cup peeled, sliced garlic (about ⅛ inch thin)

1 teaspoon turmeric

Let's get cooking

Heat the oil in a small skillet. Add the garlic and turmeric, and fry while stirring until you have golden garlic chips. There should be enough oil to completely cover the garlic. (Rather than adding more oil and cooling the temperature, fry the garlic in batches.) Remove from heat and strain the chips, reserving the oil for other uses. The garlic oil can be labeled and stored in the refrigerator. Dry the chips flat on a plate with a paper towel. I keep mine in the fridge, though some folks store theirs in a cupboard. Don't put them in a plastic bag or container until they have cooled and crisped; otherwise they will become soggy and disagreeable in taste and texture.

Fried, Crispy Broad Beans Mixed with Peanuts

Ingredients
½ cup peanut oil
⅓ cup dried broad beans
⅓ cup peanuts

Let's get cooking
Heat the oil and when hot, fry the beans until they are golden brown. Remove the beans from the pan, straining off the oil. Set them aside on a plate with a paper towel to cool and crisp. Next, fry the peanuts until they are also golden brown. Remove from the oil and dry on a paper towel to cool and crisp. I usually mix the beans and peanuts and store them together in the refrigerator, but some people store them in their cupboard. I discard this oil. (If you can't find dried broad beans, don't worry about it. These are for the salad, and you can simply use a few more peanuts, sesame seeds, and garlic chips instead.)

Lephet Thote *(Fermented Green Tea Salad)*

This dish calls for a particular Burmese item: fermented tea leaves. You can find it in Burmese markets—if you have one nearby. Some Cambodian or even Thai markets may carry it too, if you are lucky. (In the appendix, I have suggested some online resources as well.) I am told this is an acquired taste, but I acquired it upon first bite. If you can't get this tea—or don't want to—you could simply soak a few tablespoons of green tea leaves overnight in cool water with a pinch of salt to soften, rather than using dubious tea substitutes, I suggest a delicious alternative: ¼ cup thinly sliced, freshly peeled, slightly pickled ginger.

To pickle the ginger, slice the ginger the thickness of a matchstick, then cut the slices again crosswise to produce pieces that are about ½ the length of a matchstick. For ¼ cup ginger, cover with 6 tablespoons water and 4 tablespoons rice vinegar, and stir in 1 teaspoon sugar and ¼ teaspoon salt. Let this sit in an airtight container overnight. (I usually pickle the ginger in large quantities, as it keeps for several weeks in the marinade.) Rinse off the marinade before use. If you like the kick of raw ginger, by all means, skip the pickling. You can also buy sliced ginger in jars at many supermarkets, and this works reasonably well. However, I find that I need to dump out the liquid, then pour in water and vinegar in equal quantities and let the stuff sit at least overnight. Do not buy the pink Japanese pickled ginger—it's a different concept altogether.

Ingredients

1½ cups finely shredded cabbage

2 Roma tomatoes (Wash and cut off the tops. Slice each tomato lengthwise into 4 pieces, then finely slice each crosswise to produce delicate wedges.)

¼ cup fried garlic chips (See condiment recipe on p. 185.)

2 tablespoons roasted sesame seeds (Buy at an Asian market or roast the white sesame seeds yourself in a small dry skillet on medium-high heat, frequently agitating the seeds to prevent burning, until they are light brown.)

¼ cup fried broad bean and peanut mixture (See condiment recipe on p. 186. If you couldn't find the broad beans, just use a bit more peanuts, garlic chips, and sesame seeds.)

2 teaspoons shrimp powder (Hispanic markets sell shrimp powder, or you can buy dried shrimp from an Asian market and grind it yourself using a small coffee grinder.)

4 teaspoons lime juice (I prefer key lime.)

2 tablespoons onion oil (See condiment recipe on pp. 184–85.)

3–4 teaspoons *lephet* (fermented tea leaves) or more to taste, *or* ¼ cup lightly pickled ginger

3–5 teaspoons fish sauce (Go cautiously with this and use per your taste.)

1 teaspoon salt (Add this last and in portions, tasting as you go.)

For garnish:

2 green chiles, finely chopped (Use a mild serrano or a spicier small Asian chile, if available. If you want the flavor without the heat, *carefully* remove the seeds and veins. You can also discard the bottom-most part of the chile, as that is where the heat is concentrated.)

Lime wedges

Red pepper flakes

Let's get tossing

Toss everything in a bowl except the fermented tea leaves, fish sauce, salt, and garnish. Mix in 3 teaspoons tea leaves and 3 teaspoons fish sauce. Taste. If you like the fish sauce, you can add more in ½-teaspoon increments. Similarly, if you like the fermented tea, feel free to add more in ½-teaspoon increments. (Each packet of the tea differs in pungency, so treat it carefully until you get to know a brand and your tastes.) Once you have adjusted the tea and fish sauce, finally adjust for salt. The fish sauce has salt in it, so you want to add salt only after you are pleased with the fish sauce content. (Each fish sauce has a different salt content.) Mix and serve on a lovely serving platter. Your guests can personalize their salads with green chiles, lime, and even red pepper flakes.

Ohn-no Kaukswe *(Chicken-Coconut Soup Served with Egg Noodles)*

The list of ingredients may appear daunting, but like most Burmese recipes, it's easier than it looks. In Burma, the "soup" is frequently served separately from the noodles. One reason for this is that the Burmese make enormous vats of the broth and eat it for days. The longer the broth sits around (in the fridge), the tastier it gets. You boil the noodles as you need them, then place the desired amount in your bowl and ladle the broth over the noodles. The soup gets its color and texture not from the coconut milk, but from the chickpea flour that is used to thicken it. Chickpea flour, also known as gram flour or *besan,* is available in Asian specialty markets and even in some supermarkets. This dish also requires hard-boiled eggs, so do yourself a favor and boil them the day or night before.

Ingredients

8 cups chicken broth (I use nonfat, low-sodium broth.)
½ cup chickpea flour (I advise against using a substitute for this flour.)
2 tablespoons peanut oil
½ teaspoon turmeric powder
1 teaspoon sweet paprika
4 cloves garlic, finely chopped
1 small yellow onion, finely chopped

1-inch piece of fresh ginger, sliced very thin and chopped into slender strips
   Note: If you have a chopper or blender, the best way to go is to blend the
   onion, garlic, and ginger into a paste.
2 pounds skinless chicken, sliced in thin 1-inch-long pieces (You don't want
   big chunks of chicken in this soup. I use white meat to make the dish
   healthier, but you can use any combination of white and dark.)
1–3 tablespoons fish sauce (Start with 1 tablespoon and add more if you
   wish.)
1 can coconut milk (12-ounce or 13.5-ounce) (I use the healthier reduced-
   fat kind, and it is perfectly delicious. If you have doubts, use the more
   lethal full-fat milk.)
¼ pound shallots, peeled and thinly sliced
3 hard-boiled eggs, coarsely chopped
1 teaspoon sea salt
1 16-ounce bag Chinese noodles (Use egg or wheat noodles, *not* rice noodles.)

For garnish:
Finely chopped cilantro
Finely sliced ginger
Fried onions (See condiment recipe.)
Lime wedges (I find key limes to be more flavorful and prefer to use them.)
Red pepper flakes and sliced green chiles, for those who want some spice

Let's get cooking
1. Bring 7 cups of the chicken broth to a boil.
2. In a small bowl, whisk the remaining cup of broth and the chickpea flour
   until smooth. Slowly pour the lump-free mixture into the boiling broth.
   Stir occasionally to ensure that the chickpea flour does not burn, which it
   does effortlessly.
3. While that boils, heat the peanut oil in a skillet. When hot, add turmeric
   and paprika and fry for 30 seconds. Add the garlic, onions, and ginger,
   and fry for another 5 minutes or so until the onions are somewhat dry.
4. Add the chicken pieces and cook throughout. This should only take about
   3–4 minutes if the chicken is sliced thinly enough.
5. Add the fish sauce and stir. (If you are afraid of it, use just 1 tablespoon.
   You can add more later.)

6. Pour the chicken mixture into the pot with the broth and chickpea flour.

7. Add the coconut milk, shallots, and hard-boiled eggs.

8. Let simmer on low heat for at least 45 minutes, preferably 1 hour. Stir periodically to ensure that nothing is sticking and burning. Add salt and fish sauce to taste. (Be conservative: Once it's in, you can't take it out!) You can remove the broth from the heat and let it stand for several hours before your guests arrive, or you can even make it the day before and store it in the fridge. You need only reheat to serve. (You can do this in the microwave when serving only a few folks, but with all 10 cups, you'll probably need to reheat on the stove.)

9. Right before serving, bring a large pot of water to a boil. Boil the noodles for about 3 minutes until cooked throughout. (They are not served al dente, so cook them thoroughly!) Strain the noodles and place them in a serving bowl or on a platter. (I toss them with a bit of onion or garlic oil to keep them from clumping and to flavor them up a bit. I doubt this is authentic, but I hate clingy noodles and the oil-coated noodles look appealing and are tasty.)

10. To serve, put the soup in a large tureen and place it on the table, adjacent to the bowl of noodles. Encourage your guests to put some noodles in the bottom of their bowls and ladle some of the broth over them. (Alternatively, you can assemble the bowls and serve.) In separate little bowls, provide fresh cilantro, ginger, fried onions, lime wedges, red pepper flakes, and sliced green chiles for your guests to customize their dish.

Wata Majeedi (Pork Curry with Tamarind)

This dish calls for tamarind. I have tried dried tamarind soaked in water, tamarind paste soaked in water, and tamarind juice from my local Hispanic market. I do not recommend the latter since it has too much sugar, so I suggest one of the first two methods. For the first, just soak a whole piece of dried tamarind (without its shell) in ½ cup plus 2 tablespoons warm water for 30 minutes. For the second, soak a 2-inch cube of tamarind paste in ½ cup plus 2 tablespoons warm water for 30 minutes. For both preparations, squeeze out as much tamarind juice as you can and toss out the tamarind solids. (Strain before use to remove all solids.)

Traditionally, this dish calls for a three-layered pork belly. That's not my thing, and there's no need for all that fat, but you can use the traditional route if you want. This dish also requires the pork to marinate before cooking. Do this the night before the party or the morning of. This entire dish can actually be made a day or two ahead of the party and reheated. In fact, the longer the pork sits in its spices, the better!

Ingredients

½ cup tamarind water

1–3 teaspoons fish sauce (Start with 1 teaspoon and add more later if you find you like it.)

1-inch piece of ginger, grated (This should wind up being about 1 teaspoon.)

5 cloves garlic, crushed

1 medium yellow onion, finely chopped

1–3 serrano chiles or small, slender Asian chiles (Remove seeds and veins carefully, as this is where the hot stuff is. Use 1 if you don't like much heat and up to 3 if you like spicy food.)

Note: If you have a blender, you can blend the ginger, garlic, onion, and chiles into a paste. This is actually the best technique, consistent with old ladies banging away with a mortar and pestle to make a paste.

1 teaspoon turmeric powder

2 teaspoons paprika

½ teaspoon salt

1 pound pork loin or shoulder, chopped into ¾-inch cubes

3 tablespoons onion oil (see condiment recipe) or peanut oil, *or* 2 tablespoons canola oil and 1 tablespoon sesame oil

2½ cups water (or more as needed)

For garnish:

Finely chopped cilantro

Fried onions (See condiment recipe.)

Let's get cooking

1. Make the tamarind water per instructions above, which should produce about ½ cup of liquid. (Don't worry if it's a little more or less than this amount.)

2. In a ziplock bag or a bowl, whisk the fish sauce, ginger, garlic, onions, chiles, turmeric, paprika, and salt. Add the pork pieces and mix in with your hands to thoroughly coat. If marinating overnight or for several hours, store in the fridge. If you are letting it sit for only 15 minutes or so, you can leave it out on the counter. (Tip: In the spirit of being environmentally conscious, I wash and reuse those ziplock bags that I love so much.)

3. Once the pork has marinated, heat the onion oil in a pot. When hot, add the pork mixture and fry until the pork is thoroughly cooked.

4. Add 2½ cups water to the pork and bring to a boil. Lower the temperature, cover the pot, and let simmer for about 30 minutes. If after 30 minutes the pork is not tender, add another ½ cup water and let simmer for another 20 minutes or until it is tender.

5. Transfer to a serving bowel, garnish with cilantro and fried onions, and serve with plain jasmine rice.

Phazun Hin Asa *(Spicy Shrimp Curry)*

This is not a dish that stores well, so I make it right before my guests are ready to eat. The sauce can be made in advance, but once the shrimp is added, the half-life of this dish is short, so get it on the table fast.

Ingredients

1 pound medium shrimp, peeled with tail on

1–4 teaspoons fish sauce (If you are afraid, leave it out or start with 1 teaspoon.)

1 teaspoon sea salt

4 tablespoons peanut oil

1 teaspoon turmeric

2 teaspoons sweet paprika

1½-inch piece of ginger, finely chopped or grated

5 cloves garlic, crushed

1½ medium yellow onions, finely chopped

1–4 serrano chiles or slender Asian chiles, with seeds and veins carefully removed (Use 1 chile if you or your guests are pepperphobic, or up to 4 if you want some spice.)

Note: If you have a chopper or blender, the best technique is to blend ginger, garlic, onion, and chiles into a paste.

4 Roma tomatoes, finely sliced

2 cups water (or more as needed)

For garnish:

Sprigs of cilantro

Fried onions (See condiment recipe.)

Let's get cooking

1. Peel and clean the shrimp (remove the heads and devein). In a bowl, toss the shrimp with the fish sauce and salt and let sit for 15 minutes. (They can marinate longer if convenient, but keep them in the fridge.)

2. Heat the oil in a pot. When hot, add the turmeric and paprika and fry for 30 seconds. Add the ginger, garlic, onions, and chiles and fry until the onions are translucent (about 5 minutes) and the moisture gone.

3. Add the tomato slices and cook for another 5 minutes or so.

4. Add 2 cups water to the spice mixture and mix well to incorporate into a broth. (If it is too thick, add another ½ cup water). Bring to a boil.

5. Add the shrimp and cook while stirring. The shrimp will curl up and turn pink within about 5 minutes. Continue cooking, allowing the broth to reduce to a gravy. Adjust salt and fish sauce to taste if needed.

6. Transfer to a serving dish and garnish with sprigs of cilantro and fried onions. Serve with jasmine rice.

Plain Jasmine Rice

I use a rice cooker, but you don't have to. Instructions for both the cooker and the stove-top method are given below. You can also follow the instructions for your rice cooker or those on the rice package.

Ingredients

4 cups jasmine rice

4 cups water if using a rice cooker, *or* 6 cups water if using stove-top method

1 teaspoon salt

Let's get cooking

1. Inspect the rice for things that don't belong (rocks, for example). Rinse the rice with cold water *once* to remove the starch. (Burmese rice is on the sticky side.) Drain the water.

2. If using a rice cooker, add the water, salt, and rice to the cooker and turn it on. The rice cooker will automatically shut off when done. Don't open the lid during cooking, and let it sit for at least 5 minutes after it shuts off.

3. If using the stove-top method, in a heavy-bottomed pot, bring the water and salt to a boil. Stir in the rice and return to a boil. Cover, reduce heat to a simmer, and let cook until finished (about 20 minutes). Try not to open the cover while cooking. It's done when the rice is tender and the water is absorbed.

DESSERT

Sanwinmakin (Semolina Cake)

Ingredients

1¼ cups semolina (Cream of wheat will do in a pinch.)

2 13.5-ounce cans coconut milk (I use the light kind, as noted in the soup recipe.)

⅔ cup sugar

2 eggs, well beaten

2 tablespoons ghee (clarified butter) or butter, softened to room temperature (Ghee is found in the Asian and/or Middle Eastern sections of larger grocery stores.)

½ cup raisins

1 teaspoon ground cardamom

1 teaspoon salt

3 tablespoons poppy seeds or toasted sesame seeds

Let's get cooking

1. Preheat the oven to 325 degrees.

2. In a large heavy saucepan, mix the semolina and coconut milk. Whisk to ensure that the mixture is free of lumps.
3. Add the sugar, beaten eggs, softened ghee, raisins, cardamom, and salt. Cream together with the whisk until smooth.
4. Cook on medium heat and bring the mixture to a boil, stirring constantly to avoid burning or clumping. Cook until the mixture becomes very thick, bubbles, and pulls away from the sides of the pan. It's ready when it sticks together like dough.
5. Prepare a cake pan or oven-proof dish by either using a nonstick baking spray or lightly buttering the bottom and sides. (You will want to use an 8x8-inch square pan or an 11x7-inch rectangular pan.)
6. Pour the mixture into the pan and smooth the surface with a spatula.
7. If using sesame seeds, toast them in a dry pan over medium heat until they are golden. Agitate constantly to avoid burning.
8. Sprinkle the sesame or poppy seeds liberally over the mixture.
9. Bake at 325 degrees for 45 minutes to 1 hour until solid. (It's done when you insert a toothpick in the middle and it comes out clean.) Put the oven on broil and broil it about 8 inches from the flame for a few minutes, turning the pan as needed to ensure a golden brown, crispy top. (The surface begins to ripple and turn brown when it's done.) Watch this like a hawk or it will burn and catch on fire.
10. Let cool. When cool, cut diamond-shaped pieces and serve with sweetened iced coffee or tea.

Sweetened Iced Coffee (or Tea)

Southeast Asians make this beverage with a cute stainless-steel coffee filter, which is filled with coarsely ground coffee and set atop a glass of ice and sweetened condensed milk. You are given a pot of boiling water to pour over the grounds, and when about ½ cup of water filters through into the glass, you have your coffee. I am imagining that you don't have one of these contraptions, much less enough for all your guests. Instead, you can use French-pressed coffee for this recipe or brew a pot of good, strong coffee. (You can also use brewed black tea.)

Ingredients (per glass)

½ cup ice

2 tablespoons sweetened condensed milk

½ cup freshly brewed *strong* coffee (or black tea, if you prefer)

Let's get mixing

1. In a tall glass, add about ½ cup ice. Pour the sweetened condensed milk over the ice.
2. Pour in the coffee.
3. Serve unmixed, because it is lovely to see the coffee slowly mingling with the milk. Stir before drinking.

Dossier of Chinese Perfidy

The People's Republic of China (PRC) is by any definition an authoritarian state. Its own constitution states that the Chinese Communist Party (CCP) is the paramount source of power in the PRC. Naturally, party members dominate all of the choice positions in the government, police, and military, among the other sprawling bureaucracies. The constitution refers to its government not as an authoritarian state, but as a "people's democratic dictatorship." [212]

All power of any import rests in the tentacles of the twenty-four-member Politburu of the CCP and the nine-member "standing committee." General Hu Jintao, naturally, sits upon the three most plumb positions as the Secretary General of the CCP, the President of China (aka "the people's dictator"), and the Chairman of the Central Military Commission. To keep such a stifling system in place, the state has to resort to all sorts of coercion, shameless appeals to notions of nationalism to guilt folks into complying, and various means of appeasing the poor, teeming masses. [213]

According to the U.S. Department of State's Bureau of Democracy, Human Rights, and Labor, the laundry list of China's offenses is *loooong* and includes the following:

- There is no right to change the government, which is deeply and pervasively corrupt.
- Arbitrary arrest or detention (which often includes physical abuse and/or death in custody), torture, coerced confession, reeducation-through-labor, forced labor, psychiatric detention, and extended or incommunicado pretrial detention can befall any person adjudged to be a threat to the Communist Party or government. All of this is made worse by a politically controlled judiciary and a lack of due process, especially for folks deemed "dissidents."
- China is the biggest executioner state. Human Rights Watch believes that it executes at least ten thousand persons a year—although "official figures" are a fraction of that.[214]
- Citizens' mail is monitored, as are telephone and electronic communications.
- China has a coercive birth limitation policy, often resulting in forced abortion and even sterilization.[215]
- The Chinese are increasing restrictions on freedom of speech and the press: shutting newspapers and journals, banning politically sensitive publications and films, and even jamming some broadcast signals. Naturally, they restrict freedom of assembly and freedom of travel as well—especially for folks who are deemed "politically sensitive."
- The Chinese communists ("Chicoms") have no concept of religious freedom in any form and even actively harangue and detain folks who are members of "unregistered religious groups." To be a Tibetan or a Muslim from Xinjiang (Uyghur) is definitely suboptimal.
- They forcibly repatriate North Koreans, whom they don't see as "refugees" but as "economic migrants."
- The Chinese scrutinize and harass domestic and foreign nongovernmental organization operations.
- The government passively or actively engages in trafficking in women, children, and organs (often courtesy of state executions).[216]

China gets away with this crap—and Iraq didn't—because it's big, powerful, and loaded. In fact, it's one of the world's biggest economies.[217] But despite the size of China's economy ($9.9 trillion), it's still largely poor. This is in part because of its massive population. When you take that huge gross domestic product (GDP) and break it down per person, China's per capita GDP is about one-fifth that of the United States when measured in purchasing power parity and only one-twentieth of that of the U.S. when using market exchange rates.[218] But most folks don't look at China's economy in per capita terms: They only see a huge honkin' economic powerhouse, and this is the source of much ambivalence about China's vast perfidiousness—both domestic and international. Few countries are willing to put their diplomacy and money where their moralizing mouths are, and the United States is no exception. There's money to be had in China, and that gives China considerable leeway to do whatever the hell it wants.

While U.S. officials note China's economic might, they charge it with unfair trade tactics, citing the $232.5 *billion* trade deficit. U.S. officials opine that this deficit is due to China's refusal to adjust its currency (yuan) to reflect its market value and claim that China artificially suppresses the value of its currency—perhaps as much as 40 percent below market price. This means that cheap Chinese products flood the U.S. market, which penny-pinching U.S. consumers are happy to buy. Conversely, U.S. goods are much more expensive when they land in China and therefore are of less appeal to Chinese consumers who also want a bargain.[219]

Whether or not China commits fiscal crimes upon the free world may be debatable, but there is little doubt that China *is* behind the sickening and painful deaths of beloved canine and feline associates alike, because Chinese firms sold melamine-tainted grain glutens to pet food manufacturers. The poisonous, melamine-doped grain products precipitated the largest recall of pet food in the United States. The melamine was likely added to the gluten on purpose because it has high nitrogen content. Since nitrogen is a backbone element in proteins, melamine-tainted glutens test with desirable high-protein content. This in turn permits pet food manufacturers to tout the "high protein" content of their feeds to unsuspecting consumers.[220] After initially denying visas to inspectors from the U.S. Food and Drug Administration, the Chinese finally relented and let them in to do their jobs. The Chinese also arrested *one* person, Mao Lijun, head of the Xuzhou Anying Biologic Technology Development Company.[221]

Of course, poisoned pet food is not the only tainted, purportedly "edible" product the Chinese ship off to the United States. In April 2007 the FDA reported that it found hundreds of tainted food products and more than "1,000 shipments of tainted Chinese dietary supplements, toxic Chinese cosmetics and counterfeit Chinese medicines."[222] This isn't new, of course, and it's been going on for years. In fact, China has flooded the United States with foods that are not fit for human—or obviously canine or feline—consumption. Unfortunately, FDA inspectors can only inspect a small fraction of the lethal goods. Typically, the inspectors just send the stuff back to China, but with the ever-deepening realization of how much of the food chain is contaminated with this Chinese crap, some members of Congress are demanding stronger action.[223]

But it's not just food products, alas. Throughout the summer of 2007, Americans were sent for a loop when they learned (gasp!) that the Chinese are also exporting children's toys painted with lethal lead paint. China produces 80 percent of the world's toys, whipping up apparently killer amusements for big brands like Mattel. That August, Mattel had to recall 1.5 million Chinese-made products with excessive amounts of lead paint.[224] Who knows when these revelations will end. On October 31, 2007, U.S. authorities recalled another tranche of 440,000 Chinese-made toys due to "high levels of lead, just hours before U.S. children were set to use some of them while celebrating Halloween."[225]

Chicom Military Menace

If it were just human rights abuses, tainted food, poisonous vitamins, dangerous toys, and killer makeup in which China specialized, maybe it would be less menacing. But China is a threat to freedom lovers everywhere for myriad other reasons. Militarily, the United States wrings its hands about China because of the opacity surrounding its military modernization, including its nuclear weapons program. China has the largest armed forces in the world, with over 2.3 *million* active personnel in the army, air force, and navy.[226] While it may be the world's largest military, it may not be the best. In fact, some folks speculate that the Chicom armed forces are—by the standards of million-person militaries—pretty lousy, with poorly trained soldiers and aging equipment. Yet China has exploited its economic success these past several years to funnel cash into its military modernization plans, which just keep going and going and going. U.S. officials are vexed because they can't figure out just what the Chinese are up to and how much they should be concerned about it.[227]

Chicom watchers, with considerable doom and gloom, opined fearfully about China's January 2007 launch of an antisatellite weapon.[229] They note that countries don't waste the time, money, and other resources to develop a capability they see no prospect of using. U.S. officials are also discomfited by what they see as a growing arsenal of missiles and other systems targeting the much-beloved Taiwan.[230]

China is an important "strategic competitor" (diplomatese for "scary friggin' threat") for the United States. It is a permanent nuclear weapons state under the Nuclear Nonproliferation Treaty (NPT), having conducted its first successful nuclear test in 1964. Since then, China has conducted forty-five tests, including a thermonuclear device and a neutron bomb. Apparently, it was motivated to get the bomb out of fear of the United States and a desire to protect itself from U.S. coercion. In July 1950—just as the Korean War was getting under way—President Truman ordered ten B-29s, configured to carry nukes, to the Pacific Ocean, threatening that the United States would "take whatever steps are necessary" to halt Chinese intervention and furthered that the use of nuclear weapons was under active consideration. In 1952 President-elect Eisenhower also hinted quite publicly that he would authorize the use of nuclear weapons against China if the Korean War Armistice talks continued to languish. And if that weren't enough, General Curtis LeMay, commander of the U.S. Strategic Air Command, publicly said that he supported nuking China if it resumed fighting in Korea. He said, and I joke not, "There are no suitable strategic air targets in Korea. However, I would drop a few bombs in proper places like China, Manchuria and Southeastern Russia."[231]

Confronted with such abject lunacy, the Chicoms had little choice but to develop some nukes themselves, and that's what they did. Since its beginnings in the winter of 1954–55, the program relied upon foreign help, indigenous capabilities, and espionage. In 1957 the Soviets gave them a sample bomb and manufacturing data. Between 1955 and 1960 over 250 Chinese nuclear scientists and engineers went to the Soviet Union to learn the secrets of manufacturing nukes and an equal number of Soviet scientists and engineers went to China to work on the nascent program. But that relationship didn't last. By 1959 the two began having spats that became so significant that Russia walked out, leaving the Chinese to make their own bombs. But if you do the math, this is crazy progress. Only a few years after the program began, China tested its first nuclear weapon. Later, in 1967, it tested its first thermonuclear device. Some folks attribute such speed of progress to espionage and accuse the Chinese of pilfering U.S. designs.[232]

While it is impossible to know the full size of their program, most educated guessers believe that China now has about four hundred strategic and tactical nukes and stocks of fissile material that would allow it to make a much larger arsenal. It also has stocks of ballistic missiles ranging from short-range ones all the way up to intercontinental ballistic missiles (ICBMs). China can nail virtually any nemesis it wants, including Taiwan with its Dong Feng-11s (DF-11s) and DF-15s; Japan, India, and Russia with its medium-range DF-3s, DF-4s, and DF-21s; and Europe and the United States with its stock of the ICBM DF-5.[233]

Even though China is a signatory to major international agreements on biological weapons and publicly claims to comply, the U.S. government believes that it has a small-scale offensive bio-weapons program and has transferred controlled bio-weapons technology to countries as scary as Iran. In response, the United States slapped a bunch of sanctions on the Chinese entities involved. In 1996 China ratified the Chemical Weapons Convention and declared that it had two facilities that made mustard gas and lewisite. It has permitted more than a dozen on-site visits to demonstrate that it is in compliance, but Washington is dubious and suspects that China hasn't really divulged the true scope of its chemical weapons program.[234]

China Is a Friend with Benefits

China is also at the crux of nuclear and missile proliferation, despite being a signatory to the NPT and despite agreeing to abide by the Missile Technology Control Regime (MTCR). China sold *five thousand* ring magnets, which are used in gas centrifuges to enrich uranium, to Pakistan's eponymous Khan Research Laboratory (run by the black marketer A. Q. Khan). But that's not all: The Chinese also gave the Pakistanis a high-temperature furnace for molding uranium and plutonium for bomb manufacture and helped them build a nuclear reactor and heavy-water production plant as well as a plutonium-producing facility. [235]

But this is all really small change. In 1997 the director of U.S. Central Intelligence claimed that China was the principle supplier to Pakistan's nuclear weapons program. In fact, the Chicoms gave the Pakistanis a tested and verified weapon design! And . . . that's *still* not all. The Chinese transferred its M-11 short-range ballistic missile (SRBM) to Pakistan as well as related production technology. In 1991 the Bush Sr. administration spanked China for these transfers with sanctions, but they were waived in March 1992. In August 1993 the Clinton White House caught China again transferring M-11 equipment to Pakistan and imposed a new round of sanctions. The parties came to a gentlemen's agreement whereby Washington would waive those unsightly sanctions and Beijing would resist exporting "ground-to-ground-missiles" capable of delivering a 500-pound warhead 186 miles. (This language was crafted to permit China to skate around its commitments on the MTCR, which imposed limits on missile payload and distance.)[236]

In fact, the sanctioning and not sanctioning was a huge drawn-out drama that obfuscated the basic fact that China gave Pakistan M-11s on several occasions, that the specifications of the M-11s come under purview of the MTCR, and that China and Pakistan should have been more heavily and consistently sanctioned under the MTCR. But Washington has tied itself in knots trying to minimally enforce provisions of the MTCR when it comes to China Daddy Big Bucks. To date, a small number of Pakistani entities remain sanctioned under the MTCR for these transfers. Indeed, despite China's various promises that it would not sell *missiles,* it has helped Pakistan develop the *technology* to make medium-range ballistic missiles (MRBM) all by itself. China is the gift that keeps on giving. [237] Predictably, there were no sanctions for this bout of missile proliferation.

China not only satisfies Pakistan's needs for big missile and nuclear love, it also allegedly serviced Iran in some measure. While China canceled a planned sale of nuclear reactors to Iran in 1995, there were other controversial engagements such as the "calutron" built by Chinese technicians, which would permit electromagnetic isotope separation for uranium enrichment. The Chinese seemed to have backed away from further deals for the time being—although the interest in helping Iran's "civilian" program persists. To Beijing's chagrin, the Russians seem to have displaced China in that market, and Israel—a key supplier to China's military—told the Chicoms to back off from helping Iran, one of Tel Aviv's more virulent nemeses. (Savvy readers should wonder why the Israelis—who enjoy ample subsidy from the United States—chose to arm Washington's only strategic competitor.) But China did sell a slew of missile guidance systems and computerized machine tools to Iran in the 1990s, and several Chinese entities sold Iran numerous other missile-related technologies.[238]

I think you get the idea. China is a big, bad, scary place that probably deserves to be in the Axis of Evil (AoE) or at least among the Outposts of Tyranny (OoT) just as much—if not more so—than the charter members of those shameful groups. But unlike the struggling AoE or OoT states, China can buy its way out. In fact, it's busy buying U.S. debt, which is akin to grabbing Uncle Sam by the family jewels: China—after Japan—is now the United States's second-largest lender. Between 2000 and 2005 China's investment in U.S. government debt has more than tripled, from $71 billion in 2000 to $242 billion in 2005.[239]

"I'll Have the Starfish on a Stick, Please"; or, "Do You Have a Spare Monkey?"[240]

In case you didn't know, China is a huge-ass place. Its 1.3 billion folks are busting out of the seams of its nearly 3.6-million-square-mile landmass. Across the expanse of land, its climate is diverse and includes tropical climes in the south and subarctic hell in the north. China's topography is mostly mountains, high plateaus, and deserts in the west and plains, and delta and hills in the east. It shares borders with a dizzying number of disparate countries including Afghanistan, Bhutan, Burma (or Myanmar if you hate freedom), India, Kazakhstan, North Korea, Kyrgyzstan, Laos, Mongolia, Nepal, Pakistan, Russia (both in the northeast and northwest), Tajikistan, and Viet-

I'll Take That Kidney If You Aren't Using It

China's death vans are controversial because organizations like Amnesty International (AI) believe they help that country's burgeoning black market for organs. Mark Allison of AI believes that in these vans, the organs "can be extracted in a speedier and more effective way than if the prisoner is shot." His organization has collected "strong evidence" that the Chinese police, courts, and hospitals are all involved in the illicit organ trade. The lucrative organ market provides a huge financial incentive to keep the death penalty. Fueling that speculation is the fact that the Chicoms don't let the family or other folks view the bodies after execution. Allegedly they are driven straight to the crematorium—how convenient.[241] Dr. Thomas Diflo, director of the renal transplant program at New York University Medical Center, has seen a half-dozen Chinese Americans who have had kidney transplants that they freely admit were bought for about $10,000 from executed prisoners in China.[242]

nam. Lovers of freedom would also note that it shares "borders" with Hong Kong and Macau.[243]

With a wacky geography like this, you'd expect a lot of variation in how folks prepare their victuals, and China lives up to every possible expectation in that regard. Cookbooks and Chinese food enthusiasts will gush that traditionally, China has four principle "culinary schools":

The Northern school. Inclusive of the northern provinces of Liaoning, Shandong, Hebei (which includes Beijing, or Peking in old-speak), Shanxi, Shaanxi (no, that's not a typo), Gansu, Henan, and Inner Mongolia.

The Eastern school. Composed of the provinces of Shanghai, Jiangsu, Anhui, Zhejiang, Jiangxi, Fujian, Hubei, and Taiwan.

The Southern school. Claims the provinces of Guangxi and Guongdong (which you may know as "Canton," derived from a bad French transliteration of the real name).

The Western school. Reflects the food of Hunan, Guizhou, Sichuan, and Yunnan.

Those who know China like the back of their hand may be wondering about the other *ginormous* provinces of Qingha, Gansu, Xinjiang (home of the Uyghur Muslims and their halal cuisine), and Tibet in the west and

Heilongjiang and Jilin in the north. Well, I can't tell you why, but they don't have a home in any of those four "schools." While there may be some historical nasty reason(s) for their exclusion, I am going to resist speculating about the assumptions being presumed.

As you may have guessed, each school has its own characteristics. The Northern school embraces the chow of the Imperial Palace and "Peking" dishes (while Peking is now known as Beijing, "Beijing Duck" just sounds less interesting), but it also claims Mongolian grub and some Muslim varietals as well. Thus, the Northern school hosts a slew of delicious beef and lamb dishes keeping with the Muslim dietary restrictions. As you may have guessed, it also claims the eponymous Mongolian Barbecue and Mongolian Fire Pot.

Given the cool climate of the north, rice does not thrive there. The major agricultural superstars are wheat, barley, millet, corn, and soybeans as well as cabbages and different gourds. Pears, apples, grapes, and the gnarly persimmons are also abundant. As such, folks don't eat a lot of rice in the north and instead nosh on wheat-based products like noodles, steamed buns, and pancakes for everyday fare. And given the long coastline, there's quite a bit of seafood in the Northern school.

The region of the Eastern school is sometimes called "paradise on earth" or "the land of fish and rice," designating its fecundity and concomitant good eats. This area is subtropical, with a large coastline and a year-round growing season, and has it all. Wheat, barley, rice, corn, sweet potatoes, and soybeans are huge successes, but it also hosts bamboo, melons and gourds, beans, leafy things, and the like. The Yangtse River snakes its way through here too—along with a number of tributaries, streams, ponds, and lakes—giving rise to all sorts of waterfowl and fish. The regional cuisine uses a yellow-grain wine (Shaohsing), soy sauce (for which the region is famous), and black Chinkiang vinegar (used as dipping sauce). The Eastern school of cooking relies upon stir-frying, steaming, and blanching to get the job done. They also pickle and cure meat and vegetables.

The Southern school is considered China's haute cuisine, and you likely know of it under the name "Cantonese." While numerous Chinese sayings and proverbs attest to the superiority of Cantonese cuisine, I have my unshakable doubts. While in graduate school, I lived with a couple from China who introduced to me some wonderful—and not so wonderful—cooking. Richard (whose real name was Wong Dong) shared with me some of the delicacies of Canton, including "baby mouse soup" and a table specially designed to allow one to restrain a monkey, crack open its head, and eat its brains—all while the hapless primate is alive. Richard was himself a bit appalled by these delicacies and recounted his own experience of a Canton feast he attended that featured the fetal mouse soup and other Canton specialties—but mercifully excluded the monkey stuck in a torture table.

I will confess that I thought that Wong Dong was pulling my leg and taking advantage of my Midwestern naïveté about the world. It all seemed so preposterous and needlessly cruel to do that to a perfectly good monkey, with whom we share 98 percent of our DNA! That struck me akin to strapping a dimwitted cousin to a table and helping ourselves to his gray matter. I have since learned to my dismay that Richard was, in fact, truthful. Here is how one travelogue writer sums up his dalliance with Canton cuisine, describing a popular restaurant in Hong Kong that specializes in dog meat:

> The menu, thoughtfully printed in both English and Chinese, includes such mouth-watering dishes as "grainy dog meat with chili and scallion sauce" and "dog meat ready to be cooked in earthen pot over charcoal stove at table." If you're unhappy at the idea of canine cuisine, there are plenty of other things to go for: braised python, civet cat, bear's paw, "steamed old cat" or perhaps "braised guinea pig (whole)." Most meals at the Wild Game Restaurant begin with Dragon-Tiger-Phoenix Soup, a concoction of snake meat, cat meat and chicken. Monkey dishes are a regular item, and for those with hearts of stone, it is possible to go and view the ingredients cowering in cages near the main door. Just in case you

ever have a spare monkey and feel like having a go, one waiter said that the animal should be drowned and then boiled for three to four hours. Cantonese cuisine used to be famous for live monkey brains served straight out of the monkey's skull on to your plate, but it is now rarely heard of. "Eating live monkey brains is very cruel," the waiter said. "But we do serve them boiled."[245]

I'm a bit squeamish and hopelessly American when it comes to what slides down my gullet, so this is all too much for me—and my dogs would seriously not speak to me if I tried the canine concoctions, and they'd be only slightly less pissed if I ate "steamed old cat" without sharing it with them. But you can knock yourself out the next time you show up in Canton with a spare monkey.

The Western school hosts the stuff that loads of folks love and know: Sichuan and Hunan cuisine (and their variously butchered transliterated variants) as well as panda bears. Unlike the chilly north, this area is steamy—even subtropical—with hot, humid summers and mild winters. This is the "rice bowl" of China, and as you may expect in Panda Land, the lovable-looking bear isn't the only one nibbling away on bamboo. Folks here appreciate a good plate of bamboo shoots and other novelties like "tree ears" and Sichuan peppercorns (which are unrelated to peppercorns and, in fact, come from the prickly ash tree), as well as ginger, garlic, onions, and dried tangerine peel. Like many tropical/subtropical cuisines, this stuff is hot—as some of you may know. Stir-frying and steaming are the most popular cooking methods in these parts.

All of these culinary factoids notwithstanding, you *can* make a living complicating a basic truth. Yes, there are four schools and, yes, they differ in what they eat and how they eat it. But I have to be honest (and perhaps this reflects my general ignorance of Chinese cuisine at home and abroad): Much of the Chinese foods I've seen involve a lot of oil and heavy use of animals and parts of animals that I do not consider tasty. In Beijing I passed a "food street" where you could buy virtually every member of the animal kingdom impaled upon a stick and grilled to perfection—whatever that may mean. The most startling was not the snakes or scorpions in abundance, but the enormous starfishes on a stick.

When the Chinese cook at home, they use peanut oil, loads of salt, and monosodium glutamate (MSG). As for the oil thing, we have all been subjected to the mantra that a low-fat/low-cholesterol diet will help stave off ill health, and in that sense, Chinese food gets a bum rap. You would think that all that oil would mean a diminished life span, but, in truth, the Chicoms don't score too badly: Life expectancy at birth in China is about seventy-one years of age. In contrast, Americans who gorge themselves on "big slam" breakfast troughs and "super-size" fast-food feasts are expected to live, on average, to seventy-seven.[246]

MSG is another issue altogether. It's a flavor enhancer, and folks love it because it is cheap and allows them to use lower quality food that, when cooked up, still tastes good. However, glutamate is also an "excitatory neurotransmitter" (chemicals found in your brain), and too much of the stuff can kill brain neurons. For that reason, MSG is labeled an "excitotoxin," which has been inculpated in neurodegenerative diseases, migraines, and chronic pain sensitization.[247]

In this menu, I try to keep the peanut oil to a minimum and omit the headache-inducing, neuron-slaying MSG. (So in this sense, the menu may not be all that authentic.) In putting together this menu for you, there were two enduring challenges: First, what parts of China should be represented? And, second, what can I include that will be "authentic" yet considered to be edible among my target demographic? Mind you, I know China and its cuisines not nearly as well as others in this book, so this represents my best effort given the themes of this volume and my limited experience with this enormous culinary culture.

The first challenge was easily met. China is the number one nuclear nemesis of the United States and likely of free nations everywhere. The Chinese have an ICBM capable of hitting the United States, the Dong Feng-5 (DF-5). It is housed in hardened tunnels buried deep beneath the mountains in the central provinces of Henan, Hunan, and Shanxi and in the northern province of Hebei, where Beijing is located. Thus, to remind ourselves of the ever-present Chicom threat, our feast will draw from the foods of the regions hosting the fear-inspiring DF-5. With reference to China's culinary schools, this means that we have represented here three provinces of the Northern school and one from the Western school. With respect to the second challenge, I tried to pick standard critters that are welcome additions to the plates of most North American palates.

The Plan of Attack

With the exception of General Tso's chicken, I'm going to guess these dishes will be new to you, so have some fun. I've taken a few liberties here and there in the interest of general palatability and ease of ingredients, but I think you'll enjoy them nonetheless.

As always, I recommend you do the chopping, cutting, and marinating in advance to save you time and grief. Chinese marinades do not need to sit around for long, and are usually good to go in less than an hour. Most of these dishes are easy to make and can sit in a warm oven while you finish up stuff. The Chinese are not huge on appetizers, although they often put out nuts and pickles for folks to snack on while waiting for the food to come. You can certainly do so if you choose, but try to avoid the tainted stuff that the FDA should have tossed out but didn't because they test too little of the poisoned products sneaking over our borders from China.

Some of these dishes have ingredients that are not in your local grocery store. You can give it a shot online (see suggested online vendors in the appendix) or use the substitutes that I suggest. *No one* will know if you simply used cider vinegar instead of the tasty dark stuff. Similarly, if you can't find dark soy sauce, use what you know, and if you can't find Chinese rice wine, use the commonly available Japanese version or, barring that, any white wine you have. I do recommend, however, that you at least try to find rice wine and rice vinegar, as most grocery stores carry them. Your supermarket will likely carry the Japanese versions of these items and they are perfectly fine—there is just no need to knock yourself out looking for the *Chinese* versions. Yes, there are differences, but none that we need to care about! As always, this plans for a feast of eight, but there will likely be leftovers.

Note: Different brands of Chinese condiments such as soy sauce and bean paste vary in their salt content. Where possible, I provide a salt range and suggest you adjust the salt content right before serving, depending upon the soy sauce and condiments you use and your personal taste.

Main course

- *Niu Rou* (braised beef, from Shanxi)
- *Tso Chung Gai* (General Tso's chicken; the general was from Hunan!)
- *Zheng Qie Zi* (steamed spiced eggplant, from Hebei)

- *Jeung Bau Yuk See* (shredded pork, Beijing style—or maybe not[248])
- Steamed short-grain rice

Dessert

- Fried sweet potatoes in ginger syrup (Henan style), or poached pears stuffed with dates (Northern style)

Beverages

- Tsingtao beer
- Green tea with dessert

PREPARATION

⭐⭐⭐⭐⭐⭐⭐⭐⭐⭐⭐⭐⭐⭐⭐⭐⭐⭐⭐⭐⭐⭐⭐⭐⭐⭐⭐⭐⭐⭐⭐⭐
⭐⭐⭐⭐⭐⭐⭐⭐⭐⭐⭐⭐⭐⭐⭐⭐⭐⭐⭐⭐⭐⭐⭐⭐⭐⭐⭐⭐⭐⭐

MAIN COURSE

Niu Rou *(Braised Beef, from Shanxi)*

As noted, beef is not terribly common in China, so its use makes this recipe distinctive, as does the fennel. This dish can be parked in a warm oven (200 degrees) for 20 minutes or so. If you do this, garnish it *after* you yank it out of the oven.

Ingredients

For the meat:
1 pound boneless beef (e.g., sirloin)
2 tablespoons sesame oil
1 teaspoon fennel seeds

For the marinade:
¼ cup soy sauce

1 tablespoon cornstarch

½ teaspoon finely chopped fresh ginger

For the sauce:

½ cup chicken stock (I prefer the low-sodium, no-fat kind.)

2 tablespoons rice wine

¼ teaspoon sea salt (Start with this amount; you can add more to taste before garnishing.)

For the garnish:

8–10 scallions, cleaned with tips and bottoms removed and sliced on a diagonal into 3-inch pieces

Let's get cooking

1. Remove all the fat and gristle from the meat. Cut it across the grain into ⅛-inch-thick strips about 3 inches long. (Cutting it while it is partially frozen may help you get the desired thinness.) You can also use "fajita" cuts if your local store sells them.

2. In a bowl, mix the soy sauce and cornstarch together, ensuring that there are as few clumps of cornstarch as possible. Clumping of the cornstarch can be avoided by sprinkling it onto the soy sauce and mixing with a fork. (The cornstarch ensures that the marinade sticks to the meat like glue.) Add the ginger last and stir thoroughly. Next, add the meat and toss to coat well. Let marinate for about 1 hour in the fridge. (There is no need to mix it around while it marinates.)

3. Heat the sesame oil in a wok on medium-high heat (or in a skillet if you don't have a wok). When the oil smokes, add the fennel seeds and stir for about 20 seconds. Add the beef with marinade and cook until the beef is nearly done.

4. Add the sauce ingredients. Bring to a boil and let the sauce reduce to the point where the meat is coated and most of the sauce clings to the meat. (There should be only a small amount of runny sauce in the pan. Some folks like to cook it until all of the sauce clings to the meat.) Taste and add salt as needed.

5. Garnish by tossing in the scallion before serving.

Tso Chung Gai *(General Tso's Chicken, from Hunan)*

Ingredients

For the meat:

1 pound boneless, skinless chicken thighs

1 cup cornstarch for dusting

3–4 cups peanut oil for cooking

4–8 small, dried red chile peppers (Traditionally this is a hot dish. If you want the flavor without the heat, use 4 peppers. You could use more than 8, but you would be braver than most.)

For the marinade:

2 eggs, beaten

2 tablespoons cornstarch mixed with 2 tablespoons water

¼ teaspoon sea salt (I usually use ½ teaspoon, but this makes it quite salty.)

¼ teaspoon ground *white* pepper

For the sauce:

½ cup dark soy sauce (If you can't find this, don't stress out—just use the standard-issue variety. They inevitably vary by brand, style, and origin.)

4 tablespoons hoisin sauce (This is widely available at most supermarkets in the Asian foods section.)

3 teaspoons honey

2 tablespoons rice vinegar (You will most likely find the Japanese variety, and that's just fine.)

1 tablespoon rice wine (Again, you will likely find the Japanese variety at your supermarket, which will do.)

2 teaspoons minced garlic

2 tablespoons finely chopped fresh ginger

For garnish:

8 scallions, cleaned with tips and bottoms removed and sliced into very thin, lovely ringlets

Let's get cooking

1. Set your oven to about 200 degrees and place a heat-proof plate or pan in it. As you finish frying the dredged chicken pieces in batches, you will place the cooked pieces here to keep them warm. Place a few absorbent paper towels on the plate to soak up excess oil.

2. Cut the chicken thighs into approximately 1-inch cubes.
3. Mix the marinade ingredients together. Add the chicken and toss to coat thoroughly. Let marinate for about 30 minutes.
4. While the chicken marinates, mix the sauce ingredients together and set aside.
5. Heat the oil to about 350 degrees and prepare the chicken for frying. Each piece of chicken must be dredged individually. Dredging in cornstarch *is not* similar to dredging in wheat flour. Cornstarch is fine and, when wet, acts like glue, which can make the chicken pieces stick together in a messy tangle. I find it helpful to put some of the cornstarch on a plate and plop down about 6 pieces in individual places. Flip each piece around to coat using chopsticks. (I have to rinse off the clumpy, wet cornstarch periodically.)
6. Once each batch is coated, carefully add the chicken pieces to the hot oil with chopsticks or tongs and cook throughout, turning them in the oil to cook all sides. The chicken may not turn golden brown if you are using "clean" oil, but the pieces will cook in about 5 minutes at this temperature. (Break one open to test for doneness to banish doubts.) Remove each batch with a Chinese strainer and let as much oil drain off as possible. Place the chicken pieces on the hot plate or pan (with absorbent paper towels) in the oven. While one batch of chicken cooks, coat the next batch for frying. Repeat until all pieces are dredged and fried to completeness. I usually like to shake all of the pieces around on a fresh paper towel to remove as much of the excess oil as possible, which helps ensure that they are crispy and not soggy.
7. Strain the oil from the wok and discard the solids that accumulated. (I reuse oil a few times before discarding. The used oil gives a nice warm brown color due to its impurities.) Add 2 tablespoons back to the wok and heat. When a wisp of white smoke appears, add the red chiles and fry for about 30 seconds. (Be brave: This will likely send the pepper oils into the air and it will smite you mightily if you are not steeled for it.)
8. Add the fried chicken nuggets back to the wok and stir them around in the pepper-infused oil. Add the sauce mixture and stir well to coat each chicken piece. Let this cook for about 2 minutes or until the sauce thickens and clings to the chicken. I like to have a bit of gravy, so I cook until the chicken is coated but a small amount of sauce remains, but others will keep cooking it until the sauce is just a coating. The choice is yours.
9. Transfer to a serving plate and garnish by tossing in the scallion slices. This

dish can sit in the warm oven while you prepare the other items. If you do so, toss in the scallions only after removing it from the oven.

Zheng Qie Zi *(Steamed Spiced Eggplant, from Hebei)*

You can steam this healthy eggplant dish in advance and let it sit in the fridge. It can be served warm or cold. To reheat, zap in the microwave.

Ingredients
For the vegetable:
1 pound eggplant (Try the slender Asian kind if you want, but I find it easier to use the big monster variety, and the taste is not perceptibly different.)
2 teaspoons sea salt (More can be added later to adjust for taste.)

For the sauce:
⅛ cup soy sauce
1 tablespoon sesame oil
1½ teaspoon rice vinegar
2 teaspoons finely minced garlic (about 2 or 3 cloves)

For garnish:
1 teaspoon chopped chives (or scallions if more convenient)

Let's get cooking
1. Peel the eggplant and cut into strips about ½ inch wide, ½ inch thick, and a few inches long. Add the salt and toss thoroughly. Let this sit for about 1 hour. (Adding salt to the eggplant draws the water out of its flesh.) After 1 hour, drain off the liquid that accumulates in the bowl. I also squeeze out as much water as possible, which additionally helps to remove some of the 2 teaspoons of salt.
2. Place the eggplant in a heat-proof dish and steam for 20 minutes or until it is very soft. I put it in a small metal bowl stuck in a large covered pot with water up to about ⅓ of the bowl's height. (You could also use a double-boiler.) Obviously, you don't want the boiling water to leap into your pan with the eggplant, so don't overfill it with water! That would render

pointless your efforts to get the water out. For the same reason, avoid using a veggie steamer with holes.

3. While the eggplant steams, mix the sauce ingredients in a serving bowl.
4. When the eggplant is done, drain off the excess water and mash to a paste-like consistency. (You could use a small chopper for a creamier texture.) Add to the serving bowl with the prepared sauce and toss.
5. Adjust for salt content.
6. Garnish with the chives or scallions and serve.

Jeung Bau Yuk See *(Shredded Pork, Beijing Style)*

This dish is very easy to make, and you can substitute a different meat if you prefer. Chicken thighs work nicely, if you keep kosher or halal or otherwise turn your snout up to the other white meat.

Ingredients

For the meat:
1 pound boneless pork (preferably loin)
2 tablespoons peanut oil
Sea salt to taste, if desired

For the marinade:
¼ cup dark soy sauce (You can use regular soy sauce if you can't find this.)
2 tablespoons rice wine
1 tablespoon sesame oil
1 tablespoon cornstarch

For the sauce:
2 teaspoons sugar
2 tablespoons rice wine
4 tablespoons bean paste mixed with 4 tablespoons water

For garnish:
8 scallions, cut on a diagonal into 2-inch slices

Let's get cooking

1. Cut the pork into slices that are about ⅛ inch thick and about 2 inches

long. (This will be easier if the pork is still slightly frozen.)

2. Mix the marinade. And the pork slices and marinate for about 30 minutes or longer.
3. While this marinates, combine the sauce ingredients. Set aside.
4. Heat the oil in a wok or large skillet and fry the pork until it's nearly cooked.
5. Carefully add the sauce ingredients to the hot skillet. Stir to coat the pork and simmer until the sauce thickens and the meat is cooked throughout. Taste and add salt if needed. (Some soy sauces are saltier than others, and for this reason I omit salt completely from this recipe until the end.)
6. Arrange the scallions on a plate. Turn the pork out on top of the scallion bed and serve.

Steamed Short-Grain Rice

I use a rice cooker when making most kinds of plain rice, but you don't have to. Instructions for both the cooker and the stove-top method are given below.

Ingredients
4 cups short-grain rice
4 cups water if using a rice cooker, *or* 6 cups water if using stove-top method
1 teaspoon sea salt

Let's get cooking
1. Examine the rice for things that don't belong (rocks, for example). Rinse the rice with cold water *once* to remove the starch. (Short-grain rice is on the sticky side.) Drain the water.
2. If using a rice cooker, add the rice, water, and salt and turn it on. The cooker will automatically shut off when done. Don't open the lid during cooking, and let it sit for at least 5 minutes after it shuts off.
3. If using the stove-top method, in a heavy-bottomed pot, bring the water and salt to a boil. Stir in the rice and return to a boil. Cover, reduce the heat to a simmer, and let cook until finished (about 15–20 minutes). Try not to open the cover while cooking, as this lets the steam escape. The rice is done when it is tender and the water is absorbed. When done, remove the rice from the heat and let it sit covered for a few minutes.

DESSERT

★★★★★★★★★★★★★★★★★★★★★

You have two dessert options. The first, which features sweet potatoes, is from a special area in Henan (Kaifeng) that is renowned for its cuisine. The original recipe calls for a garnish of "haw jelly." Haw is a cousin of the crab apple, and haw "jelly" is not a spreadable condiment despite the name. It is made by reducing the juice of the haw berry with a truckload of sugar and two truckloads of pectin to create a product that has the consistency of the innards of a jelly bean. I couldn't find this stuff anywhere, much to my relief. In the original preparation, the sauced-up fried sweet potatoes are tossed with cubes of haw jelly. I am dubious that the combination of textures would work—even though the flavor of the haw jelly might be tasty. So, like the other dishes in this chapter, I've taken some liberties with this recipe. I omit the suspect haw condiment, add fresh ginger to the syrup, and garnish the thing with sliced almonds. But the spirit remains: fried sweet potatoes in yummy sugary goo.

The second dessert option is a poached pear stuffed with dates. It draws from my favorite elements of several poached pear dishes in the north (Shanxi and environs). Both of these scrumptious desserts can be served with green tea. There is no special tea preparation, so just follow the instructions on the box and use the green tea of your choice.

Fried Sweet Potatoes in Ginger Syrup (Henan Style)

This dish is served hot. The sweet potatoes can be fried in advance and kept at room temperature covered with a paper towel. Don't put them in a plastic bag or airtight container, or keep them in a warm oven, because they will just get soggy if you do.

Ingredients
2 pounds sweet potatoes or yams (In the United States at least, things labeled "yams" are almost always sweet potatoes.)
3 cups peanut oil for frying
1 cup warm water
½-inch fresh ginger, thinly julienned

½ cup sugar

2 tablespoons honey

2 tablespoons cornstarch mixed with 4 tablespoons water

For garnish:

2 tablespoons finely sliced (and preferably toasted) almonds

Let's get cooking

1. Peel the sweet potatoes and julienne into pieces that are about 3 inches long and ¾ inch thick.
2. Heat the oil in a large skillet or wok.
3. When the oil is hot, fry the sweet potatoes until they are crisp and brown. Remove them as they cook with a Chinese strainer. Allow as much oil as possible to drip off into the wok, then transfer the sweet potatoes to a plate with a paper towel to absorb excess oil.
4. Drain the oil and quickly wipe the skillet or wok with a paper towel, leaving a thin layer of oil. Add 1 cup warm water along with the ginger slices. Bring to a rapid boil and let the ginger boil for about 3 minutes. This will help extract the flavor from the ginger into the water.
5. Add the sugar and stir to dissolve. When the sugar has dissolved, add the honey and stir until incorporated while maintaining a rumbling boil. Add the cornstarch and water mixture, and reduce the heat to a simmer. Stir until the syrup has thickened. Return the sweet potatoes to the skillet and mix to coat.
6. Turn out onto a serving plate and garnish with almond slices. Serve with the green tea of your choice.

Pears Stuffed with Dates and Poached in Syrup *(Northern Style)*

This dish can be served hot or cold. If you want to serve it cold, be sure to make it several hours in advance so that the pears can chill. I like to serve these pears—hot or cold—with a scoop of vanilla ice cream, which is probably not terribly authentic but delicious nonetheless. Whether you serve them hot or cold, reserve the cooking fluid to reduce into a syrup that can be served hot, cold, or at room temperature. If you are serving these pears hot, try to time their cooking so that they begin poaching when folks start eating. This way, the pears are ready by the time your guests have finished their dinners. (I save excess syrup for pancakes or waffles!)

Ingredients

For the pears:

8 firm pears (preferably Asian or Bosc)

1½ cups coarsely chopped dates

Zest from 2 large oranges (Reserve small amounts of zest for garnish, and finely chop the rest.)

For the poaching fluid:

6 cups water

2 cups rice wine (or any other sweet white wine you may have)

½ inch ginger, peeled and finely sliced

2 large pieces of cinnamon stick

2 star anise

2 cups sugar

For garnish:

Orange zest in long, lovely pieces

Let's get cooking

1. Cut the tops off the pears and core them. I keep the peels on them for texture, but some people remove them for aesthetic purposes. If the pears cannot sit upright, cut off a small portion from the bottom so that they will sit up straight in the poaching pot.
2. Mix the dates and finely chopped orange zest.
3. Pack the date mixture into the pears. I pack them hard so that the ingredients don't fall out while poaching.
4. In a pot that is adequately large enough to hold all the pears (sitting upright in one layer), add the water, wine, ginger, cinnamon sticks, and star anise. Bring to a boil. Add the sugar and stir to dissolve. When all of the sugar has dissolved, carefully arrange the stuffed pears upright in the pot. (If you have stuffed them well, the stuffing should not fall out during poaching.)
5. Turn down the heat and cover. Simmer the pears until they are thoroughly cooked. With a good firm pear, this should take about 40 minutes. Keep

an eye on them and poke periodically with a fork or a toothpick to check for doneness. They should be soft when completely cooked through.

6. When completely cooked, move the pears to serving dishes. Turn up the heat and let the syrup reduce slightly for a few minutes, then transfer to a cool bowl so that the syrup cools faster. If serving hot, spoon on a bit of the slightly cooled syrup, garnish with a few pieces of orange zest, and serve, preferably with a scoop of vanilla ice cream. If you are making this in advance, the pears can chill in the refrigerator. The syrup will become thick like maple syrup when it cools and may need to be zapped in the microwave for a few seconds before serving. Chilled pears are also yummy with the ice cream and, of course, the syrup.

PART IV

The Great Satan Barbecue

THE GREAT SATAN BARBECUE

Americans are frequently treated to lengthy expositions about the perfidy of other nations. But, as my fellow Americans have come to learn (the hard way, alas) in recent years, we really seem to irritate most of the world. Thus, in the spirit of embracing our inner hegemons and in the hope that Americans will wake up and smell the enmity and demand better leadership and saner policies, I offer this sarcastic glimpse into what the data say about "why they hate us." (Hint: It's definitely not our freedoms.) Ladies and gentlemen, pick up your pitchforks with patriotic pride and fire up those coals!

Dossier of American Perfidy

Let me say up front that I *love* being American. As a country, we have much to offer the world apart from, inter alia, interfering in other sovereign states' domestic affairs, propping up and funding (often military and/or right-wing) dictators,[249] toppling democratically elected folks we dislike, waging unpopular preemptive wars against countries that posed no real threat before being invaded, supporting countries that oppress all or parts of their populations, and bankrolling states that occupy people and appropriate their lands.

There are probably any number of *good* things we *could* do that wouldn't foster global enmity—or at least as much as our current suite of policies. For example, if we took the cash that we squandered on these morally and ethically questionable programs and deployed those resources to educate folks, provide health care and robust feeding programs, and underwrite civil society institutions working within their legal structures for change, the U.S. of A. may have been spared the "Great Satan" moniker. Hell, we'd probably be in a better place than we are right now had we spent those same greenbacks educating *American*s and providing sustainable and affordable health care rather than engaging in such dubious adventurism abroad.

I'd guess based upon my Midwestern experiences in Indiana and Chicago that prior to planes crashing into our buildings and suicide nutters attacking our embassies and naval vessels and before we saw our countrymen and allies being beheaded on the Internet, many Americans probably didn't know how hated we are outside of our porous borders that are so easily crossed by the millions of illegal immigrants who still want to come here despite all the bad things said about us. In fact, some may say, if we are so bad, why is that anywhere between 400,000 and 700,000 poor sons of bitches make their way illegally to the Great Satan *every year*? As they say, 10.3 million "unauthorized" immigrants since 2004 can't be wrong![250] If I were to be adventurous and hazard a guess, I'd say this collective obliviousness to global animosity and its possible origins is likely due, in part, to the fact that Americans don't travel that much. In fact, according to data from 2005, 80 percent of the American citizenry and 30 percent of U.S. congresspersons don't even have passports.[251] This is weird, given that we are the world's only global superpower. This is even stranger when you consider how rich we are. Depending upon how you measure per capita wealth, the United States is either fourth or tenth out of 209 countries so ranked.[252]

"Lies, Damned Lies, and Statistics"

Those of you who are convinced that Uncle Sam is a benign, avuncular man loved by all may be suspicious of my premise that Americans *really* are disliked and dismiss the claim as just a bunch of tree-hugging clap-trap. However, dear suspicious reader, I fear that the preponderance of data—regrettably—confirms that we are, in fact, disliked and, in some places, we are downright loathed. And, it's not just the terrorists who have bones to pick with us. The Pew Global Attitudes Project has collected scads and reams of data over several years that illuminate the ignominious truth that the United States has few friends in the world and we lost many that we had before 9/11. While cookbooks don't typically have charts, the gravity of our "dislikedness" necessitates one.

Take a gander at the chart on the next page, lovingly crafted with the aforementioned Pew data. Before 9/11 most of the below-noted countries had healthy majorities who saw the United States favorably, but by 2006 only

Percentage of Folks with Favorable Opinions of the Great Satan

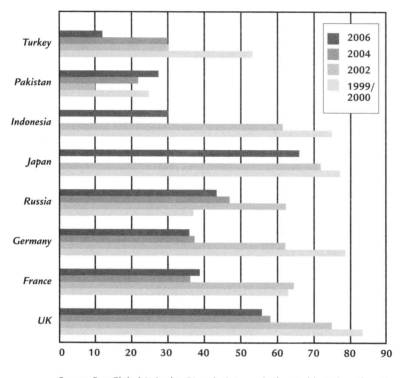

Source: Pew Global Attitudes, "America's Image in the World: Findings from the Pew Global Attitudes Project"

in the UK and Japan was there a majority of folks so inclined.[253] Take a look at Pakistan, to which the United States has given something on the order of *twenty billion* bucks since 9/11 in overt and covert funds. Now, to be sure, a few Pakistanis like us more than they did before that infusion of cash, but still only one in four view us approvingly. Of course, Pakistanis rightly ask, who got the cash and for what purposes?[254]

I know some of you don't trust survey data, and why should you? As the wise British statesman Benjamin Disraeli famously quipped, "There are three kinds of lies: lies, damned lies, and statistics." Maybe Pew is incompetent, you say, or even a foe of freedom. I doubt it, but I understand your concerns.

Unfortunately, there are slews of other data that paint the same ugly American picture.

In March 2007 U.S-based WorldPublicOpinion.org, paired up with the British BBC to survey more than 28,000 respondents in twenty-seven countries who were given a list of twelve countries (including the United States) and asked whether the countries in question had a "mostly positive or mostly negative influence in the world." Here's the heartache: There were four countries that received mostly negative responses, and the land of the free and the home of the brave was among them. Of course, Israel topped the list with 56 percent of surveyed folks opining negatively about that state's swagger. Iran trundled in with 54 percent of those 28,000 folks having largely negative views of the mullahcracy's influence. The United States got the bronze medal in the execrableness contest, with 51 percent espousing unfavorable views of its role in the world. In comparison, only 48 percent of those 28,000 viewed North Korea so hostilely. Worse yet, there were only four countries wherein majorities thought the U.S. role in the world was a *good* thing: the United States (only 57 percent thought their own country's influence was mainly positive); Nigeria (72 percent); Kenya (70 percent); and the Philippines (72 percent). The folks in Canada even disliked us too, by and large, with only one in three standing up for us.[255]

So, it seems to me that it's pretty clear that folks are irked by the United States. The question, of course, is why. On September 20, 2001, President Bush famously addressed the nation and offered these prairie oysters of wisdom:

> "Americans are asking, why do they [presumably terrorists and their supporters] hate us? They hate what they see right here in this chamber—a democratically elected government. Their leaders are self-appointed. They hate our freedoms—our freedom of religion, our freedom of speech, our freedom to vote and assemble and disagree with each other."[256]

Now a smart-arse person not unlike myself would note snidely that the U.S. government has consistently supported "self-appointed" leaders when expedient, such as oil-purveying sheikhs and military and other right-wing dictators. But the Bush crowd is pretty fond of the bromide "They hate us fer [*sic*] our freedom," and they have hocked this canard like hot dogs on the DC Mall on the Fourth of July for years.

Osama bin Laden was so irritated with this persistent nonsense that he "hates us for our freedom" that he drug his ass out of his cave and made a video on the eve of the 2004 elections in an effort to put all that silliness to rest. While bin Laden is a murderous, loathsome, scraggy-bearded aspirant despot, it is worth looking at why *he* says he hates us:

> Before I begin, I say to you that security is an indispensable pillar of human life and that free men do not forfeit their security, contrary to Bush's claim that we hate freedom.
>
> If so, then let him explain to us why we don't strike, for example, Sweden? And we know that freedom-haters don't possess defiant spirits like those of the 19—may Allah have mercy on them. No one except a dumb thief plays with the security of others and then makes himself believe he will be secure. Whereas thinking people, when disaster strikes, make it their priority to look for its causes, in order to prevent it happening again. But I am amazed at you. Even though we are in the fourth year after the events of September 11th, Bush is still engaged in distortion, deception and hiding from you the real causes. And thus, the reasons are still there for a repeat of what occurred.[257]

Clearly, bin Laden has a different explanation for why *he* hates the United States, and his views should count for something, as he is the arch-hater of the United States and evil terrorist mastermind that would like to drive our fine country into the Atlantic Ocean, the Pacific Ocean, *and* the Gulf of Mexico if he could. There are a few important takeaways from his minimus opus. The first is the utter nonsense of the "they hate our freedom" narrative. The

We Are What We Eat

Americans are fat, fat, and fat, and we're kind of famous for that in the same way that the French are notorious for their marital infidelities. While bin Laden hasn't named it (yet), McDonald's has been accused of being a global public health menace and it is probably what people think of most readily when they ponder the effects of globalization.[258] While the Big Mac can be scarfed in about 100 different countries, Americans lead the pack by chomping down about 550 million of those bad boys each year. Given that each sandwich contains 29 grams of fat, Americans eat 17,582 tons of fat annually from Big Macs alone. Some wise-ass journalist calculated that this amounts to 40 fully loaded Boeing 747 passenger jets.[259]

man may be maniacal, but he's right: Al-Qaeda didn't target Sweden. In fact, Sweden is even *freer* than the United States, according to data from Freedom House.[260] So if terrorists are anti-freedom-seeking missiles, then those freedom-dripping Swedes would be royally screwed. Second, bin Laden seems to be pointing out the obvious: The United States is a big bully, and there's loads of evidence that suggest that publics—who are neither terrorists nor their supporters—may agree with him on this score. Third, he implies that we are not "thinking people" because some of us still believe they hate us "fer our freedom."

Instead, we should embrace the fact that we are the world's only global hegemon. The Soviet Union has gone. The United States is the only superpower standing, which means the United States gets to do whatever the hell it wants with scant regard to what other sovereign states think, as evidenced by our Cuba, Iraq, and Israel policies.

Anti-Americanism Is a Global Phenomenon

To state the obvious, anti-Americanism is a global phenomenon, but as the Pew nerds note, "It is clearly strongest in the Muslim world."[261] Within the five predominantly Muslim countries they polled in 2006, fewer than one in three persons queried had good things to say about the United States. More to the point, the Pew folks contend that with the Iraq war, anti-Americanism spread to Muslim countries that *used* to like us, such as Turkey and Indonesia.[262] Muslims, like many people in the world, don't seem to be buying the bull that Washington is selling. One T-shirt hawker on the Internet found a better formulation more in line with the empirics of the antipathy but retaining the pith: "They Hate US for Our Freedom . . . to Dominate Them or Kill Them Trying."[263]

Curiously, Americans are also dubious about many of the same issues as their fellow global citizens. Most Americans disapprove of our mess in Mesopotamia and Washington's approach to global warming. One in two Americans mercifully reject the way detainees are treated in Gitmo and other prisons as well. Americans are also split in their assessment of the way their government has dealt with Iran. A bit less than half (47 percent) of Americans are not fond of the way the United States handled the "Israel-Lebanon" war, and 43 percent disagree with Washington's approach to Pyongyang's nuclear hankerings. More than half (53 percent) even think the U.S. military presence in the Middle East makes more messes than it prevents.[264] Moreover, most of my fellow Americans think we are "policing" the world more than we ought to be.[265] So the question, of course, remains: If Americans don't like this crap and ostensibly no one else does either, why is our purportedly elected government engaging in these shenanigans and why can't we stop them?

U.S. efforts to put democracy on the march at gunpoint strikes some folks as curious given recent electoral follies in the world's "oldest democracy." When I wrote this chapter, I knew loads of sensible, educated folks of all class and ethnic backgrounds who still questioned the legitimacy of the 2000 *and* 2004 presidential rumbles. The issues stem from the ways in which the voters' list is, or at least can be, manipulated and some of the groups of people who appear to be disproportionately disenfranchised either by not letting them vote in the first place or by excluding their vote once cast. African Americans—who are not typically Republican—seem particularly screwed over. Writing in 2004 for the *San Francisco Chronicle,* Greg Palast explained that in the 2000 presidential election, there were 1.9 million Americans whose votes were not counted because they were deemed "spoiled votes." Curiously, 1 million of them (more than half of the rejected ballots) were cast by African-American voters, even though they comprise only 12 percent of the electorate![266]

Of course, the vote shenanigans didn't end in Florida in 2000. In the 2004 presidential contest, Ohio was the flashpoint of criticism, though relatively muted in comparison to the Florida hoopla. In several vastly Democratic and majority African-American districts, voters had to wait in lines for hours in the rain to cast their ballot, and many just aborted their electoral missions. Meanwhile, in vastly Republican and majority white neighborhoods, folks waited fifteen minutes or so to vote. One observer explained that it was "poor planning" and that "county officials knew they had this huge increase in registrations, and yet there weren't enough machines in the city." In fact, these electoral dysfunctions disenfranchised 5,000 to 15,000 frustrated would-be voting Columbus residents on November 2.[267]

While those "lost" votes would not have made a ding in Bush's 118,000-vote margin, similar problems took place throughout state, galvanizing protest marches and hollering for a recount. Fueling doubts about Republican intentions, the foul-ups seemed to be most acute in Democratic-leaning districts. In Cleveland, for example, nincompoop poll workers reportedly provided bogus instructions to voters, resulting in the disqualification of thousands of provisional ballots. As one would expect in this tale of intrigue, several hundred votes were transferred to third-party candidates. In Youngstown twenty-five electronic machines moved some unknown number of votes cast for the distinguished Vietnam War vet and senatorial "flip-flopper" John F. Kerry to the incumbent George W.[268]

Many people around the world—including bin Laden himself—were baffled by the American polity's willingness to reelect (or *elect,* if you are really riled up by the 2000 election) the Shrub. In his 2004 pugnacious diatribe, bin Laden ignominiously explains to the citizens of the United States that there indeed have been winners in this war, namely "shady Bush administration-linked mega-corporations, like Halliburton and its kind . . . And it all shows the real loser is . . . you."[269] Later, in 2007, in his oddest video yet, bin Laden expressed incredulity that the Americans, in spite of his various screwups, "permitted Bush to complete his first term, and stranger still, chose him for a second term, which gave him a clear mandate from you—with your full knowledge and consent—to continue to murder our people in Iraq and Afghanistan."[270] What can you say to this? Sometime the world's nastiest terrorist mastermind makes good points.

It's Definitely Not Bad To Be American

There are a few things remaining that I don't quite understand about my nation's predicament. As noted, by per capita measures of wealth, it's not bad to be American. Measured by human development standards, we are not poorly off either. Using the United Nations Development Program's notion of Human Development Indicators, the U.S. of A. is ranked eighth among 177 nations so ranked.[271] So we are rich and well developed, but we are oddly just clueless. I suspect that part of the problem could be the way in which we Americans get our news. Profit-motivated media, which has increasingly been consolidated in the hands of a few, have produced a sense of uniform, sensationalistic, dread-mongering "infotainment," with little actual news content and plenty of genuflecting to advertisement revenues. The über-liberal *Mother Jones* magazine estimated that there are only eight firms that dominate the huge U.S. media market.[272]

It is bizarre how all of the mainstream American media remain so captivated by Anna Nicole Smith in the backdrop of two wars and mounting casualties, while Iran gets nuttier, Pakistan melts down and the Palestinians still suffer under Israel's metal-toed boot. If buxom blondes or purposeless "reality TV shows" are not hogging up your HDTV despite the hundreds of channels on cable, then it seems like any source of fright will do to lure in our channel-flipping attentions. Infotainment news programs have all perfected the formulaic fear-hocking with their freaky titles, such as "Terror in your medicine cabinet," "Could terrorists be plotting to buy the Washington Redskins?" "Could terrorists be running your HMO?" and "Terrorists in your septic tank."

Who cares, you ask, if American media are mind-numbing? Well, I care, because there is evidence that Americans who get their news from commercial media sources are more likely to be wrong on important issues, and this state of "wrongness" permits politicians to do things that are not in our interests. In November 2003 researchers published an essay titled "Misperceptions, the Media and the Iraq War," wherein they found that in the run-up to the pointless invasion of Iraq and subsequent occupation-related quagmire, a significant chunk of the electorate held several wrongheaded ideas germane to the Bush administration's justification for its warmongering.[274]

First they asked, "Is it your impression that the U.S. has or has not found clear evidence in Iraq that Saddam Hussein was working closely with the al Qaeda terrorist organization?" (The answer, dear reader, is "*has not.*") Large percentages, 45 to 52 percent, got that question *wrong.* Second they asked,

"Since the war with Iraq ended, is it your impression that the U.S. has or has not found Iraqi Weapons of Mass Destruction?" (Again, the answer is *"has not,"* although suggesting that the "war had ended" was, in hindsight, absurd.) Americans did better on this question than on the first: Between 21 and 34 percent failed. Third they asked Americans, "Thinking about how all the people in the world feel about the U.S. going/having gone to war with Iraq, do you think the majority of people favor it, oppose it, or are views evenly balanced?" (Correct answer: "Mostly the world *opposed* it.") Anywhere between 24 and 31 percent mistakenly believed that the majority supported the war, and another one in three incorrectly opined that international views were evenly mixed. (The good news is that 35 to 42 percent got the question right, depending upon when the poll was fielded.) Across all three of these incredibly basic, rudimentary, and straightforward questions, only one in three got *all* of them correct.[275]

How does this advance my contention that this widespread misinformation is related to the source of crappy news? That team also looked at the source of news consumed, asking respondents, "If one of the networks below is your primary source of news please select it." The options given were ABC, CBS, NBC, CNN, Fox News, PBS, and NPR. They were also allowed to identify "print media." Lamentably, PBS and NPR had so few responses that the team combined them into one category, "public networks," for analysis. They then examined those who got the above-three questions correct or incorrect and correlated their responses to the source of news. They found that the folks who had all three questions correct overwhelmingly relied on NPR and PBS for their news. In what will no doubt *not* come as an earth-shattering surprise, only 20 percent of Fox's viewership got them all right, which means that (shock!) 80 percent of consumers of Fox's "fair and balanced" news got at least one of the questions wrong.[276]

Apart from the public networks, people who relied mostly upon print media were second most likely to get all items correct and second less likely to get one of the questions wrong. For those who think CNN walks on water, 45 percent of the folks who identified CNN as their primary news source had no mistakes, while a majority (55 percent) got at least one item wrong. CNN was actually tied with NBC, but viewers of CBS and ABC were more likely to be wrong and less likely to get a perfect score than either.[277]

The final point that I'd like to share with you is the irony that the United

States is dedicated (purportedly) to fighting "religious extremism" abroad—*but* we have a strong population of religious extremists at home. In November 2004 CBS did a poll of Americans to query their views on evolution. Astonishingly, a slim majority (13 percent) believed in evolution as most legitimate scientists would define it (e.g., no god involved). The biggest slice of folks (55 percent) said that they believe that "God created humans in their present form." Another 27 percent said that they believe that humans evolved, but "God guided the process."[278] Note that since this involves a supernatural explanation (God's involvement), it is not, strictly speaking, evolution. Overwhelmingly, white evangelicals, weekly churchgoers, and conservatives were most likely to say "God created humans in their present form." Not surprisingly, that same poll found that a majority (71 percent) of people think that both creationism and evolution should be taught in U.S. schools.

The Men vs. the Monkeys

To be fair, there have been other studies of acceptance of evolution among Americans, and the answer differs depending on how you ask the question. In 2006 Pew found that one in four believed that humans evolved through natural selection and one in five believed that humans evolved under the guidance of a "supreme being," while the largest chunk (four in ten) believed that humans and other living things have always existed only in their current form.[279]

In 2006 a study was published in *Science* magazine that measured the acceptance of evolution by Americans and the residents of Japan and thirty-two European countries. Folks in that study were asked whether they agreed with, disagreed with, or were uncertain about the statement "Human beings, as we know them, developed from earlier species of animals." Whereas among most European countries, 80 percent or more agreed and 7 to 15 percent said it was "false," in the United States, 40 percent agreed and as almost many disagreed. When Americans were asked about the same statement but were given a different set of choices (the statement is "definitely true," "probably true," etc.), only 14 percent said that evolution is "definitely true," and one in three outright rejected it. The researchers, trying to figure out why Americans seemed to have more in common with (Muslim) Turkey than with the other countries examined, summarized their findings in the following terms: "The acceptance of evolution is lower in the United States than in Japan or Europe, largely because of widespread fundamentalism and the politicization of science in the United States."[280] In fact, American opponents of evolution are so gung-ho about creationism, they even built a "museum" dedicated to it in Petersburg, Kentucky, in May 2007.

Pew's polls offer some more frightening, data-driven insights in the U.S. of A., which if evangelical Christians get their way, could be renamed Jesustan. Let's begin with the scary fact identified by the reliable bean counters at Pew who found that Americans overwhelmingly consider the country to be a "Christian nation." (That's scary stuff for the Atheists, Jews, Muslims, Sikhs, Hindus, Buddhists, and other non-Christian Americans who are destined to burn in hell.) Fortunately, most Americans still believe that citizen preference should trump the Bible when it comes to law, except those white evangelicals, who comprise about one in four of the Pew sample. The majority of those wannabe citizens of Jesustan (60 percent) believe that the Bible should be the guiding principle in drafting laws. In partial explanation of the insane U.S. policies toward Israel, nearly 70 percent of white evangelicals believe that God *gave* Israel to the Jewish people and nearly 60 percent believe that Israel is the fulfillment of biblical prophecy—a view that is rejected by other Protestant and Catholic groups. Not surprisingly, those who see Israel as a gift to Jewry and a fulfillment of biblical soothsaying are more likely to sympathize with Israel in its "dispute" with the Palestinians.[281]

Obviously, evangelical and other religious Americans are also nuts over abortion, fetal rights (endowed with rights taken away from women), physician-assisted suicide, and the like. Evangelicals, along with their political and judicial proxies, have coined a moniker for their collective of purportedly Bible-based beliefs and efforts to stamp out the above-noted practices. They call depriving women of health care and stripping humans of the same dignity in death as afforded house pets and horses as "creating a culture of life," embraced by the purported evangelical in chief, George W. Bush, who even publicly worked to found it from the Oval Office.[282] Incidentally, there is no reference to abortion in the Bible and there are loads of examples demonstrating that God is not kind to children (killing all firstborn in Egypt, among other gruesome examples) and certainly not thoughtful toward women (damning them to painful childbirth and governance of husbands who can beat them).[283]

Our president seems to value fetuses over born children. In the fall of 2007 he vetoed a law that would provide the actual children of working, but poor, parents with health care. And I won't even remind you of the huge of loss of life in Iraq. Apparently that culture of life *excludes* Iraqi lives and that of armed service personnel dying there daily. Indeed, every Republican presidential hopeful was out there demonstrating that every gamete is sacred. Monty Python couldn't spoof these debates better than they spoofed themselves. But once again, I'd like to point out why this is so funny to folks watching the American fish bowl.

While we decry grotesque practices of governments and wrangle them into apposite categories like Axis of Evil and Outposts of Tyranny, we are, in fact, criticized by many governments and international human rights organizations because we use the death penalty and have embraced torture in the war on terrorism, which are not terribly consistent with a "culture of life." Across the world in 2006, Amnesty International says that at least 1,591 people are known to have been executed and 91 percent of these known executions took place in six countries: China (1,010), Iran (177), Pakistan (92), Iraq (65), Sudan (65), and the *USA* (53). The good news is if you divide the execution counts by population, the United States has the least per capita executions of these six states.[284] Texas is the biggest American user of the "punishment": Out of 1,099 executions in the United States since 1976, Texas accounts for a whopping 405![285]

While many Americans have moral qualms about the death penalty's use,[286] it is appalling that the world's oldest democracy still uses capital punishment given the risk of killing innocent people, which often happens as DNA-based exculpatory evidence has shown, and given that race and class determine access to justice, as does the ability to afford a decent defense attorney.[287]

Folks, I love my country. But we can—and must—do better. We can all start by reading, demanding better news, and insisting upon accountability for stupid and deadly policies that advance anyone's interests but our own. And with that lengthy, contumely, and outright intemperate outburst, let's get back to food.

Welcome to the Great Satan Barbecue[288]

America is a big place, and its cuisines are varied. Notwithstanding the city slickers in L.A. and "The City" (as New Yorkers are wont to say), the United

States and its foreign policies are driven by the Bible-thumpers in the "heartland." Thus, being a daughter of the soil of Jesustan, I am going to bring to you the food of *my* people—albeit a "reconstructed" variation. Traditionally, Middle Americans eat horrid "appetizers," which tend to rely heavily on cream cheese, shoddy imitations of salsa, ranch dressing, "cheez" balls, and deli platters that include the oddity "pickle loaf." In fact, they should not be called "appetizers" at all because they are not remotely appetizing.

Since I actually want folks to eat this food, I have had to innovate or at least improve upon the Tupperware platters of inedibles that I recall from my sordid youth. I wish I could say I am sharing with you the recipes of the women of my family, lovingly handed down from generation to generation. That did not happen. My mother unloaded trucks for a living in Indiana, and began her day at o'dark thirty. When she came home sweaty and exhausted, feeding the family—me, my brothers, and my step-monster—was a chore akin to slopping hogs. It was a duty to be performed with the greatest ease, minimal time, and the least cleanup. She preferred things that cooked themselves. This usually involved perpetrating various culinary crimes with cooking bags, canned mushroom soup, and cheez products. Mother had many talents—swearing, speeding, decking obnoxious husbands—but cooking was simply not in her repertoire.

Understandably, I went through college with the belief that stirring a can of tuna into a mix of macaroni and cheese teetered on sophistication and that special occasions called for wrapping cream cheese and a pickle in a piece of dried beef and slicing the roll into swirled wedges, each pierced with a plastic-fringed toothpick and arranged thoughtfully on a Tupperware platter. Mom made a mean corn dog—oddly, however, without cornmeal, which is the hallmark ingredient of the "dish." She also made a wonderful breakfast called "shit on a shingle," which was constructed by boiling thinly sliced chipped beef in water to impart flavor and mixing in milk and flour to make a delicious gravy. This delicacy was often served hastily over usually singed white bread. On special occasions, Mom would make my favorite, sausage gravy and biscuits. Of course, she did not make her own biscuits—that would be absurd. She used the handy "biscuits in a tube" that you find in the margarine section of your supermarket. When she died, I unsuccessfully scoured her kitchen for the cornless-corn dog recipe. They really were delicious—especially with French's mustard.

While you more sophisticated folks may be cringing, I love the food I grew up on. When I come across a restaurant that serves up fried green tomatoes or okra, I am overcome with nostalgia and twenty minutes after consuming the same, implacable heartburn. I squeal with delight if I see dandelion greens on a menu. As a child, I helped my grandmother pick the greens from behind her trailer, and she'd wilt them with bacon fat and season them with a bit of vinegar. I can still remember the smell of those greens breaking down and the pungent aroma of real pig fat sizzling in the pan. Grandma made cornmeal mush—a hilljack's take on polenta. She even poured leftover cream of wheat into a buttered loaf pan and kept it in the fridge until the next morning, when she would slice it, fry it up in butter, and serve with (faux) maple syrup. To this day, a gussied-up TFC (as I call tuna fish casserole) is my comfort food of choice—and you can't go wrong with a fried Spam sandwich on white bread with mustard.

Family reunions, while not enjoyable, were always memorable. On my grandmother's side, the family farmed pigs. I mostly recall the succulent roasted pig and the hideous and strange fruits of the pawpaw trees that grew along the Wabash River. Salads consistently were dressed in Miracle Whip with frozen peas and bacon. Sometimes someone would get fancy and substitute spinach for the lettuce, which left some folks disgruntled. Cakes were reliably made with Jell-O stirred into the batter to make funny colored swirls. And the beer was invariably Pabst Blue Ribbon. I considered myself lucky if someone made a tuna fish casserole with real cheddar cheese—not Velveeta— or if someone bothered to make a real macaroni and cheese.

The folks on my first step-monster's side were also pig farmers of German heritage. Great-grandma Weber would cook anything that moved. She would fry up rabbit caught in her own garden, make a "Swiss steak" out of anything rendered into her kitchen, and seemed to have a personal philosophy that if it grew, she could pickle it. Grandpa Weber—her son—was and is fond of making strudels and schnitzels and eating them in one sitting. He also had a distinct sense of humor. Loads of people in Indiana hunt deer, and while it's commonplace to get the "rack" mounted, Grandpa Weber had the ass of a doe mounted. The "deer ass" hangs proudly in my home, both shocking and amusing guests at once.

This meal is centered on the Beer Butt Chicken barbecue. Yes, as the name suggests, it involves cooking a chicken with a beer can. You simply insert said can (appropriately sized for the bird in question) and stabilize the chicken atop it. You cook the bird upright, as if it were sitting on the can. While you may be dubious, the science of this is impeccable. It steams the bird from the inside while allowing it to get crispy on the outside. You can cook the bird on the barbecue or in your oven. (Since I have generally been a city girl since leaving Indiana, I generally use my oven for this. Although I did grill up a mess of these birds in Kabul.)

The Plan of Attack

This plan of attack presumes you are feeding a crowd of eight esurient diners. Adjust accordingly. As noted, the star of this dinner is the Beer Butt Chicken, preferably cooked on your barbecue for theatrical effect. (Otherwise, it's the Great Satan *Dinner Party,* which is equally fun but doesn't involve playing with hot coals, which is Satan's signature medium, no?) We'll also serve up corn, blackened on the grill or any other hot surface (preferably with a flame) such a broiler. (When it's just me and the spouse, I cautiously do this over the gas flame on my stove top.) Once slightly blackened, the corn will be slathered with lime and chile pepper. (The wimps can stick with butter and rock salt.) If your wingding is in the spring or summer, I suggest you go with the mustard/buttermilk mashed baby red potatoes. If you have a fall or winter shindig, I recommend the roasted sweet potatoes with sage butter. I am going to give you a road map to an Indiana-inspired salad suitable for family reunions throughout the heartland. (I'll also provide an alternative for those who think Miracle Whip is something that makes your spouse or significant other perform better.) We'll wrap this up with a homemade apple-pear crumble with an easy homemade vanilla frozen ice. (If you don't want to make the vanilla ice yourself, you can substitute your favorite store-bought.)

The beverage of choice is beer. Pick your favorite for drinking, but for the birds, you could and should use a cheap beer. It's authentic and there is no point trying to get sophisticated with this: What makes a good beer different from a bad beer is the solutes, which don't evaporate anyway. Go ahead and swallow your shame and pick up some PBR or whatever is the local cheap brew at your market. It's no worse than doing the walk of shame, familiar to college co-eds.

Some of this stuff can be done before the evening of your soiree. You can make the potatoes and the crumble a day in advance, and you *must* make the vanilla ice mixture the day before (or at the earliest, the morning of your dinner party) and tuck it into your fridge. If your ice-cream maker is like mine, you cannot put anything remotely warm in that sucker and expect it to work. I usually pour the mixture into the ice-cream maker about 45 minutes before anticipated dessert time—that usually means a few minutes before my guests begin to arrive. But you need to take cues from your ice-cream maker's instruction manual (and your own experience with the appliance) with respect to prepping the mixture for freezing, time needed to freeze the confection, and what preparation the device needs to do its job.

Main course

- Beer Butt Chicken (chickens, sitting atop *open* beer cans with some beer decanted, barbecued or baked)
- Mashed potatoes with mustard and buttermilk, *or* roasted sweet potatoes with sage butter
- Roasted ears of sweet corn with red chile pepper and lime juice
- Reworked Hoosier salad, *or* if you prefer something lighter, mixed baby greens with goat cheese and pomegranate vinaigrette

Dessert

- Apple-pear crumble with homemade vanilla ice

Beverages

- Beer!
- Coffee

PREPARATION

★ ★
★ ★

MAIN COURSE

Beer Butt Chicken

Ingredients

2 organic chickens, about 4–5 pounds each (I prefer these birds because
    they taste better than the monster mutant ones.)
Salt and freshly ground pepper to season
20 cloves garlic, peeled
2 lemons, sliced
Several sprigs rosemary
2 cans beer (Pabst Blue Ribbon, Miller Genuine Draft, or whatever you
    have. It need not be and should not be a fancy beer.)

For garnish:
Who needs garnish for a dish like this? But if you are purist and like the aes-
    thetics of garnish, use some of those rosemary sprigs.

Let's get cooking

1. Get your coals going and ready to cook, or preheat the oven to 350 degrees
   if you are roasting these guys in your oven.
2. Remove and discard the gizzards and rinse the birds in cold water. Pat dry.
   Season with salt and pepper. Set aside.
3. Prepare the chickens. Make 10 incisions throughout each bird and insert
   10 cloves of garlic into the holes. Get the legs, breast, and back. Don't be
   shy. (Don't be worried either: The alcohol will evaporate and help distribute the flavors throughout the birds.)
4. Loosen up the skin around the breast of each bird and stuff several slices
   of lemon and sprigs of rosemary between the skin and the breast.

U . S . A .

5. Open the beer cans and pour out a bit of the brew.
6. If you are cooking your chickens on the grill, sit them atop the beer cans before putting them on the grill. (They should look like they're sitting on those cans.) Arrange them on your grill to maximize their stability. I cover them with foil for about half of their anticipated cooking time, which is about 1½ hours, depending on the size of your birds. I remove the foil to let them brown up before serving. I suggest you check for doneness using a meat thermometer, which will read 180 degrees when the birds are done. Remove from the grill, transfer to a plate, and let them sit covered.

   If you are using the oven, put the birds upright into the oven but stand them up in a pan in case they fall over. The pan is also a more stable surface to keep them sitting up than the grids on a baking rack. As above, I cover them with foil for the first half of their cooking time of about 1½ hours. When the above-noted meat thermometer reads 180 degrees, the birds are done. Pull the birds out, remove them from the pans, and let them sit covered (tented in foil) for about 10 minutes.

   (For those of you who are afraid of uncooked birds, remove them when the temperature is 180 degrees. However, I remove them when they are between 170 and 175 degrees. The temperature will increase while the birds sit. But suit yourself.)
7. Here's the hard part: removing them from the cans. This is a two-person job. Wearing oven mitts, have your assistant hold the beer can from the bottom while you pull the chicken up off of it. (Children and adults alike seem to enjoy this spectacle.) You can use foil, gloves, or tongs to pull it off. It's not easy.
8. Keep the chickens covered until ready to serve, as this will keep them warm and diminish the likelihood of drying out. Carve and arrange nicely on a serving platter. (By the way, carving these birds may feel odd because they don't have the shape that a chicken cooked horizontally would have.) Garnish if you must with sprigs of rosemary, and serve as soon as possible after carving.
9. Please, discard the beer cans used for cooking.

Mashed Potatoes with Whole-Grain Mustard and Buttermilk

I use baby red potatoes because I hate peeling potatoes and the baby reds can be cleaned, boiled, and then on with the show. You can use Yukon Gold or russet or even some of the sexy fingerling potatoes that are increasingly on the market. The advantage of the fingerlings—like the reds—is that they need not be peeled. This dish can be made a day in advance and reheated in a microwave oven.

Ingredients

3 pounds potatoes (I use baby reds with the peel on, but use whatever potato you like best and feel comfortable with.)
4 cloves garlic, peeled
1 teaspoon salt
1–1½ cups buttermilk, or more as needed (I use reduced fat buttermilk, as it has the flavor without the bad stuff.)
¾ cup unsalted butter
¼ cup whole-grain or coarse-grain mustard (My friends in the heartland, please do not reach for the yellow stuff that you put on hot dogs.)
Salt and white pepper to taste

Let's get cooking

1. Clean the potatoes. If you are using baby reds and you want to keep the peel on, clean them well and simply cut them in half. If you are using big potatoes that must be peeled and cut up, do so. Stick the potatoes, along with the garlic, in a 5-quart pot and add cool water to cover the spuds by about 2 inches. Add 1 teaspoon salt and bring the potatoes to a simmer. Cook until tender. Depending on the kind of potato that you have chosen, this could take 35–45 minutes.

2. While the potatoes are simmering, take the butter and buttermilk out of the fridge to remove the chill. When the potatoes are almost finished, in a small saucepan heat up 1 cup buttermilk. Slice up the butter into small pieces and add to the buttermilk.

3. Drain the potatoes and garlic, then return to them to the same hot pot in which they were cooked. Finish the preparation over low heat. I find that this helps mash the potatoes while preventing sogginess.

U . S . A .

4. Once the potatoes and garlic are back in the still-warm pot, add the mustard and about ⅓ cup of the warm buttermilk/butter mixture. Mash the potatoes and garlic with a potato masher until you have the desired consistency. (You can also whip these if you like. Folks in Indiana *love* whipping their taters with a mixer.) If they are too dry, slowly add more milk—remember, you can't take it out once you add it! When the consistency is right, adjust the salt and pepper. I use white pepper because I like it better visually, but you could use the black stuff.
5. When ready to serve, transfer to a serving bowl.

Roasted Sweet Potatoes with Sage Butter

Some folks get all up in a swivet over the difference between "yams" and "sweet potatoes." I believe that for the most part, we don't get real yams in the United States. Real yams are dioecious tubers from West Africa and Asia, have rough and scaly outsides, and are dry and mealy to the mouth. So even things that are called "yams" in U.S. markets are, I think, really sweet potatoes. But I am not a botanist, so who knows? Just pick the variety from your store that you know is delicious and moist. This dish can be made a day in advance and reheated in the microwave.

Ingredients
3 pounds sweet potatoes
½ stick unsalted butter
3 tablespoons finely chopped fresh sage
Salt and white pepper to taste

For garnish:
Whole leaves of sage

Let's get cooking
1. Preheat your oven to 400 degrees.
2. Scrub the sweet potatoes and place them on a foil-lined baking sheet.
3. Bake the potatoes until they are soft, about 50 minutes. (Hint: I sometimes put a small pan of water in the oven to keep things moist.) Meanwhile, let the butter warm up to room temperature and finely chop the sage.

4. When the sweet potatoes are done, transfer them to a cooling rack and slice in two to help them cool more efficiently. Let them cool just until they can be handled without burning your hands.
5. Spoon out the soft flesh and transfer to a dish. Cover to retain the heat.
6. In a saucepan large enough to accommodate the sweet potatoes, melt the butter over medium heat. When the butter melts and begins to turn brown, add the chopped sage and fry for about 30 seconds. Add the sweet potatoes and incorporate the sage-butter mixture into the potatoes. You can use a potato masher or even a hand mixer if you prefer, as I do, to get a creamer texture. Adjust salt and pepper to taste.
7. When ready to serve, transfer to a serving bowl and garnish with whole sage leaves.

Roasted Sweet Corn with Red Chile Pepper and Lime Juice

Commensurate with this being a barbecue, you can grill this corn right on the barbie. It will take about 15-20 minutes, and they will need some turning. Put them on the grill during the last 5-10 minutes of the bird's cooking time. They can finish up after the bird is off the grill and resting.

Ingredients
8 ears sweet corn (husk and floss removed)
Olive oil (I often cheat and use spray-on olive oil.)
8 teaspoons red chile pepper
8 key limes, cut into halves
Salt to taste

For garnish:
Finely chopped fresh cilantro

Let's get cooking
1. Remove the husk and fibers from the ears of corn. Grease up your hands with some olive oil and rub each ear of corn with the oil. (You can also use a spray-on oil if you like.)
2. Grill the corn until it is nicely blackened all over. The corn should have a nice

black char on their surface. You can do this in the broiler if you prefer, which takes about 10 minutes. Turn as needed to get a uniform, gorgeous char.

3. While the corn cooks, place a couple teaspoons of red chile pepper in small bowls, 1 bowl for every 2 guests, at sensible places on your table. (I use 2-ounce glass prep bowls for this.) Cut the key limes in half and set aside.

4. When the corn is done, transfer it to a serving platter. Garnish with the key lime halves by squeezing some juice all over the ears. Sprinkle with small amounts of salt and finely chopped cilantro.

5. Guests should be encouraged to coat a piece of lime with chile pepper and run the pepper lime up and down the ear of corn. Wimps can stick with butter, but they should be lampooned for doing so.

Gooey Indiana Family Reunion Salad

When I was a child, every salad was served limp and dripping wet with salad dressing. If you want to go native, I'll give you a road map. It's actually delicious, if you can get your head around it and stop thinking of it as a salad, with crisp, refreshing flavors. Instead think of it as a "salad product."

Ingredients
1 large head lettuce, cut into shreds (You can also buy the bagged iceberg lettuce.)
1 cup frozen peas, thawed
1 cucumber, thinly sliced
1 red onion, thinly sliced
1 red radish, thinly sliced
1 cup *or more* Miracle Whip (Yes, you must use this product if you are taking this course of action. Real mayo isn't a bad option, though.)
2 tablespoons apple cider vinegar

For garnish:
At least 4 huge, thick pieces of country-style bacon, fried until crisp, cooled, and crumbled

Let's get tossing
1. Toss all of the vegetables into a bowl.

2. Whisk together the Miracle Whip and cider vinegar.
3. Dress the salad until that salad is gooey, wet, and slimy. Garnish with crumbled bacon. This will be the only thing that crunches in this "salad."

Baby Greens with Goat Cheese and Pomegranate Vinaigrette

Now that I did my duty and gave you a typical salad of my youth (which is assuredly delicious), I'll give you the salad that I actually eat as an adult when I have control over the menu.

Ingredients

For the salad:

1 box organic mixed greens (Get the pre-washed kind to save yourself grief.)

Seeds of 1 fresh pomegranate (If you can't find a pomegranate or if they are out of season, substitute ½ cup dried sour cherries, barberries, or even currants.)

½ cup pecan halves

3 ounces goat cheese, gently baked at 275 degrees for about 10 minutes to warm (It's done when the top slightly browns and the cheese is fluffy and airy.)

For the vinaigrette:

½ cup grape seed oil

½ cup cider vinegar

¼ cup pomegranate syrup, or more to taste

Honey to taste

Pinch of salt

Pinch of white pepper

Let's get tossing

1. Toss the greens, pomegranate seeds (or dried fruit substitute), and pecan halves in a bowl.
2. Whisk together the vinaigrette ingredients. Every pomegranate syrup brand is different in terms of sweetness and tang, so add more if it needs more tang. Adjust sweetness and balance by adding small amounts of honey (1 teaspoon at a time).

U . S . A .

3. Right before serving, dollup the warm goat cheese over the salad.
4. Dress the salad right before serving, or allow your guests to determine how much they want on their greens—which is what I do.

DESSERT

The crumble can be made in advance and reheated in the oven if you want to serve it warm. If you chose to make it the same day as the party, be sure to give it 1 hour to cook and *at least* 15 minutes to cool. This cooling time is important because it allows the fruit to set up with the sugar. The mixture for the vanilla ice should be made the day before or the morning of the party to give it time to cool. If you are using an ice-cream maker that requires a chilled bowl, be sure that it's chilled adequately and ready to go. (I keep mine in my freezer at all times in the event that we are inspired to concoct a frozen confection.) As with all small appliances, refer to the instructions and your own experience with your gadget.

Apple-Pear Crumble

Ingredients
For the crumble topping:
1½ cups unbleached flour
1 cup old-fashioned oats
1 cup lightly packed brown sugar
2 teaspoons cinnamon
½ teaspoon nutmeg
¼ teaspoon salt
¼ cup finely chopped walnuts
1 cup (2 sticks) unsalted butter, cut into ½-inch pieces

For the yummy apple-pear goo:
4 Granny Smith apples (or any other firm, tart apple)
2 firm Bartlett (or Bosc) pears

Juice of 1 fresh lemon (about ¼ cup)

1 cup demerara or raw cane sugar (Yes, as elsewhere, you can use the lousy white granulated stuff if you must.)

¼ cup unbleached flour

1 teaspoon cinnamon

½ teaspoon nutmeg

¼ teaspoon salt

½ cup dried currants (You can also use dried barberries, chopped dried cherries, or, less optimally, raisins. The preference here is a dried berry with a tart kick.)

Let's get cooking

1. Preheat the oven to 350 degrees.
2. Make the crumble topping. Mix all of the dry crumble ingredients, then using your fingertips, incorporate the butter into the mixture until you get moist clumps, which is the basis of the crumble. (I have tried using less butter to make it not so lethal, but, regrettably, it just doesn't work. This is the minimum butter you can use and get the topping to be moist and delicious.)
3. Peel and slice the apples and pears into ¼-inch pieces and transfer to a large mixing bowl. Coat thoroughly with the lemon juice to help the dry mixture adhere to the sliced fruit.
4. In a separate bowl, thoroughly mix all of the dry ingredients for the apple-pear goo, including the dried berries.
5. Add the dry ingredients to the lemon-coated fruit and toss thoroughly to ensure that the fruit slices are evenly coated.
6. Prepare a 13x9x2-inch rectangular baking dish either by coating with the cooking spray of your choice or with butter. (I use canola oil spray.)
7. Turn out the fruit mixture into the dish. Sprinkle the crumble topping all over the fruit.
8. Bake for about 1 hour or until the fruit bubbles at the edge and the topping crisps.
9. Remove from the oven and let sit for *at least 15 minutes* before serving with the vanilla ice (or a yummy store-bought ice cream).

U . S . A .

Vanilla Ice

This is a very easy "ice cream" recipe that is more in the tradition of the Mexican *nieve* and, as such, is a lot lighter than some of the other ice-cream recipes out there. I like this recipe because its texture reminds me of the "snow ice cream" that Grandpa Weber made when we were kids.

Ingredients
4 cups milk (I usually use 1 percent milk, but some folks prefer their ice to be richer, which means a higher fat content.)
2 vanilla beans
1 cup sugar (You can use the white granulated stuff here.)
¾ cup peeled blanched almonds

Let's get cooking
1. Pour the milk into a heavy-bottomed saucepan.
2. Using a knife, carefully slit open the vanilla bean pods and scrape the black seeds into the pot of milk. Dump the pods into the milk, but remember to remove them before blending.
3. Add the sugar and the almonds.
4. Carefully and with your fullest attention, bring the mixture to a gentle boil and let it simmer for 5 minutes. Stir it frequently and adjust the heat if you fear the possibility of scorching the milk.
5. Remove the mixture from the heat and remove the vanilla bean pods. Pour into a heat-resistant vessel. (This stops the cooking, as the pan retains heat and you are unlikely to keep stirring it once you remove it from the stove. This also helps cool the mixture more effectively.) Let it cool until it can be safely stuck in a blender. Transfer to a blender and blend to ensure that the almonds are finely ground.
6. Put the mixture in the fridge (not the freezer) and let it chill.
7. Follow the instructions for your ice-cream maker. This ice really can't be made in advance, and it needs to be served as soon as it is made unless you want to undertake a huge inconvenience, per your ice-cream maker's instructions. My gadget takes about 45 minutes to produce the frozen delicacy. This means that by the time we are all eating dinner (or even in the

minutes before my guest arrives if eating is the immediate order of business), I sneak into the kitchen to get the vanilla goop stirred and dumped into the machine. After 45 minutes of agitation in the machine, the vanilla ice is good to go. Serve with the crumble and coffee, made as you like.

APPENDIX: ADDITIONAL RESOURCES

The Charter Members of the Axis of Evil

North Korea

Further Reading

Albright, David, and Paul Brannan. "The North Korean Plutonium Stock, February 2007," Institute for Science and International Security, February 20, 2007. www.isis-online.org/publications/dprk/DPRKplutonium FEB.pdf.

Arms Control Association. "The U.S.-North Korean Agreed Framework at a Glance," August 2004. www.armscontrol.org/factsheets/agreed framework.asp.

BBC News Online, "N. Korea Wages War on Long Hair," January 8, 2005. http://news.bbc.co.uk/2/hi/world/asia-pacific/4157121.stm.

Brooke, James. "Kim Jong Il's Ex-Chef Lifts Lid on Ruler's Fancy Tastes." *New York Times*, October 20, 2004.

Carlson, Peter. "Sins of the Son: Kim Jong Il's North Korea Is in Ruins, But Why Should That Spoil His Fun?" *Washington Post*, May 11, 2003. www.washingtonpost.com/ac2/wp-dyn/A40505-2003May10?language =printer.

Chun, Injoo, Jaewoon Lee, Youngran Baek, et al. *Authentic Recipes from Korea* (North Clarendon, VT: Periplus, 2004).

Crossland, David. "Monster Bunnies for North Korea." *Spiegel Online*, January 10, 2007. www.spiegel.de/international/0,1518,458863,00.html.

———. "No More Monster Bunnies for North Korea." *Spiegel Online*, April 2, 2007. www.spiegel.de/international/zeitgeist/0,1518,475218,00.html.

The Economist. "Faces Saved All Around," February 15, 2007. www .economist.com/world/displaystory.cfm?story_id=8706148.

Faiola, Anthony. "The Dear Leader, On a Platter: Sushi Chef's Book Details Kim Jong Il's Many Purported Indulgences." *Washington Post,* March 16, 2004.

Federation of American Scientists. "Nuclear Weapons Program: Current Status," November 16, 2006. www.fas.org/nuke/guide/dprk/nuke/index.html.

Furlanis, Ermanno. "I Made Pizza for Kim Jong-il." *Asia Times Online,* August 4, 11, and 18, 2001. http://dirkburgdorf.com/Pizza-for-Kim.pdf.

GlobalSecurity.org. "Six-Party Talks." www.globalsecurity.org/wmd/world /dprk/6-party.htm.

The Guardian, "The Producer from Hell," April 4, 2003.

Hepinstall, Hi Soo Shin. *Growing Up in a Korean Kitchen: A Cookbook.* Berkeley, CA: Ten Speed Press, 2001.

Human Rights Watch. "North Korea," January 2007. http://hrw.org/eng-lishwr2k7/docs/2007/01/11/nkorea14755.htm.

Hwang Jang-yop. *Hwang Jang Yop Kaikoroku: Kim Seinichi eno Sensen Fukoku* (Hwang Jang-yop's Memoir: Declaration of War on Kim Jong-il). Translated by Toru Ogiwara. Tokyo: Bungei Shunju, 1999.

International Crisis Group. *After the North Korea Nuclear Breakthrough: Compliance or Confrontation.* Seoul/Brussels: ICG, April 30, 2007.

———. *North Korea's Nuclear Test: The Fallout.* Seoul/Brussels: ICG, November 13, 2006.

———. *Perilous Journeys: The Plight of North Koreans in China and Beyond.* Seoul/Brussels: ICG, October 26, 2006.

International Herald Tribune, "U.S. Keeping North Korea on Its List of Terror Sponsors," September 4, 2007.

Kahn, Herman. *Thinking about the Unthinkable in the 1980s.* New York: Touchstone, 1985.

Lee, Cecilia Hae-Jin. *Eating Korean: From Barbecue to Kimchi, Recipes from Home.* Hoboken, NJ: Wiley, 2005.

Marks, Copeland. *The Korean Kitchen: Classic Recipes from the Land of the Morning Calm.* San Francisco: Chronicle Books, 1993.

Mount Holyoke College. "Documents on the Korean War," including "Memoirs of Kim Il Sung." www.mtholyoke.edu/acad/intrel/korea /korea.htm.

Niksch, Larry A. *North Korea's Nuclear Weapons Development and Diplomacy,* Congressional Research Service Report RL 33590. Washington, DC: CRS, January 3, 2007.

Niksch, Larry, and Raphael Perl. *North Korea: Terrorism List Removal?* Congressional Research Service Report RL 30613. Washington, DC: CRS, April 6, 2007.

Oberdorfer, Don. *The Two Koreas: A Contemporary History.* New York: Basic Books, 1997.

O'Neill, Tina-Maire. "Kim Jong-il's North Korean empire prepares for war." *Sunday Business Post Online,* January 12, 2003. http://archives.tcm.ie/businesspost/2003/01/12/story218812528.asp.

Pollack, Jonathan D. "North Korea's Nuclear Weapons Program to 2015: Three Scenarios." *Asia Policy* 1, no. 3 (January 2007): 105–23.

Samore, Gary. "Dear Leader: Inside the North Korean Nuclear Deal," *Global Asia* 2, no. 1 (April 5, 2007): 66–68. www.globalasia.org/pdf/issue2/Dear_Leader.pdf.

Squassoni, Sharon A. *Weapons of Mass Destruction: Trade Between North Korea and Pakistan,* Congressional Research Service Report FL 31900. Washington, DC: CRS, November 28, 2006.

Stueck, William. *Rethinking the Korean War.* Princeton, NJ: Princeton University Press, 2002.

U.S. Central Intelligence Agency. *The World Factbook—North Korea.*

World Food Programme. "Where We Work—Korea (DPR)." www.wfp.org/country_brief/indexcountry.asp?country=408.

Where to Shop

I have been fortunate to live within driving distance of good Korean groceries. You can try your luck with the sites below, but do so at your own risk. I am not vouching for these guys!

www.ikoreaplaza.com
www.kgrocer.com
www.koreanfeast.com/korean_markets_in_the_us.htm.
http://en.wikipedia.org/wiki/Asian_supermarket

Iran

Further Reading

Ansari, Ali. *Confronting Iran: The Failure of American Foreign Policy and the Next Great Crisis in the Middle East.* London: Perseus Book Group, 2006.

———. *Iran, Islam and Democracy: The Politics of Managing Change.* London: Royal Institute of International Affairs, 2000.

———. *Modern Iran Since 1921: The Pahlavis and After.* London: Pearson Education Limited, 2003.

Argetsinger, Amy, and Roxanne Robe. "POTUS iPod: Totally Random." *Washington Post,* December 16, 2005.

Coll, Steven. *Ghost Wars: The Secret History of the CIA, Afghanistan, and Bin Laden, from the Soviet Invasion to September 10, 2001.* London: Penguin Books, 2004.

Cronin, Richard P., Alan Kronstadt, and Sharon Squassoni. *Pakistan's Nuclear Proliferation Activities and the Recommendations of the 9/11 Commission: U.S. Policy Constraints and Options.* Washington, DC: Congressional Research Service Report, January 25, 2005. www.fas.org/spp/starwars/crs/RL32745.pdf

The Daily Show with Jon Stewart. Demetri Martin's "Trend Spotting" segment on hookahs. July 25, 2006. www.comedycentral.com/shows/the_daily_show/videos/demetri_martin/index.jhtml.

Galbraith, Peter W. *The End of Iraq: How American Incompetence Created a War Without End.* New York: Simon and Schuster, 2006.

GlobalSecurity.org. "Mahmoud Ahmadinejad." www.globalsecurity.org/military/world/iran/ahmadinejad.htm.

Hen-Tov, Elliot. "Understanding Iran's new Authoritarianism." *Washington Quarterly* 30, no. 1 (Winter 2006–2007): 163–79.

Human Rights Watch. "Iran," January 2007. www.hrw.org/englishwr2k7/docs/2007/01/11/iran14703.htm.

International Atomic Energy Agency. "In Focus: IAEA and Iran." www.iaea.org/NewsCenter/Focus/IaeaIran/index.shtml.

International Crisis Group. *Iran: Ahmadi-Nejad's Tumultuous Presidency.* Tehran, Brussels: International Crisis Group, February 2007.

———. *Iran: Is There a Way Out of the Nuclear Impasse?* Brussels, Washington, Tehran: International Crisis Group, February 2006.

———. *The State of Sectarianism in Pakistan.* Brussels, Islamabad: International Crisis Group, 2005.

Iran News and Iranian Cultural Journal, "Iran, China and Pakistan lead 'capital punishment,'" April 27, 2007. http://iranian.ws/iran_news/publish/article_21680.shtml.

Kerr, Paul. "UN Security Council Sanctions Iran," January 2007. www .armscontrol.org/act/2007_01-02/SecurityCouncilIran.asp.

Leverett, Flynt. *Dealing with Tehran: Assessing U.S. Diplomatic Options Towards Iran.* Washington, DC: Century Foundation Report, 2006. www.tcf.org.

Nafisi, Azair. *Reading Lolita in Tehran: A Memoir in Books.* New York: Random House, 2003.

Nasr, Vali R. "International Politics, Domestic Imperatives, and Identity Mobilization: Sectarianism in Pakistan, 1979–1998." *Comparative Politics* 32, no. 2 (January 2000): 175–79, 183–87.

Pollack, Kenneth. *The Persian Puzzle: The Conflict Between Iran and America.* New York: Random House, 2004.

President of the Islamic Republic of Iran (in Farsi), "Official Biography of Mahmoud Ahmadinejad." http://president.ir/eng/ahmadinejad/bio.

Squassoni, Sharon. *Iran's Nuclear Program: Recent Developments.* Washington, DC: Congressional Research Service, October 2, 2005.

"Treaty on the Non-proliferation of Nuclear Weapons." Federation of American Scientists. www.fas.org/nuke/control/npt/text/npt2.htm.

U.S. Directorate of National Intelligence, *National Intelligence Estimate Iran: Nuclear Intentions and Capabilities* (Washington: DNI, November 2007). dni.gov/press_releases/20071203_release.pdf.

Where to Shop

There are a number of directories for Persian supermarkets, including the following Web sites. As always, shop wisely on the Internet.

www.farsinet.com/baghghali
www.persianmirror.com/community/biz.cfm
www.persianbazaar.com/food
www.sadaf.com/newbazar
www.persiangrocery.com/us

Iraq

Further Reading

Amnesty International. *Amnesty International Report 2003,* "Iraq." www.amnesty.org/report2003/Irq-summary-eng.

ArabicNews.com. "Two new novels by Saddam Hussein," from Iraqi local news translated and published by ArabicNews.com, March 22, 2002. www.arabicnews.com/ansub/Daily/Day/020322/2002032202.html.

Bamford, James. *A Pretext for War: 9/11, Iraq, and the Abuse of America's Intelligence Agencies.* New York: Anchor Books, 2005.

BBC News, "Iraq death toll 'soared post-war,'" October 29, 2004. http://news.bbc.co.uk/2/hi/middle_east/3962969.stm.

———, "Saddam 'pens two more novels,'" March 20, 2002. http://news.bbc.co.uk/2/hi/entertainment/1884051.stm.

Bilmes, Linda, and Joseph Stiglitz. "The Economic Costs of the Iraq War: An Appraisal Three Years after the Beginning of the Conflict." NBER Working Paper 12054, February 2006. www.nber.org/papers/w12054.

Bottéro, Jean. "The Cuisine of Ancient Mesopotamia." Translated in *Biblical Archeologist* (March 1985): 36–47.

———.*The Oldest Cuisines in the World: Cooking in Mesopotamia.* Chicago: University of Chicago Press, 2002.

Bounds, Gwendlyn. "Green Beans Comes Marching Home: Mobile Coffee Supplier to U.S. Troops Opening Retail Cafés Stateside." *Wall Street Journal*, January 2, 2007. www.online.wsj.com/public/article/SB116769083722664270-9fgpXLGYlJvqK9Ff7l5pBBbr8Q_20070131.html?mod=tff_main_tff_top.

Bsisu, May S. *The Arab Table: Recipes and Culinary Traditions.* New York: Harper Collins, 2005.

Burnham, Gilbert, Riyadh Lafta, Shannon Doocy, and Les Roberts. "Mortality after the 2003 invasion of Iraq: a cross-sectional cluster sample survey." *The Lancet* 368: 1421–28.

Bush, George W. "The President's State of the Union Address," January 28, 2003. www.whitehouse.gov/news/releases/2003/01/20030128-19.html.

——. "The President's State of the Union Address," January 29, 2002. www.whitehouse.gov/news/releases/2002/01/20020129-11.html.

Crincione, Joseph, Jessica T. Mathews, and George Perkovich, with Alexis Orton. *WMD in Iraq: Evidence and Implications.* Washington, DC: Carnegie Endowment for International Peace, 2004.

Farrey, Tom. "The horrors of Saddam's 'sadist son,'" ESPN.com, December 22, 2002. www.espn.go.com/oly/s/2002/1220/1480103.html.

Fox News, "Alleged Mistress Recalls Life with Saddam," September 12, 2002. www.foxnews.com/story/0,2933,62558,00.html.

Galbraith, Peter W. *The End of Iraq: How American Incompetence Created a War Without End.* New York: Simon and Schuster, 2006.

GlobalSecurity.org. "Qusay Saddam Hussein al-Tikriti." www.globalsecurity .org/military/world/iraq/qusay.htm.

Grimmett, Richard F. *U.S. Use of Preemptive Military Force.* Washington, DC: Congressional Research Service, September 2002.

Haldane, Sir Aylmer. *Insurrection in Mesopotamia 1920.* Nashville, TN: Battery Press, 2005. Reprint of Imperial War Museum/Battery Press original 1922 edition.

Human Rights Watch. *World Report 2003—Events of 2002*, "Iraq and Kurdistan." New York: Human Rights Watch, 2003. www.hrw.org/wr2k3/ pdf/iraqandiraqikurdistan.pdf.

Independent Inquiry Committee into the United Nations Oil-for-Food Program. *Report on the Manipulation of the Oil-for-Food Programme*, October 27, 2005. www.iic-offp.org/story27oct05.htm.

International Institute for Strategic Studies. *IISS Strategic Dossier—Iraq's Weapons of Mass Destruction: A Net Assessment.* London: International Institute for Strategic Studies, September 9, 2002.

Iraq Body Count. www.iraqbodycount.org/database.

Karim, Kay. *Iraqi Family Cookbook: From Mosul to America.* Self-published, 2006.

Khalifé, Maria. *The Middle Eastern Cookbook.* Northampton, MA: Interlink Books, 2007.

Kosiak, Steven M. *The Cost of US Operations in Iraq and Afghanistan and for the War on Terrorism through Fiscal Year 2007 and Beyond.* Washington, DC: Center for Strategic and Budgetary Assessments, September 12, 2007. www.csbaonline.org/4Publications/PubLibrary/U.20070913.The_Cost_ of_US_Ope/U.20070913.The_Cost_of_US_Ope.pdf.

Mallos, Tess. *Middle Eastern Home Cooking.* London: Parkway, 2002.

Marr, Phebe. *A Modern History of Iraq.* Boulder, CO: Westview Press, 2004.

Mostert, Mary. "87% fewer violent deaths annually in Iraq now than under Saddam Hussein." *Renew America,* January 17, 2005. www.renewamerica .us/columns/mostert/050117.

Murali, D. "Why get past the present that has all future." *Hindu Business Line,* December 1, 2003. www.thehindubusinessline.com/bline/mentor /2003/12/01/stories/2003120100361000.htm.

Nasrallah, Nawal. *Delights from the Garden of Eden: A Cookbook and History of the Iraqi Cuisine.* Self-published, 2003, 2004.

O'Hanlon, Michael E., and Jason H. Campbell. *Iraq Index: Tracking Variables of Reconstruction & Security in Post-Saddam Iraq.* Washington, DC: Brookings Institution, 2007. www.brookings.edu/iraqindex.

Richelson, Jeffrey. "Iraq and Weapons of Mass Destruction: National Security Archive Electronic Briefing Book No. 80," February 26, 2003. www.gwu.edu/~nsarchiv/NSAEBB/NSAEBB80.

Roberts, Les, Riyadh Lafta, Richard Garfield, Jamal Khudhairi, and Gilbert Burnham. "Mortality before and after the 2003 invasion of Iraq: cluster sample survey." *The Lancet* 364: 1857–64.

Salloum, Habeeb, and James Peters. *From the Lands of Figs and Olives.* New York: Interlink Books, 2004.

Slavin, Barbara, and Gregg Zoroya. "Miscalculations from start to finish in Saddam's career." *USA Today,* December 14, 2006. www.usatoday.com/ news/world/iraq/2003-12-14-saddam-profile_x.htm.

Tripp, Charles. *A History of Iraq.* Cambridge: Cambridge University Press, 2000.

U.S. Senate, Select Committee on Intelligence. *Report of the Select Committee on Intelligence on the U.S. Intelligence Community's Prewar Intelligence Assessments on Iraq.* Washington, DC: Government Printing Office, July 2004. www.gpoaccess.gov/serialset/creports/iraq.html.

Wolk, Martin. "Cost of Iraq war could surpass $1 trillion." MSNBC.com, March 17, 2006. www.msnbc.msn.com/id/11880954.

Woodward, Bob. *Bush at War.* New York: Simon and Schuster, 2002.

———. *Plan of Attack.* New York: Simon and Schuster, 2004.

———. *State of Denial: Bush at War (Part III).* New York: Simon and Schuster, 2006.

Where to Shop

There are a number of directories for South Asian supermarkets and online vendors, listed below. Shop online carefully and with your wits about you!

www.thokalath.com/grocery/index.php
   (directory of Indian groceries in the United States)
www.thokalath.com/india_grocery_store.php
www.spicesofindia.co.uk/?referrer=mamtaskitchen
www.indianfoodsco.com
www.ethnicgrocer.com/c-174-india.aspx
www.indiaspicehouse.shopclassic.com
www.indiaplaza.com/sf.aspx
www.searchindia.com/search/groc.html

The NPT+3 States

Israel

Further Reading

Abu-Lughod, Ibrahim, and Baha Abu-aban. *Settler Regimes in Africa and the Arab World: The Illusion of Endurance*. Wilmette, IL: Medina University Press International, 1974.

Advisory Group on Public Diplomacy for the Arab and Muslim World. *Changing Minds, Winning Peace: A New Strategic Direction for U.S. Public Diplomacy in the Arab and Muslim World*. Report submitted to the Committee on Appropriations, U.S. House of Representatives, October 1, 2003.

AIPAC. "The United Nations and Israel," December 5, 2006. www.aipac.org/Publications/AIPACAnalysesMemos/United_Nations_and_Israel.pdf.

Ansky, Sherry. *The Food of Israel: Authentic Recipes from the Land of Milk and Honey*. Boston: Periplus, 2000.

Barkat, Amiram. "Majority of Israelis Are Opposed to Intermarriage, Survey Finds." *Ha'aretz*, September 15, 2003.

Ben-Gurion, David. *The Jews in Their Land*. London: Aldus Books, 1966.

Bill, James A., and Robert Springborg. *Politics in the Middle East,* 4th ed. New York: Harper Collins College Publishers, 1994.

Black, Ian, and Benny Morris. *Israel's Secret Wars: A History of Israel's Intelligence Services.* New York: Grove Press, 1991.

Blackburn, Nicky. "Better a Jew." *Ha'aretz,* April 21, 2004.

B'tselem. "Forbidden Families: Family Unification and Child Registration in East Jerusalem," January 2004. www.btselem.org/Download/ 200401_Forbidden_Families_Eng.rtf.

Burr, William. "National Intelligence Estimates of the Nuclear Proliferation Problem: The First Ten Years, 1957–1967." National Security Archive Electronic Briefing Book No. 155, June 1, 2005. www.gwu.edu/ ~nsarchiv/NSAEBB/NSAEBB155/index.htm.

Carter, Jimmy. *Palestine: Peace Not Apartheid.* New York: Simon and Schuster, 2006.

Christian Action for Israel. "The U.N.'s Record vis à vis Israel." www .christianactionforisrael.org/un/record.html.

Clarke, Duncan L. "Israel's Economic Espionage in the United States." *Journal of Palestine Studies* 27, no. 4 (Summer 1998).

Cohen, Avner. "The Bomb That Never Is." *Bulletin of the Atomic Scientists* 56, no. 3 (May/June 2000).

———. *Israel and the Bomb.* New York: Columbia University Press, 1998.

Congedo, Isaac. "The Case of Jaffa Oranges." TED Case Studies No. 778, 2005. www.american.edu/ted/jaffa.htm.

Drogin, Bob, and Greg Miller. "Israel Has Long Spied on U.S. Say Officials." *Los Angeles Times,* September 3, 2004.

Farr, Warner D. "The Third Temple's Holy of Holies: Israel's Nuclear Weapons," in *The Counterproliferation Papers.* Future Warfare Series No. 2. USAF Counterproliferation Center, September 1999.

Federation of American Scientists. "Israel: Nuclear Weapons." www.fas .org/nuke/guide/israel/nuke.

Findley, Paul. *Deliberate Deceptions.* Washington, DC: American Education Trust, 1995.

Flapan, Simha. *The Birth of Israel: Myths and Realities.* New York: Pantheon Books, 1987.

Foundation for Middle East Peace. www.fmep.org.

Gaffney, Mark. *Dimona: The Third Temple? The Story Behind the Vanunu Revelation.* Brattleboro, VT: Amana Books, 1989.

Galili, Lily. "Hitting Below the Belt." *Ha'aretz,* August 8, 2004.

Goldberg, Jeffrey. "Real Insiders: A Pro-Israel Lobby and an F.B.I. Sting." *New Yorker* 81, no. 19 (July 4, 2005).

Goldmann, Nahum. *The Jewish Paradox.* Translated by Steve Cox. New York: Grosset and Dunlap, 1978.

Hersh, Seymour H. "The Traitor: Why Pollard Should Never Be Released." *New Yorker* 74, no. 42 (January 18, 1999).

Herzl, Theodor. *The Diaries of Theodor Herzl.* Edited by Marvin Lowenthal. New York: Grosset & Dunlop, 1962.

———. *The Jewish State.* Miami, FL: BN Publishing, 2007. Reprint of original 1896 edition.

Human Rights Watch. "Israel: Don't Outlaw Family Life," July 28, 2003. www.hrw.org/press/2003/07/israel072803.htm.

International Herald Tribune, "US says Israel cluster bomb use possible violation," January 29, 2007.

Israel Democracy Institute. *The 2006 Israeli Democracy Index.* Jerusalem: Israel Democracy Institute, 2006.

Israeli Democracy Institute. *The Democracy Index: Major Findings 2003.* www.idi.org.il/english/article.asp?id=1466.

Jewish Virtual Library. "Israel's Nuclear Weapons." www.jewishvirtual library.org/jsource/Society_&_Culture/nukes.html.

———. "Mordechai Vanunu." www.jewishvirtuallibrary.org/jsource/ biography/Vanunu.html.

Kaufman, Sheilah. *Sephardic Israeli Cuisine: A Mediterranean Mosaic.* New York: Hippocrene Books, 2002.

Lewisohn, Ludwig, ed. *Theodor Herzl.* Cleveland, OH: World Publishing Co., 1955.

Loftus, John, and Aarons, Mark. *The Secret War Against the Jews: How Western Espionage Betrayed the Jewish People.* New York: St. Martin's Griffin, 1994.

MacAskill, Ewen. "US questions Israel's use of cluster bombs in a rare rebuke." *The Guardian,* January 30, 2007.

Masalha, Nur. *Expulsion of the Palestinians: The Concept of Transfer in Zionist Political Thought, 1882–1948.* Washington, DC: Institute for Palestine Studies, 1992.

McCarthy, Justine. *The Population of Palestine: Population History and Statistics of the Late Ottoman Period and the Mandate.* Institute for Palestine Studies Series. New York: Columbia University Press, 1990.

Mearsheimer, John J., and Stephen M. Walt. "The Israeli Lobby and U.S. Foreign Policy." John F. Kennedy School of Government Working Paper, RWP06-011, March 2006. A version was published in *London Review of Book* 28, no. 6 (March 2006), available at www.lrb.co.uk/v28/n06/mear01_.html.

Migdalovitz, Carol. "Israeli United States Relations," Issue Brief for Congress. Washington, DC: Congressional Research Service, November 14, 2006.

Morris, Benny. *The Birth of the Palestinian Refugee Problem, 1947–48.* Cambridge: Cambridge University Press, 1988.

———. *Righteous Victims: A History of the Zionist-Arab Conflict, 1881–1999.* New York: Alfred Knopf, 1999.

Nathan, Joan. *The Foods of Israel Today.* New York: Alfred A. Knopf, 2005.

Permanent Mission of Israel to the United Nations. "Israel and the United Nations—An Uneasy Relationship." www.israel-un.org/israel_un/uneasy relation.htm.

Pew Global Attitudes Project. *Views of a Changing World 2003: War With Iraq Further Divides Global Publics.* Washington, DC: Pew Research Center for the People and the Press, June 3, 2003.

PIPA and Globescan. "Israel and Iran Share Most Negative Ratings in Global Poll," March 5, 2007. www.worldpublicopinion.org/pipa/articles/home_page/325.php?nid=&id=&pnt=325&lb=hmpg1.

Pry, Peter. *Israel's Nuclear Arsenal.* Boulder, CO: Westview, 1984.

Rodinson, Maxime. *Israel: A Colonial-Settler State?* New York: Pathfinder Press, 1973.

Snetsinger, John. *Truman, the Jewish Vote, and the Creation of Israel.* Stanford, CA: Hoover Institution Press, 1974.

Sunday Times (London), "Revealed: The Secrets of Israel's Nuclear Arsenal," October 5, 1986.

Tveth, Shabtai. *Ben-Gurion and the Palestine Arabs.* Oxford: Oxford University Press, 1985.

United Nations General Assembly. www.un.org/documents/resga.htm.

United Nations Security Council. www.un.org/documents/scres.htm.

Van Creveld, Martin. *The Sword and the Olive: A Critical History of the Israeli Defense Forces.* New York: Public Affairs, 1998.

Weizmann, Chaim. *Trial and Error: The Autobiography of Chaim Weizmann.* New York: Harper & Row, 1959.

Zogby, John. *How Arabs View America, How Arabs Learn about America.* Utica, NY: Zogby International, 2004.

———. *The Ten Nation Impressions of America Poll.* Utica, NY: Zogby International, April 11, 2002.

Where to Shop

Most of the ingredients in this chapter can be obtained at any large supermarket, either in the Middle East or kosher sections. Below are a number of online options for Middle Eastern groceries. I can't vouch for them so, as always, use caution when buying online.

www.cedarsky.com
www.daynasmarket.com
www.shamra.com
www.zamourispices.com

India

Further Reading

Behera, Navnita Chadha. *Demystifying Kashmir.* Washington, DC: Brookings Institution Press, 2006.

Bladhold, Linda, and Neela Paniz. *The Indian Grocery Store Demystified.* Los Angeles, Renaissance Books, 2000.

Central Chronicle, "Pictures of the Day," May 6, 2006. www.centralchronicle.com/20060506/PicDay.htm.

Conrod, Carol S. "Chronic Hunger and the Status of Women in India." The Hunger Project, June 1998. www.thp.org/reports/indiawom.htm.

Dugger, Cecilia. "Kerosene, Weapon of Choice for Attacks on Wives in India." *New York Times,* December 26, 2000.

Evans, Alexander. "The Kashmir Insurgency: As Bad as it Gets." *Small Wars and Insurgencies* 11, no. 1 (Spring 2000).

Fair, C. Christine. "Learning to Think the Unthinkable: Lessons from India's Nuclear Test." *India Review* 4, no. 1 (January 2005).

Ganguly, Sumit. *The Crisis in Kashmir: Portents of War, Hopes of Peace.* Cambridge: Woodrow Wilson Center Press and Cambridge University Press, 1997.

HIMAL South Asia, "Scientists as shamans," July 2002. www.himalmag.com/2002/july/southasiasphere.htm.

Human Rights Watch. *"Everyone Lives in Fear": Patterns of Impunity in Jammu and Kashmir.* Human Rights Index No. C1811, September 12, 2006. www.hrw.org/reports/2006/india0906.

———. *"With Friends Like These . . .": Human Rights Violations in Azad Kashmir.* Human Rights Index No. C1812, September 21, 2006. www.hrw.org/reports/2006/pakistan0906.

Mehra, Chander. "The Dowry Disease." *India Currents,* February 16, 2004.

Nuclear Nonproliferation Treaty. Text available at Federation of American Scientists Web site, www.fas.org/nuke/control/npt/text/npt2.htm.

Perkovich, George. *India's Nuclear Bomb: The Impact of Global Proliferation.* Berkeley, CA: University of California Press, 1999.

Popham, Peter. "Why can't Hindus and Muslims get along together? It's a long story." *The Independent* (London), June 1, 1998.

Tellis, Ashley J. *India as a New Global Power: An Action Agenda for the United States.* Washington, DC: Carnegie Endowment for International Peace, 2005.

———. *India's Emerging Nuclear Posture: Between Recessed Deterrent and Ready Arsenal.* Santa Monica, CA: RAND, 2001.

Tellis, Ashley J., C. Christine Fair, and Jamison Jo Medby. *Limited Conflicts Under the Nuclear Umbrella—Indian and Pakistani Lessons from the Kargil Crisis.* Santa Monica, CA: RAND, 2001.

United Nations Development Program. *Human Development Report 2006—Beyond Scarcity: Power, Poverty and the Global Water Crisis.* www.hdr.undp.org/hdr2006/statistics.

U.S. Central Intelligence Agency. *The World Factbook.* www.cia.gov/cia/publications/factbook/geos/su.html.

Walker, William. "India's Nuclear Labyrinth." *The Nonproliferation Review* (Fall 1996): 65.

Wirsing, Robert. *India, Pakistan, and the Kashmir Dispute: On Regional Conflict and Its Resolution.* New York: St. Martin's Press, 1994.

Where to Shop

Below are a number of directories for South Asian supermarkets and online vendors. As always, be careful when shopping online.

www.thokalath.com/grocery/index.pho

(directory of Indian groceries in the United States)

www.thokalath.com/india_grocery_store.php

www.spicesofindia.co.uk/?referrer=mamtaskitchen

www.indianfoodsco.com

www.ethnicgrocer.com/c-174-india.aspx

www.indiaspicehouse.shopclassic.com

www.indiaplaza.com/sf.aspx

www.searchindia.com/search/groc.html

Pakistan

Further Reading

Ahmed, Akbar S. *Jinnah, Pakistan and Islamic Identity: The Search for Saladin.* London: Routledge, 1997.

Behera, Navnita Chadha. *Demystifying Kashmir.* Washington, DC: Brookings, 2007.

Bose, Sumantra. *Kashmir: Roots of Conflict, Paths to Peace.* Boston: Harvard University Press, 2005.

Cloughley, Brian. *A History of the Pakistan Army: Wars and Insurrections.* Oxford: Oxford University Press, 2000.

Cohen, Stephen P. *The Pakistan Army.* Berkeley and Los Angeles: University of California Press, 1984.

Coll, Steve. *Ghost Wars: The Secret History of the CIA, Afghanistan, and Bin Laden, from the Soviet Invasion to September 10, 2001.* New York: Penguin Press, 2004.

Crile, George. *Charlie Wilson's War: The Extraordinary Story of How the Wildest Man in Congress and a Rogue CIA Agent Changed the History of Our Times.* New York: Grove Press, 2003.

Das, Veena. "National Honor and Practical Kinship: Unwanted Women and Their Children." In Faye D. Ginsburg and Rayne Rapp, *Conceiving the New World Order: The Global Politics of Reproduction.* Berkeley, CA: University of California Press, 1995.

Evans, Alexander. "The Kashmir Insurgency: As Bad as It Gets." *Small Wars and Insurgencies* 11, no. 1 (Spring 2000): 69–81.

Federation of American Scientists. "Pakistan Nuclear Weapons: A Brief History of Pakistan's Nuclear Program." www.fas.org/nuke/guide/pakistan/nuke/index.html.

Ganguly, Sumit. *The Crisis in Kashmir: Portents of War, Hopes of Peace.* New York: Cambridge University Press, 1997.

———. *The Origins of War in South Asia: The Indo-Pakistani Conflicts Since 1947.* Boulder, CO: Westview Press, 1998.

Jaffrelot, Christophe. "Introduction: Nationalism without a Nation; Pakistan Searching for Its Identity." In *Pakistan: Nationalism without a Nation?* edited by Christophe Jaffrelot. New Delhi: Manohar, 2002.

Kile, Shannon N., Vitaly Fedchenko, and Hans M. Kristensen. *"World Nuclear Forces," SIPRI Yearbook 2006: Armaments, Disarmament and International Security.* Oxford: Oxford University Press, 2006.

Koch, Andrew, and Jennifer Topping. "Pakistan's Nuclear Weapons Program: A Status Report." *The Nonproliferation Review* (Spring–Summer 1997): 109–13.

Kukreja, Veena. *Contemporary Pakistan: Political Processes, Conflicts and Crises.* New Delhi: Sage Publications, 2003.

Lawrence Livermore National Laboratory. "Monitoring Clandestine Nuclear Tests." www.llnl.gov/str/Walter.html.

Matinuddin, Kamal. *The Taliban Phenomenon: Afghanistan, 1994–1997.* Oxford: Oxford University Press, 1999.

McKibben, Bill. "George Harrison and the Concert for Bangladesh." Salon.com, December 1, 2001. www.archive.salon.com/people/feature/2001/12/01/harrison_concert/index.html.

Rashid, Ahmed. *Taliban: Islam, Oil and the New Great Game in Central Asia.* London: I. B. Taurus, 2000.

Rizvi, Hasan Askari. *Military, State and Society in Pakistan.* London: Milton Press, 2000.

Schofield, Victoria. *Kashmir in Conflict: India, Pakistan and the Unending War.* London: I. B. Taurus, 2003.

———. *Kashmir in the Crossfire.* London: I. B. Taurus, 1996.

Tellis, Ashley. *Stability in South Asia.* Santa Monica, CA: RAND, 1997.

Wirsing, Robert G. *India, Pakistan, and the Kashmir Dispute: On Regional Conflict and Its Resolution.* New York: St. Martin's Press, 1997.

———. *Kashmir in the Shadow of War.* New York: M. E. Sharpe, 2003.

Wright, Lawrence. *The Looming Tower: Al-Qaeda and the Road to 9/11.* New York: Knopf, 2006.

Ziring, Lawrence. *Pakistan in the Twentieth Century: A Political History.* Oxford: Oxford University Press, 1997.

Where to Shop

Several directories for South Asian supermarkets and online vendors are given below. Note that these are identical to the section for India; most South Asian grocery stores cater to the folks from India, Pakistan, and Bangladesh, and occasionally even the odd Sri Lankan. As elsewhere, I cannot personally vouch for these vendors.

www.thokalath.com/grocery/index.php (directory of Indian groceries in the United States)
www.thokalath.com/india_grocery_store.php
www.spicesofindia.co.uk/?referrer=mamtaskitchen
www.indianfoodsco.com
www.ethnicgrocer.com/c-174-india.aspx
www.indiaspicehouse.shopclassic.com
www.indiaplaza.com/sf.aspx
www.searchindia.com/search/groc.html

The Dashers of Democracy

Cuba

Further Reading

Amnesty International. *Amnesty International Report 2007: State of the World's*

Human Rights. www.thereport.amnesty.org/eng/Regions/Americas/Cuba.

———. "Cuba: 'Essential Measures'? Human Rights Crackdown in the Name of Security," June 3, 2003. www.web.amnesty.org/library/Index/ENGAM R250172003.

———. "Death Penalty: Executions Fall as Pressure Grows for Universal Moratorium," press release, April 27, 2007. www.web.amnesty.org/library/Index/ENGACT500132007.

Campbell, Duncan. "638 ways to kill Castro." *The Guardian*, August 3, 2006.

Committee on Monitoring International Labor Standards, National Research Council. *Monitoring International Labor Standards: Techniques and Sources of Information*. Washington, DC: National Academies Press, 2004.

The Economist. "The Good Terrorist," April 26, 2007.

Escalante, Fabian. *Executive Action: 634 Ways to Kill Fidel Castro (Secret War)*. Melbourne: Ocean Press, 2007.

Fair, C. Christine. "India and Iran: New Delhi's Balancing Act." *Washington Quarterly* 30, no. 3 (Summer 2007).

Franklin, Jane. *Cuba and the United States: A Chronological History*. Melbourne: Ocean Press, 1997.

Gott, Richard. *Cuba: A New History*. New Haven, CT: Yale University Press, 2005.

Horley, Morris H. *Imperial State and Revolution: The United States and Cuba, 1952–1986*. Cambridge: Cambridge University Press, 1987.

Human Rights Watch. "Cuba Country Summary, January 2007." www.hrw.org.

Independent, The, "The Castropedia: Fidel's Cuba in facts and figures," July 30, 2007. http://news.independent.co.uk/world/americas/article2160411.ece.

International Labor Organization. *Labour Practices in the Footwear, Leather, Textiles, and Clothing Industries*. Geneva: ILO, 2000.

Lafray, Joyce. *Cuba Cocina: The Tantalizing World of Cuban Cooking*. New York: William Morrow Cookbooks, 2005.

Llamasm, Beatriz. *A Taste of Cuba*. Northampton, MA: Interlink Books, 2005.

Luscombe, Richard. "World's Longest Serving Leader Gets 100% Approval." *The Scotsman*, March 8, 2003.

Moran, Theodore. *Beyond Sweatshops*. Washington, DC: Brookings Institution, 2002.

Ospina, Hernando Calvo. "Cuba Exports Health." *Le Monde Diplomatique*, August 2006. www.mondediplo.com/2006/08/11cuba.

Pérez, Louis A. *Cuba and the United States: Ties of Singular Intimacy*. Athens, GA: University of Georgia Press, 2003.

Ravi, N. "Memorable Meeting: Manmohan." *The Hindu*, September 19, 2006.

Simons, Geoff. *Cuba: From Conquistador to Castro*. Chippenham, Wiltshire, UK: Antony Rowe, 1996.

Snow, Anita. "CIA Plot to Kill Castro Detailed." *Washington Post*, June 27, 2007.

Sullivan, Mark P. *Cuba: Issues for the 110th Congress*. Congressional Research Service Report No. 33819. Washington, DC: CRS, January 2007.

Thomas, Hugh. *Cuba: The Pursuit for Freedom*. New York: Harper Collins, 1971.

Three Guys From Miami. *Cook Cuban*. Salt Lake City, UT: Gibbs Smith, 2004.

U.S. Department of State, Office of the Coordinator for Counterterrorism. *Country Reports on Terrorism 2006*, April 30, 2007. www.state.gov/s/ct/rls/crt/2006/.

U.S. Senate. "Communist Threat to the United States through the Caribbean." Hearings before the Subcommittee to Investigate the Administration of the Internal Security Act and Other Internal Security Laws of the Committee on the Judiciary, United States Senate, Eighty-Sixth Congress, August 27, 1960. www.latinamericanstudies.org/us-cuba/gardner-smith.htm.

World Food Programme, "Where We Work—World View." www.wfp.org/country_brief/indexcountry.asp?country=192.

Where to Shop

Fortunately, this chapter doesn't require anything too exotic, and you should be able to get everything you need from your local supermarket.

Burma

Further Reading

BBC News Online, "Burma leader's lavish lifestyle aired," November 2, 2006. http://news.bbc.co.uk/2/hi/asia-pacific/6109356.stmand.

Bhumichitr, Vatcharin. *Vatch's Southeast Asian Cookbook.* New York: St. Martin's Griffin, 2000.

Black, Robin, and Christine Harmston. "Burma: The Tyranny Continues." *Peace Magazine* (March–April, 1998): 24.

"Burma's Last Mission." *The Irrawaddy* 5, no. 7 (December 1, 1997). www.irrawaddy.org/article.php?art_id=944.

Callahan, Mary P. *Making Enemies: War and State Building in Burma.* Ithaca, NY: Cornell University Press, 2003.

Chan, Susan. *Flavors of Burma.* New York: Hippocrene, 2003.

City Times (Dubai), "Suu Kyi Turns 62 in Isolation," June 20, 2007.

Haacke, Jurgen. *Myanmar's Foreign Policy: Domestic Influences and International Implications.* London: IISS Adelphi Paper, 2006.

Head, Jonathan. "Burma discusses version of democracy." *BBC News*, October 23, 2006.

Human Rights Watch. "Burma: Events of 2006." In *World Report 2007*, available at http://hrw.org/englishwr2k7/docs/2007/01/11/burma14865.htm.

———. "Rohingya Refugees from Burma Mistreated in Bangladesh," March 27, 2007. www.hrw.org/english/docs/2007/03/27/bangla15571.htm.

James, Helen. *Security and Sustainable Development in Myanmar.* London: Routledgecurzon, 2006.

Kazmin, Amy. "Burma relocates ministries to remote compound." *Financial Times*, November 7, 2005.

Khaing, Mi Mi. *Cook and Entertain the Burmese Way.* Yangon: Daw Khin Myo Chit, n.d.

McClearn, Matthew. "Stranger in a Strange Land." *Canadian Business* 75, no. 3 (February 18, 2002).

Parker, Clive. "Forcing the Issue on Myanmar Labor." *Asia Times*, March 1, 2007.

Shenon, Philip. "Burma Using Forced Labor on Tourist Projects." *New York Times*, July 16, 1994.

Soe, Khin Maung. "The Underground Revolution," Cell #5, Room #7, Insein Prison, November, 1975. www.aappb.org/article9.html.

Tesoro, Jose Manuel, and Dominic Faulder. "Changing of the Guard: SLORC fixes its name—and purges some faces." *Asiaweek.com,* November 28, 1997. www.asiaweek.com/asiaweek/97/1128/nat4.html.

Thompson, Mike. "Burma's Forgotten Rohingya." *BBC News,* March 3, 2006.

United National Development Program. *Human Development Report Statistics.* www.hdr.undp.org/hdr2006/statistics.

U.S. Central Intelligence Agency. *The World Factbook—Burma.* www.cia.gov/cia/publications/factbook/geos/bm.html.

U.S. Department of State, Bureau of Democracy, Human Rights, and Labor. "Burma." In *International Religious Freedom Report 2006,* September 15, 2006. www.state.gov/g/drl/rls/irf/2006/71335.htm.

U.S. Department of State, Bureau of Public Affairs. *Burma: A Human Rights Disaster and Threat to Regional Security,* September 16, 2006. www.state.gov/r/pa/scp/2006/72840.htm.

Where to Shop

Burmese resources online are pretty skimpy, but here are two. As elsewhere, I cannot vouch for these sellers.

www.myathayaphu.com

www.shwestore.com (They have fast delivery, even if their packaging makes little sense. They mailed a plastic jar in an envelope, which predictably broke. Fortunately, it was wrapped twice in plastic before being put in to the jar, and the tea was perfectly usable despite the mess.)

China

Further Reading

Baard, Erik, and Rebecca Cooney. "China's Execution, Inc.: The People's Republic Has Long Been Suspected of Selling Organs from Prisoners; Now One New York Doctor Knows the Rumors Are True." *The Village Voice,* May 2–8, 2001. www.villagevoice.com/news/0118,baard,24344,1.html.

Babington, Charles, and Mike Allen. "Congress Passes Schiavo Measure: Bush Signs Bill Giving U.S. Courts Jurisdiction in Case of Fla. Woman." *Washington Post*, March 21, 2005.

Baker, A. J., R. J. Moulton, V. H. MacMillan, and P. M. Shedden. "Excitatory Amino Acids in Cerebralspinal Fluid Following Traumatic Brain Injury in Humans." *Journal of Neurosurgery* 79(3) (September 1993): 369–72.

Barboza, David. "China Makes Arrest in Pet Food Case." *New York Times*, May 4, 2007.

———. "China Yields to Inquiry on Pet Food." *New York Times*, April 24, 2007.

Bergsten, C. Fred. "The U.S. Trade Deficit and China." Statement before the Hearing on U.S.-China Economic Relations Revisited, Committee on Finance, United States Senate, March 29, 2006. http://finance.senate .gov/hearings/testimony/2005test/032906CBtest.pdf.

Bhumichitr, Vatcharin. *Vatch's Southeast Asian Cookbook.* New York: St. Martin's Griffin, 2000.

Campbell, T. Colin, and Thomas M. Campbell II. *The China Study: The Most Comprehensive Study of Nutrition Ever Conducted and the Startling Implications for Diet, Weight Loss and Long-Term Health.* Dallas, TX: BenBella Books, 2004.

Crane, Keith, Roger Cliff, Evan S. Medeiros, James C. Mulvenon, and William H. Overholt. *Modernizing China's Military: Opportunities and Constraints.* Santa Monica, CA: RAND, 2005.

Crincione, Joseph. "Cox Report and the Threat from China," June 17, 1999. Washington, DC: Carnegie Endowment for International Peace, 1999.

Dickenson, A. H. "Gate Control Theory of pain stands the test of time." *British Journal of Anaesthesia* 88 (June 2002): 755–57.

Dunlop, Fuchsia. *Revolutionary Chinese Cookbook: Recipes from Hunan Province.* London: Ebury Press, 2006.

Earnshaw, Graham. *On Your Own in China,* section on Guongdon, aka Canton. www.earnshaw.com/china/ch08.html.

The Economist. "China Factsheet," May 8, 2007. www.economist.com/ countries/China/profile.cfm?folder=Profile-FactSheet.

———. "United States Factsheet," May 30, 2007. www.economist.com/ countries/USA/profile.cfm?folder=Profile-FactSheet.

Halvorsen, Francine. *The Food and Cooking of China.* New York: John Wiley & Sons, 1996.

Harvard School of Public Health. "Fats and Cholesterol—the Good, the Bad, and the Healthy Diet." www.hsph.harvard.edu/nutrition source/fats.html.

Hesketh, Therese, and Zhu Wei Xing. "Abnormal sex ratios in human populations: Causes and consequences." *Proceedings of the National Academy of Sciences of the United States of America* 103 (2006): 13271–75.

Human Rights Watch. "China: Beijing Must Disclose Execution Numbers; Death Penalty Reform Welcomed but Does Not Go Far Enough," November 1, 2006. www.hrw.org/english/docs/2006/11/01/china 14487.htm.

———. "China: Country Summary," January 2007. www.hrw.org/englishwr2k7/docs/2007/01/11/china14867.htm.

International Institute for Strategic Studies. *The Military Balance 2007.* London: IISS, 2007.

Kan, Shirley A. *China and Proliferation of Weapons of Mass Destruction and Missiles: Policy Issues.* CRS Report for Congress, No. RL31555. Washington, DC: CRS, January 31, 2007.

Keidel, Albert. *China's Currency: Not the Problem.* Washington, DC: CEIP, June 2005.

Liang, Lucille. *Chinese Regional Cooking.* New York: Sterling Publishing, 2002.

Lim, Louisa. "Cases of Forced Abortions Surface in China." *National Public Radio Morning Edition*, April 23, 2007. www.npr.org/templates/story/story.php?storyId=9766870.

Lipton, S. A., and P. A. Rosenberg. "Excitatory Amino Acids as a Final Common Pathway for Neurologic Disorders." *New England Journal of Medicine* 330(9) (March 1994): 613–22.

Lo, Eileen Yin-Fei. *The Chinese Kitchen.* New York: William Morrow, 1999.

MacLeod, Calum. "China makes ultimate punishment mobile." *USA Today*, June 15, 2006. www.usatoday.com/news/world/2006-06-14-death-van_x.htm.

Medeiros, Evan S. "Analyzing China's Defense Industries and the Implications for Chinese Military Modernization: Testimony presented to the U.S.-China Economic and Security Review Commission on February 6, 2004." Santa Monica, CA: RAND, 2004.

Milhollin, Gary. "The Pitfalls of Nuclear Trade with China: China's export record and its refusals speak of the need for US safeguards." *Boston Sunday Globe*, February 22, 1998.

Nuclear Threat Initiative. "China Profile," January 2007. www.nti.org/
e_research/profiles/China/index.html

———. "China Profile: Nuclear Overview," January 2007. www.nti.org/
e_research/profiles/China/Nuclear/index.html.

Qichen, Qian. *Ten Episodes in China's Diplomacy.* New York: Harper Collins, 2005.

Simonds, Nina. *Classic Chinese Cuisine.* Boston: Houghton Mifflin, 1994.

Sterkler, Rendi. *Guide to China: Delicious Foods.* Shanghai: Classics Press,
2002.

Swaine, Michael. "Assessing the Meaning of the Chinese ASAT Test," February 7, 2007. www.carnegieendowment.org/publications/index
.cfm?fa=view&id=19006&prog=zch.

United Nations Development Program. *Human Development Report 2006.*
www.hdr.undp.org/hdr2006/statistics/indicators/89.html.

U.S. Central Intelligence Agency. *The World Factbook—China.*
www.cia.gov/library/publications/the-world-factbook/geos/ch.html.

U.S. Department of State. "U.S.-China Relations." Thomas J. Christensen,
Deputy Assistant Secretary for East Asian and Pacific Affairs, Statement
before the House Committee on Foreign Affairs, Subcommittee on Asia,
the Pacific, and the Global Environment, March 27, 2007. www.state
.gov/p/eap/rls/rm/2007/82276.htm.

U.S. Department of State, Bureau of Democracy, Human Rights, and
Labor. "China (includes Tibet, Hong Kong, and Macau): Country
Reports on Human Rights Practices—2005," March 8, 2006.
www.state.gov/g/drl/rls/hrrpt/2005/61605.htm.

U.S. House of Representatives. "Select Committee on U.S. National Security
and Military/Commercial Concerns with the People's Republic of
China," May 1999. www.house.gov/coxreport.

Weiss, Rick. "Tainted Chinese Imports Common: In Four Months, FDA
Refused 298 Shipments." *Washington Post*, May 20, 2007.

Where to Shop

As always, use your wits when shopping online.
www.amazon.com/gp/browse.html?node=3370831
www.earthy.com
www.igourmet.com
www.orientalpantry.com

The Great Satan Barbecue

U.S.A.

Further Reading

Allard, Patricia, and Marc Mauer. *Regaining the Vote: An Assessment of Activity Relating to Felon Disenfranchisement Laws.* New York: Open Society Institute, January 2000. www.soros.org/initiatives/justice/articles_publications/ publications/regainingthevote_2000011.

Amnesty International. "Death Penalty Statistics 2006," April 2007. www.amnestyusa.org/document.php?id=ENGACT500122007&lang=e.

Barber, Benjamin R. *Jihad vs. McWorld: Terrorism's Challenge to Democracy.* New York: Ballantine Books, 1995.

BBC News Online, "Rice names 'outposts of tyranny,'" January 19, 2005. http://news.bbc.co.uk/2/hi/americas/4186241.stm.

Bin Ladin, Usama. "The Solution—A Video Speech from Usama bin Ladin Addressing the American People on the Occasion of the Sixth Anniversary of 9/11—9/2007." SITE Intelligence Group. www.counterterrorism-blog.org/site-resources/images/SITE-OBL-transcript.pdf.

——. "Speech on the Eve of the U.S. 2001 General Elections," November 1, 2004. http://english.aljazeera.net/NR/exeres/79C6AF22-98FB-4A1C-B21F-2BC36E87F61F.htm.

Bush, George W. "Address to a Joint Session of Congress and the American People," September 20, 2001. www.whitehouse.gov/news/releases/2001/09/20010920-8.html.

CBS News. "Poll: Creationism Trumps Evolution," November 22, 2004. cbsnews.com/stories/2004/11/22/opinion/polls/main657083.shtml.

Cohen, Craig, and Derek Chollet. "When $10 Billion Is Not Enough: Rethinking U.S. Strategy toward Pakistan." *Washington Quarterly* 30, no. 2 (Spring 2007): 7–19.

Critzer, Greg. *Fat Land: How Americans Became the Fattest People in the World.* New York: Houghton Mifflon, 2003.

Dean, Cornelia. "Scientific Savvy? In U.S., Not Much." *New York Times,* August 30, 2005. www.nytimes.com/2005/08/30/science/30profile.html.

Death Penalty Information Center. *Innocence and the Crisis in the American Death Penalty.* Washington, DC: Death Penalty Information Center, 2004. www.deathpenaltyinfo.org/article.php?scid=45&did=1150.

——. "Number of Executions by State and Region Since 1976," September 28, 2007. www.deathpenaltyinfo.org/article.php?scid=8&did=186.

Dieter, Richard C. *A Crisis of Confidence: Americans' Doubts About the Death Penalty.* Washington, DC: Death Penalty Information Center Report, 2007. www.deathpenaltyinfo.org/CoC.pdf.

Dobbs, Michael. "In a Global Test of Math Skills, U.S. Students Behind the Curve. *Washington Post,* December 7, 2004. www.washingtonpost.com/wp-dyn/articles/A41278-2004Dec6.html.

The Economist. "Keeping the word: The triumph of faith over experience in Kentucky," May 31, 2007. www.economist.com/world/na/displaystory.cfm?story_id=9261747.

Elsner, Alan. "America's Prison Habit." *Washington Post,* January 24, 2004.

"Felony Disenfranchisement Removes 1.4 Million Black Men from the Voting Rolls," *Journal of Blacks in Higher Education* 22 (Winter 1998–1999): 61–62.

Fletcher, Michael A. "Bush Hails Progress Toward 'Culture of Life': Limits on Abortion, Stem Cell Use Cited." *Washington Post,* January 25, 2005. www.washingtonpost.com/wp-dyn/articles/A32959-2005Jan24.html.

Freedom from Religion Foundation. "What Does the Bible Say About Abortion?" Contract #7, 2007. www.ffrf.org/nontracts/abortion.php.

Freedom House. "Freedom in the World 2007 Sub-Scores." www.freedomhouse.org/template.cfm?page=372.

Gattuso, James. "The Myth of Media Concentration: Why the FCC's Media Ownership Rules Are Unnecessary." Heritage Foundation #284, May 29, 2003. www.heritage.org/Research/InternetandTechnology/wm284.cfm.

Gove, Michael. "Putin's Bare Chest Is a Display of Power Best Kept Secret." *Times Online,* August 21, 2007. http://timesonline.co.uk/tol/comment/columnists/michael_gove/article2293856.ece.

Granitsas, Alkman. "Americans are Tuning Out the World: When the world comes to their shore, U.S. citizens are increasingly less interested in foreign affairs." *Yale Global,* November 24, 2005.

International Federation of Journalists. "Media Concentration." www.ifj.org/default.asp?Issue=OWNER&Language=EN.

Klinenberg, Eric. "Breaking the News." *Mother Jones* 49 (March/April 2007). www.motherjones.com/news/feature/2007/03/breaking_the_news.html.

Kull, Steven, Clay Ramsay, and Evan Lewis. "Misperception, the Media, and the Iraq War." *Political Science Quarterly* 118, no. 3 (2003–2004): 569–98.

Loury, Glenn C. "Ghettos, Prisons and Racial Stigma," April 4, 2007. www.econ.brown.edu/fac/Glenn%5FLoury/louryhomepage/teaching/Ec%20137/Ec%20137%20spring07/LECTURE%20I.pdf.

Masci, David. "Twenty Years after a Landmark Supreme Court Decision, Americans Are Still Fighting about Evolution." Pew Forum on Religion and Public Life, June 13, 2006. www.pewforum.org/docs/?DocID=222.

Miller, John. "Numbers Crunch—Using Sampling in Year 2000 Census Is Mistake." *National Review*, July 20, 1998. www.findarticles.com/p/articles/mi_m1282/is_n13_v50/ai_20977845-31k.

Miller, Jon D., Eugenie C. Scott, and Shinji Okamoto. "Public Acceptance of Evolution." *Science* 213, no. 5788 (August 11, 2006): 765–66.

National Center for Educational Statistics. *International Outcomes of Learning in Mathematics Literacy and Problem Solving: PISA 2003 Results from the U.S. Perspective.* Washington, DC: U.S. Department of Education, 2003. www.nces.ed.gov/pubs2005/2005003.pdf.

Owen, James. "Evolution Less Accepted in U.S. Than Other Western Countries, Study Finds." *National Geographic News*, August 10, 2006. www.news.nationalgeographic.com/news/2006/08/060810-evolution.html.

Palast, Greg. "1 Million Black Votes Didn't Count in the 2000 Presidential Election: It's Not Too Hard to Get Your Vote Lost—If Some Politicians Want It to be Lost." *San Francisco Chronicle*, June 20, 2004. www.sfgate.com/cgi-bin/article.cgi?file=/chronicle/archive/2004/06/20/ING2976LG61.DTL.

———. "Florida's 'Disappeared Voters': Disfranchised by the GOP." *The Nation*, February 5, 2001. www.thenation.com/doc/20010205/palest.

Panel on Alternative Census Methodologies, Committee on National Statistics, National Research Council. *Measuring a Changing Nation: Modern Methods for the 2000 Census.* Edited by Michael L. Cohen, Andrew A. White, and Keith F. Rust. Washington, DC: National Academy Press, 1999. http://books.nap.edu/openbook.php?record_id=6500&page=R1.

Passel, Jeffrey S., and Roberto Suro. *Rise, Peak, and Decline: Trends in U.S. Immigration 1992–2004.* Washington, DC: Pew Hispanic Center, September 27, 2005. www.pewhispanic.org/files/reports/53.pdf.

Pew Forum on Religion and Public Life. "Many Americans Uneasy with Mix of Religion and Politics," August 24. 2006. www.pewforum.org/docs/index.php?DocID=153.

Pew Global Attitudes. "America's Image in the World: Findings from the Pew Global Attitudes Project: Remarks of Andrew Kohut to the U.S. House Committee on Foreign Affairs; Subcommittee on International Organizations, Human Rights, and Oversight, March 14, 2007." www.pewglobal.org/commentary/display.php?AnalysisID=1019.

Powell, Michael, and Peter Slevin. "Several Factors Contributed to 'Lost' Voters in Ohio." *Washington Post*, December 15, 2004. www.washington post.com/wp-dyn/articles/A64737-2004Dec14.html.

Roach, John. "Fossil Find Is Missing Link in Human Evolution, Scientists Say." *National Geographic News*, April 13 2006. www.news.national geographic.com/news/2006/04/0413_060413_evolution.html.

Roberts, Alasdair. "The War We Deserve." *Foreign Policy,* November/December 2007.

Rottinghaus, Brandon. *Incarceration and Enfranchisement: International Practices, Impact and Recommendations for Reform.* Washington, DC: International Foundation for Election Systems, 2003. www.ifes.org/publication/4bbcc7feabf9b17c41be87346f57c1c4/08_18_03_Manatt_Brandon_Ro ttinghaus.pdf.

Schmitz, David F. *The United States and Right-Wing Dictatorships, 1965–1989.* Cambridge: Cambridge University Press, 2006.

Shields, Rachel. "Americans celebrate a national symbol as the Big Mac turns 40." *The Independent,* August 25, 2007. http://news.independent .co.uk/world/americas/article2893894.ece.

Simon, Roger. "Giuliani Warns of 'New 9/11' If Dems Win." Politico.com, April 26, 2007. www.politico.com/news/stories/0407/3684.html.

Telhami, Shibley. "America in Arab Eyes." *Survival* 49, no. 1 (Spring 2007): 115.

United Nations Development Program. *Human Development Report 2006.* www.hdr.undp.org/hdr2006/statistics.

U.S. Government Accountability Office. *GAO-06-770 Illegal Immigration: Border-Crossing Deaths Have Doubled Since 1995*. Washington, DC: U.S. GAO, August 2006. www.gao.gov/new.items/d06770.pdf.

U.S. White House. "Promoting a Culture of Life: The Accomplishments," November 5, 2003. www.whitehouse.gov/infocus/achievement/chap15.html.

USA Today, "The Big Mac Turns 40, Gets a Museum," August 24, 2007. www.usatoday.com/news/nation/2007-08-24-big-mac-at-40_N.htm.

Walmsley, Roy. "Global Incarceration and Prison Trends." *Forum on Crime and Society* 3, nos. 1 and 2 (December 2003): 65–78.

World Bank. "GNI per capita 2006, Atlas method and PPP." From the World Development Indicators database, World Bank, September 14, 2007. www.siteresources.worldbank.org/DATASTATISTICS/Resources/GNIPC.pdf.

WorldPublicOpinion.org. "Israel and Iran Share Most Negative Ratings in Global," March 2007. www.worldpublicopinion.org/pipa/pdf/mar07/BBC_ViewsCountries_Mar07_pr.pdf.

———. "Muslim Public Opinion on U.S. Policy, Attacks on Civilians and al Qaeda," April 24, 2007. www.worldpublicopinion.org/pipa/pdf/apr07/START_Apr07_rpt.pdf.

———. "World View of US Role Goes From Bad to Worse," January 2007. www.worldpublicopinion.org/pipa/articles/home_page/306.php?nid=&id=&pnt=306&lb=hmpg.

NOTES

Introduction

1. Indiana, in fact, has over 8,000 high-value targets, including a petting zoo. See Eric Lipton, "Come One, Come All, Join the Terror Target List," *New York Times*, July 12, 2006, www.nytimes.com/2006/07/12/washington/12assets.html.
2. Alkman Granitsas, "Americans Are Tuning Out the World: When the world comes to their shore, U.S. citizens are increasingly less interested in foreign affairs," *Yale Global*, November 24, 2005.
3. Lizzie Collingham, *Curry: A Tale of Cooks and Conquerors* (New York: Oxford University Press, 2006).

Part I: The Charter Members of the Axis of Evil

4. Some may accuse me of speaking ill about our Great Leader, but, in fact, "The Shrub" is simply the English translation of his self-appellation "Arbusto," which means "shrub," or "bush," in Spanish. He liked the name so much, he named his oil and gas company Arbusto Energy, which he started in 1978 but soon ran into the ground, as he did all of his business enterprises. See a Web site devoted to famous Texans for more info on Arbusto, www.famoustexans.com/georgewbush.htm.
5. George W. Bush, "The President's State of the Union Address," January 29, 2002, www.whitehouse.gov/news/releases/2002/01/20020129-11.html.
6. Peter W. Galbraith, *The End of Iraq: How American Incompetence Created a War Without End* (New York: Simon and Schuster, 2006), 70–71.

North Korea

7. U.S. Central Intelligence Agency, *The World Factbook—North Korea*, November 1, 2007, www.cia.gov/library/publications/the-world-factbook/geos/kn.html; William Stueck, *Rethinking the Korean War* (Princeton, NJ: Princeton University Press, 2002).
8. Peter Carlson, "Sins of the Son: Kim Jong Il's North Korea Is in Ruins, but Why Should That Spoil His Fun?" *Washington Post*, May 11, 2003, www.washingtonpost.com/ac2/wp-dyn/A40505-2003May10?language=printer.
9. Ibid.
10. Ibid.
11. Ibid.
12. "N. Korea Wages War on Long Hair," *BBC News Online*, January 8, 2005, http://news.bbc.co.uk/1/hi/world/asia-pacific/4157121.stm.
13. Pollack, "North Korea's Nuclear Weapons Program to 2015," p. 6. Also see International Crisis Group, *After the North Korea Nuclear Breakthrough: Compliance or Confrontation* (Seoul/Brussels: ICG, April 30 2007).
14. International Crisis Group, *North Korea's Nuclear Test: The Fallout* (Seoul, Brussels: ICG, November 13, 2006); Jonathan D. Pollack, "North Korea's Nuclear Weapons Program to 2015: Three Scenarios," *Asia Policy* 1, no. 3 (January 2007): 105–23; Larry A. Niksch,

North Korea's Nuclear Weapons Development and Diplomacy (Washington, DC: Congressional Research Service, January 3, 2007).

15. David Crossland, "Monster Bunnies for North Korea," *Spiegel Online*, January 10, 2007, http://spiegel.de/international/0,1518,458863,00.html; David Crossland, "No More Monster Bunnies for North Korea," *Spiegel Online*, April 2, 2007, http://spiegel.de/international/zeitgeist/0,1518,475218,00.html.

16. Niksch, *North Korea's Nuclear Weapons Development and Diplomacy*; Arms Control Association, "The U.S.–North Korean Agreed Framework at a Glance," August 2004, www.armscontrol.org/factsheets/agreedframework.asp.

17. Niksch, *North Korea's Nuclear Weapons Development and Diplomacy*; Arms Control Association, "The U.S.–North Korean Agreed Framework at a Glance," August 2004, www.armscontrol.org/factsheets/agreedframework.asp.

18. Sharon A. Squassoni, *Weapons of Mass Destruction: Trade between North Korea and Pakistan* (Washington, DC: Congressional Research Service, November 28, 2006); see also Niksch, *North Korea's Nuclear Weapons Development and Diplomacy*.

19. Squassoni, *Weapons of Mass Destruction*.

20. Jonathan D. Pollack, "North Korea's Nuclear Weapons Program to 2015: Three Scenarios," p. 106.

21. Herman Kahn, *Thinking about the Unthinkable in the 1980s* (New York: Touchstone, 1985); Pollack, "North Korea's Nuclear Weapons Program to 2015," 106; GlobalSecurity.org, "Six-Party Talks," www.globalsecurity.org/wmd/world/dprk/6-party.htm.

22. "Faces Saved All Around," *The Economist*, February 15, 2007, www.economist.com/world/displaystory.cfm?story_id=8706148.

23. It is worth reading this in its entirety to get a sense of how perfidious these jokers are. See Gary Samore, "Dear Leader: Inside the North Korean Nuclear Deal," *Global Asia*, vol. 2, no. 1 (April 5, 2007): 66–68, www.globalasia.org/pdf/issue2/Dear_Leader.pdf.

24. International Crisis Group, *After the North Korea Nuclear Breakthrough: Compliance or Confrontation* (Seoul, Brussels: ICG, April 30, 2007); Pollack, "North Korea's Nuclear Weapons Program to 2015," 6.

25. Human Rights Watch, "North Korea Country Summary," January 2007, www.hrw.org/englishwr2k7/docs/2007/01/11/nkorea14755.htm.

26. Dan Oberdorfer, *The Two Koreas: A Contemporary History*. New York, NY: Basic Books, 1997, 140–41.

27. Larry Niksch and Raphael Perl, *North Korea: Terrorism List Removal?* (Washington, DC: Congressional Research Service, April 6, 2007); "U.S. Keeping North Korea on Its List of Terror Sponsors," *International Herald Tribune*, September 4, 2007, www.iht.com/articles/2007/09/04/asia/north.php.

28. Hwang Jang-yop, *Hwang Jang Yop Kaikoroku: Kim Seinichi eno Sensen Fukoku* [Hwang Jang-yop's Memoir: Declaration of War on Kim Jong-il], trans. Toru Ogiwara (Tokyo: Bungei Shunju, 1999), cited in Carlson, "Sins of the Son."

29. Carlson, "Sins of the Son."

30. Human Rights Watch, "North Korea Country Summary," January 2007, www.hrw.org/englishwr2k7/docs/2007/01/11/nkorea14755.htm.

31. Human Rights Watch, "North Korea Country Summary"; see also World Food Programme, "Where We Work—DPRK," www.wfp.org/country_brief/indexcountry.asp?country=408.

32. International Crisis Group, *Perilous Journeys: The Plight of North Koreans in China and Beyond* (Seoul, Brussels: ICG, October 26, 2006); Human Rights Watch, "North Korea Country Summary."

33. "The Producer from Hell," *The Guardian*, April 4, 2003, film.guardian.co.uk/features/featurepages/0,4120,929182,00.html; Carlson, "Sins of the Son."

34. "The Producer from Hell," *The Guardian*, April 4, 2003, film.guardian.co.uk/features/

featurepages/0,4120,929182,00.html; Carlson, "Sins of the Son."

35. Tina-Maire O'Neill, "Kim Jong-Il's North Korean empire prepares for war," *Sunday Business Post Online,* January 12, 2003, http://archives.tcm.ie/businesspost/2003/01/12/ story218812528.asp; Niksch, *North Korea's Nuclear Weapons Development and Diplomacy;* Carlson, "Sins of the Son."

36. Anthony Faiola, "The Dear Leader, On a Platter: Sushi Chef's Book Details Kim Jong Il's Many Purported Indulgences," *Washington Post,* March 16, 2004, www.washingtonpost .com/ac2/wp-dyn/A61550-2004Mar15?language=printer; James Brooke, "Kim Jong Il's Ex-Chef Lifts Lid on Ruler's Fancy Tastes," *International Herald Tribune,* October 20, 2004, www.iht.com/articles/2004/10/19/news/norkor.php.

37. Ermanno Furlanis, "I Made Pizza for Kim Jong-il," *Asia Times Online,* August 4, 11, and 18, 2001, www.dirkburgdorf.com/Pizza-for-Kim.pdf.

38. Ibid.

39. Carlson, "Sins of the Son."

Iran

40. Flynt Leverett, *Dealing with Tehran: Assessing U.S. Diplomatic Options Towards Iran* (Washington, DC: Century Foundation Report, 2006), www.tcf.org.

41. Elliot Hen-Tov, "Understanding Iran's New Authoritarianism," *Washington Quarterly* 30, no. 1 (Winter 2006–2007): 163–79; International Crisis Group, *Iran: Ahmadi-Nejad's Tumultuous Presidency* (Tehran, Brussels: ICG, February 2007).

42. Leverett, *Dealing with Tehran.*

43. During the Iran-Iraq war, Ahmadinejad voluntarily joined the special forces of the Islamic Revolution's Guards Corps (IRGC) and reportedly was a senior officer stationed at Ramazan Garrison, which was headquarters of "Extra-territorial Operations." He is alleged to have been involved in suppressing dissidents both inside and outside of Iran, and there are reports he committed some very nasty acts in Tehran's notorious Evin prison and may have engaged in covert operations around Kirkuk, Iraq. See Global Security, "Mahmoud Ahmadinejad," www.globalsecurity.org/military/world/iran/ ahmadinejad.htm. For a less interesting account, she his official bio at president.ir/eng/ ahmadinejad/bio.

44. For an interesting take on the evolution of the revolution and the ambivalence of the folks who once fought for it, see Azair Nafisi, *Reading Lolita in Tehran: A Memoir in Books* (New York: Random House, 2003). For a more historical and analytical review of these tumultuous times, see Ali Ansari, *Iran, Islam and Democracy: The Politics of Managing Change* (London: Royal Institute of International Affairs, 2000), and Ali Ansari, *Modern Iran Since 1921: The Pahlavis and After* (London: Pearson Education Limited, 2003).

45. Galbraith, *The End of Iraq,* 14–20; Ansari, *Iran, Islam and Democracy;* Ansari, *Modern Iran Since 1921.*

46. Galbraith, *The End of Iraq,* 15–20.

47. Ibid.

48. Steven Coll, *Ghost Wars: The Secret History of the CIA, Afghanistan, and Bin Laden, from the Soviet Invasion to September 10, 2001* (London: Penguin Books, 2004).

49. For more on this senseless loss of life, see Vali R. Nasr, "International Politics, Domestic Imperatives, and Identity Mobilization: Sectarianism in Pakistan, 1979–1998," *Comparative Politics* 32, no. 2 (January 2000): 175–79, 183–87; International Crisis Group, *The State of Sectarianism in Pakistan,* Crisis Group Asia Report no. 95 (Brussels, Islamabad: ICG, 2005), 12, 19–20.

50. Galbraith, *The End of Iraq,* 23–24.

51. Human Rights Watch, "Country Summary: Iran," January 2007, www.hrw.org/english wr2k7/docs/2007/01/11/iran14703.htm; "Iran, China and Pakistan lead 'capital punishment,'" *Iran News and Iranian Cultural Journal,* April 27, 2007, http://iranian.ws/ iran_news/publish/article_21680.shtml.

52. Human Rights Watch "Country Summary: Iran," 4.

53. Ibid.

54. "Treaty on the Non-proliferation of Nuclear Weapons," available at www.fas.org/nuke/control/npt/text/npt2.htm. Also see International Crisis Group, *Iran: Is There a Way Out of This Nuclear Impasse?* (Brussels, Tehran: ICG, February 2006).

55. See Paul Kerr, "UN Security Council Sanctions Iran," January 2007, www.armscontrol.org/act/2007_01-02/SecurityCouncilIran.asp.

56. U.S. Directorate of National Intelligence, *National Intelligence Estimate Iran: Nuclear Intentions and Capabilities* (Washington: DNI, November 2007). dni.gov/press_releases/20071203_release.pdf.

57. International Crisis Group, *Iran: Is There a Way Out of This Nuclear Impasse?*

58. Also see Dimitri Martin's "Trend Spotting" segment on hookahs, on *The Daily Show with Jon Stewart,* www.comedycentral.com/shows/the_daily_show/videos/demetri_martin/index.jhtml.

Iraq

59. For an account of that shellacking, see Sir Aylmer Haldane, *Insurrection in Mesopotamia 1920* (Nashville, TN: Battery Press, 2005), reprint of Imperial War Museum/Battery Press original 1922 edition.

60. For good histories of Iraq and its messy history, see Charles Tripp, *A History of Iraq* (Cambridge: Cambridge University Press, 2000), and Phebe Marr, *A Modern History of Iraq* (Boulder, CO: Westview Press, 2004).

61. For an account of the human rights situation before the invasion, see Human Rights Watch, *World Report 2003—Events of 2002,* "Iraq and Kurdistan" (New York: Human Rights Watch, 2003), www.hrw.org/wr2k3/pdf/iraqandiraqikurdistan.pdf. Also see Amnesty International, *Amnesty International Report 2003,* "Iraq," www.web.amnesty.org/report2003/Irq-summary-eng.

62. Bush, "The President's State of the Union Address," January 29, 2002.

63. "Alleged Mistress Recalls Life With Saddam," *Fox News,* September 12, 2002, www.foxnews.com/story/0,2933,62558,00.html.

64. Barbara Slavin and Gregg Zoroya, "Miscalculations from start to finish in Saddam's career," *USA Today,* December 14, 2006, www.usatoday.com/news/world/iraq/2003-12-14-saddam-profile_x.htm.

65. Richard F. Grimmett, *U.S. Use of Preemptive Military Force* (Washington, DC: Congressional Research Service, September 2002).

66. Expression used here was developed by Jon Stewart's *The Daily Show,* reflecting his personal genius and that of his writers. The expression should be trademarked, but since it isn't, I'm using it with appropriate attribution and indeed abject genuflection.

67. For a startling live update of costs, see www.nationalpriorities.org/index.php?option=com_wrapper&Itemid=182.

68. Steven M. Kosiak, *The Cost of US Operations in Iraq and Afghanistan and for the War on Terrorism through Fiscal Year 2007 and Beyond* (Washington, DC: Center for Strategic and Budgetary Assessments, September 12, 2007), www.csbaonline.org/4Publications/PubLibrary/U.20070913.The_Cost_of_US_Ope/U.20070913.The_Cost_of_US_Ope.pdf.

69. Linda Bilmes and Joseph Stiglitz, "The Economic Costs of the Iraq War: An Appraisal Three Years after the Beginning of the Conflict," NBER Working Paper 12054, February 2006, www.nber.org/papers/w12054.

70. Bilmes and Stiglitz note that direct costs "greatly underestimate the War's true costs. After a lengthy and complex discussion of how they did their math, they conservatively estimate that the true costs of the Iraq war will exceed a trillion dollars. See Bilmes and Stiglitz, "The Economic Costs Of The Iraq War," 2.

71. "Two new novels by Saddam Hussein," from Iraqi local news translated and published by *ArabicNews.com,* March 22, 2002, www.arabicnews.com/ansub/Daily/Day/020322/2002032202.html.

72. "Saddam 'pens two more novels,'" *BBC News,* March 20, 2002, http://news.bbc.co.uk/2/hi/entertainment/1884051.stm.

73. Martin Wolk, "Cost of Iraq war could surpass $1 trillion," *MSNBC.com,* March 17, 2006, www.msnbc.msn.com/id/11880954/.

74. Joseph Crincione, Jessica T. Mathews, and George Perkovich, with Alexis Orton, *WMD in Iraq: Evidence and Implications* (Washington, DC: Carnegie Endowment for International Peace, 2004), 6; see also 47–48.

75. Ibid, 6; see also 48.

76. Ibid, 7.

77. George W. Bush, "The President's State of the Union Address," January 28, 2003, www.whitehouse.gov/news/releases/2003/01/20030128-19.html.

78. Crincione, et al., *WMD in Iraq,* 7, 48.

79. Ibid, 7. See also James Bamford, *A Pretext for War: 9/11, Iraq, and the Abuse of America's Intelligence Agencies* (New York: Anchor Books, 2005); Galbraith, *The End of Iraq;* Bob Woodward, *Bush at War* (New York: Simon and Schuster, 2002); Bob Woodward, *Plan of Attack* (New York: Simon and Schuster, 2004); Bob Woodward, *State of Denial: Bush at War (Part III)* (New York: Simon and Schuster, 2006).

80. D. Murali, "Why get past the present that has all future," *Hindu Business Line,* December 1, 2003, www.thehindubusinessline.com/bline/mentor/2003/12/01/stories/2003120100361000.htm, citing Enigma Series of Dictators, *The Enigma that is Saddam Hussein* (Mumbai: English Ed. Publ. & Distributors. 2003).

81. Crincione, et al., *WMD in Iraq,* 8; see also 52–53.

82. U.S. Senate, Select Committee on Intelligence, *Report of the Select Committee on Intelligence on the U.S. Intelligence Community's Prewar Intelligence Assessments on Iraq* (Washington, DC: Government Printing Office, July 2004), 14, www.gpoaccess.gov/serialset/creports/iraq.html.

83. For other assessments of what was or was not known about Iraq's WMD, see IISS Strategic Dossier, "Iraq's Weapons of Mass Destruction: A Net Assessment" (London: International Institute for Strategic Studies, September 9, 2002); Jeffrey Richelson, "Iraq and Weapons of Mass Destruction: National Security Archive Electronic Briefing Book no. 80," February 26, 2003, www.gwu.edu/~nsarchiv/NSAEBB/NSAEBB80.

84. See GlobalSecurity.org, "Qusay Saddam Hussein al-Tikriti," www.globalsecurity.org/military/world/iraq/qusay.htm.

85. Tom Farrey, "The horrors of Saddam's 'sadist' son," ESPN.com, December 22, 2002, www.espn.go.com/oly/s/2002/1220/1480103.html.

86. Galbraith, *The End of Iraq,* 19, 26–29.

87. Ibid, 43–44, 46–49.

88. George Herbert Walker Bush and Brent Snowcraft, *A World Transformed: The Collapse of the Soviet Empire, the Unification of Germany, Tiananmen Square, the Gulf War* (New York: Alfred A. Knopf, 1998), cited in Galbraith, *The End of Iraq,* 58.

89. Murali, "Why get past the present that has all the future."

90. Iraq Body Count, www.iraqbodycount.org/database (figure is updated routinely).

91. Michael E. O'Hanlon and Jason H. Campbell, "Iraq Index: Tracking Variables of Reconstruction & Security in Post-Saddam Iraq" (Washington, DC: Brookings Institution, 2007), 13, www.brookings.edu/iraqindex.

92. The estimates of civilian casualties are debated, and it is difficult to resolve the differences at least in part because the U.S. forces *say* that they don't bother counting. (It turns out that's not true.) For a published range of estimates, see *BBC News,* "Iraq death toll 'soared post-war,'" October 29, 2004, http://news.bbc.co.uk/2/hi/middle_east/3962969.stm. Also see the Iraqi Body Count, www.iraqbodycount.org; Les Roberts,

Riyadh Lafta, Richard Garfield, Jamal Khudhairi, and Gilbert Burnham, "Mortality before and after the 2003 invasion of Iraq: Cluster sample survey," *The Lancet* 364, 1857–64, www.thelancet.com; Gilbert Burnham, Riyadh Lafta, Shannon Doocy, and Les Roberts, "Mortality after the 2003 invasion of Iraq: A cross-sectional cluster sample survey," *The Lancet* 368, 1421–28, www.thelancet.com

93. Mary Mostert, "87% fewer violent deaths annually in Iraq now than under Saddam Hussein," *Renew America*, January 17, 2005, www.renewamerica.us/columns/mostert/050117.

94. This phrase, as noted earlier, is pilfered from *The Daily Show with Jon Stewart*, and I cannot claim to have invented this witticism.

95. For a discussion of the shamed program, see Independent Inquiry Committee Into the United Nations Oil-for-Food Program, *Report on the Manipulation of the Oil-for-Food Programme*, October 27, 2005, www.iic-offp.org/story27oct05.htm.

96. Jean Bottéro, *The Oldest Cuisines in the World: Cooking in Mesopotamia* (Chicago: University of Chicago Press, 2002); Jean Bottéro, "The Cuisine of Ancient Mesopotamia," *Biblical Archeologist* (March 1985): 36–47.

97. Nawal Nasrallah, *Delights from the Garden of Eden: A Cookbook and History of the Iraqi Cuisine* (self-published, 2003, 2004).

Part II: The NPT+3 States

98. For text of the NPT, see Federation of American Scientists Web site at www.fas.org/nuke/control/npt/text/npt2.htm.

Israel

99. Federation of American Scientists, *Israel: Nuclear Weapons*, www.fas.org/nuke/guide/israel/nuke; Avner Cohen, *Israel and the Bomb* (New York: Columbia University Press, 1998); Peter Pry, *Israel's Nuclear Arsenal* (Boulder, CO: Westview, 1984). For a defense of Israel's extra-legal program, see John Loftus and Mark Aarons, *The Secret War Against the Jews: How Western Espionage Betrayed the Jewish People* (New York: St. Martin's Griffin, 1994), 287–303.

100. Federation of American Scientists, *Israel: Nuclear Weapons*; Cohen, *Israel and the Bomb*; Pry, *Israel's Nuclear Arsenal*; Loftus and Aarons, *The Secret War Against the Jews:*

101. I kid you not. When the French dispatched the reactor tank to Israel, French customs officials were told that it was a desalinization plant that was destined for Latin America! See Federation of American Scientists, *Israel: Nuclear Weapons*.

102. Federation of American Scientists, *Israel: Nuclear Weapons*; Cohen, *Israel and the Bomb*; Pry, *Israel's Nuclear Arsenal* ; Loftus and Aarons, *The Secret War Against the Jews*, 287–303.

103. William Burr, *National Intelligence Estimates of the Nuclear Proliferation Problem: The First Ten Years, 1957–1967*, National Security Archive Electronic Briefing Book No. 155, posted June 1, 2005, http://gwu.edu/~nsarchiv/NSAEBB/NSAEBB155/index.htm; Federation of American Scientists, *Israel: Nuclear Weapons*; Cohen, *Israel and the Bomb*; Pry, *Israel's Nuclear Arsenal*; Loftus and Aarons, *The Secret War Against the Jews*, 287–303.

104. Wisconsin Project on Nuclear Arms Control. "Israel's Nuclear Weapon Capability: An Overview," *The Risk Report* 2, no. 4 (July–August 1996), www.wisconsinproject.org/countries/israel/nuke.html.

105. Jewish Virtual Library, "Mordechai Vanunu," www.jewishvirtuallibrary.org/jsource/biography/Vanunu.html.

106. Warner D. Farr, "The Third Temple's Holy of Holies: Israel's Nuclear Weapons," *The Counterproliferation Papers*, Future Warfare Series No. 2, USAF Counterproliferation Center, September 1999, http://au.af.mil/au/awc/awcgate/cpc-pubs/farr.htm; Cohen, *Israel and the Bomb*; Mark Gaffney, *Dimona: The Third Temple? The Story Behind the Vanunu*

Revelation (Brattleboro, VT: Amana Books, 1989); "Revealed: The Secrets of Israel's Nuclear Arsenal" (London) *Sunday Times,* October 5, 1986; Avner Cohen, "The Bomb That Never Is," *Bulletin of the Atomic Scientists* 56, no. 3 (May/June 2000): 22–23; Jewish Virtual Library, "Israel's Nuclear Weapons."

107. These statistics are kept by the Israeli human rights organizations B'Tselem at btselem .org/english/statistics/Casualities.asp.

108. Jimmy Carter, *Palestine: Peace Not Apartheid* (New York: Simon and Schuster, 2006). See also publications of the amazing organization B'tselem (www.btselem.org), which tracks Israel's ongoing violations of international law. The Foundation for Middle East Peace (www.fmep.org) also does a superb job keeping an eye on Israeli perfidy.

109. Christian Action for Israel, "The U.N.'s Record vis à vis Israel," www.christianactionfor israel.org/un/record.html.

110. Paul Findley, *Deliberate Deceptions* (Washington, DC: American Education Trust, 1995), 192–94.

111. Visit the United Nations Security Council (www.un.org/documents/scres.htm) and General Assembly (www.un.org/documents/resga.htm) Web sites to obtain lists and narratives of resolutions passed.

112. For some good examples of whining about how unfair it is to be Israel at the UN, see AIPAC, "The United Nations and Israel," December 5, 2006, www.aipac.org/ Publications/AIPACAnalysesMemos/United_Nations_and_Israel.pdf, and Permanent Mission of Israel to the United Nations, "Israel and the United Nations—An Uneasy Relationship," www.israel-un.org/israel_un/uneasyrelation.htm.

113. *The Economist,* "Israel Factsheet" (April 27, 2007), www.economist.com/countries/ Israel/profile.cfm?folder=Profile-FactSheet, and "Spain Factsheet" (May 1, 2007), www.economist.com/countries/Spain/profile.cfm?folder=Profile-FactSheet.

114. According to the United States Agency for International Development (USAID), Israel has received more than 140 *billion* dollars (in 2003 dollars), as cited by John J. Mearsheimer and Stephen M. Walt in "The Israeli Lobby and U.S. Foreign Policy," John F. Kennedy School of Government Working Paper RWP06-011, March 2006. A version was also published in *London Review of Book* 28, no. 6 (March 2006), http://lrb.co.uk/v28/n06/mear01_.html.

115. The United States was loath to concede Israeli violation of terms of use and did its best to bury the issue. As of this writing, Israel has faced no consequence for this viola- tion. See "US says Israel cluster bomb use possible violation," *International Herald Trib- une,* January 29, 2007, www.iht.com/articles/2007/01/29/news/israel.php; Ewen MacAskill, "US questions Israel's use of cluster bombs in a rare rebuke," *The Guardian,* January 30, 2007, www.guardian.co.uk/israel/Story/0,,2001680,00.html.

116. Mearsheimer and Walt, "The Israeli Lobby and U.S. Foreign Policy," 5–6.

117. Don't take my word for it: Go see B'Tselem's data on this at btselem.org/english/ Settlements/Settlement_population.xls.

118. *Changing Minds, Winning Peace: A New Strategic Direction for U.S. Public Diplomacy in the Arab and Muslim World,* Report of the Advisory Group on Public Diplomacy for the Arab and Muslim World, Submitted to the Committee on Appropriations, U.S. House of Repre- sentatives, October 1, 2003, cited by Mearsheimer and Walt, "The Israeli Lobby and U.S. Foreign Policy," 5.

119. Pew Global Attitudes Project, *Views of a Changing World 2003: War With Iraq Further Di- vides Global Publics* (Washington, DC: Pew Research Center for the People and the Press, June 3, 2003), www.people-press.org/reports/display.php3?ReportID=185; John Zogby, *The Ten Nation Impressions of America Poll* (Utica, NY: Zogby International, April 11, 2002); John Zogby, *How Arabs View America, How Arabs Learn about America (Six Nation Survey)* (Utica, NY: Zogby International, 2004).

120. Mearsheimer and Walt, "The Israeli Lobby and U.S. Foreign Policy," 6; Duncan L.

Clarke, "Israel's Economic Espionage in the United States," *Journal of Palestine Studies* 27, no. 4 (Summer 1998): 21; Bob Drogin and Greg Miller, "Israel Has Long Spied on U.S. Say Officials," *Los Angeles Times*, September 3, 2004; Carol Migdalovitz *Israeli United States Relations* (Washington, DC: Congressional Research Service, November 14, 2006); Seymour H. Hersh "The Traitor: Why Pollard Should Never Be Released," *New Yorker* 74, no. 42 (January 18, 1999): 26–33; Jeffrey Goldberg, "Real Insiders: A Pro-Israel Lobby and an F.B.I. Sting," *New Yorker* 81, no. 19 (July 4, 2005): 34–40.

121. Mearsheimer and Walt, "The Israeli Lobby and U.S. Foreign Policy," 6.

122. See *Forbidden Families: Family Unification and Child Registration in East Jerusalem*, January 2004, www.btselem.org/Download/200401_Forbidden_Families_Eng.rtf, and Human Rights Watch, "Israel: Don't Outlaw Family Life," July 28, 2003, www.hrw.org/press/2003/07/israel072803.htm.

123. Mearsheimer and Walt, "The Israeli Lobby and U.S. Foreign Policy," 8, 48. They cite three articles on this survey: Amiram Barkat, "Majority of Israelis Are Opposed to Intermarriage, Survey Finds," *Ha'aretz*, September 15, 2003; Nicky Blackburn, "Better a Jew," *Ha'aretz*, April 21, 2004; Lily Galili, "Hitting Below the Belt," *Ha'aretz*, August 8, 2004.

124. Israeli Democracy Institute, "The Democracy Index: Major Findings 2003," www.idi.org.il/english/article.asp?id=1466;

125. Israel Democracy Institute, *The 2006 Israeli Democracy Index* (Jerusalem: Israel Democracy Institute, 2006), www.idi.org.il/english/catalog.asp?pdid=564&did=50.

126. See PIPA and Globescan, "Israel and Iran Share Most Negative Ratings in Global Poll," March 5, 2007. worldpublicopinion.org/pipa/articles/home_page/325.php?nid=&id=&pnt=325 &lb=hmpg1.

127. Theodor Herzl, *The Jewish State* (1896; repr., BN Publishing, 2007).

128. See Bill and Springborg. *Politics in the Middle East*, 315–316.

129. Nur Masalah, *Expulsion of the Palestinians: The Concept of Transfer in Zionist Political Thought, 1882–1948* (Washington, DC: Institute for Palestine Studies, 1992), 128; Benny Morris, *Righteous Victims: A History of the Zionist' Arab Conflict, 1881–1999* (New York: Alfred Knopf, 1999), 140, 142, 168–169. Cited in Mearsheimer and Walt, "The Israeli Lobby and U.S. Foreign Policy," 9. Ben-Gurion said a number of foul things about the Palestinians and the Israeli stratagems to toss them out and fully annex their land. See Flapan, *The Birth of Israel*.

130. Cited by Bill and Springborg, *Politics in the Middle East*, 315–16.

131. Chaim Weismann, *Trial and Error: The Autobiography of Chaim Weizmann* (New York: Harper & Row, 1959), 125, 128–29, cited in Bill and Springborg, *Politics in the Middle East,* 315–16.

132. Theodor Herzl, *The Diaries of Theodor Herzl*, ed. Marvin Lowenthal (New York: Grosset & Dunlop, 1962) cited by Bill and Springborg, *Politics in the Middle East*, 317.

133. For varying estimates of Palestinians and Jews living in the area at different times, see David Ben-Gurion, *The Jews in Their Land* (London: Aldus Books, 1966), 292; and Justine McCarthy, *The Population of Palestine: Population History and Statistics of the Late Ottoman Period and the Mandate,* Institute for Palestine Studies Series (New York: Columbia University Press, 1990), 26.

134. For a good summary of the successive bad deals the Israelis have given them, see Carter, *Palestine: Peace Not Apartheid.*

135. John Snetsinger, *Truman, the Jewish Vote, and the Creation of Israel* (Stanford, CA: Hoover Institution Press, 1974); Bill and Springborg, *Politics in the Middle East,* 306–7.

136. Simha Flapan, *The Birth of Israel: Myths and Realities* (New York: Pantheon Books, 1987), 13–80.

137. David Ben-Gurion, *Memoirs*, vol. 4, 151, cited by Bill and Springborg, *Politics in the Middle East*, 307. Flapan, *The Birth of Israel: Myths and Realities*, 94–103.

138. Letter from David Ben-Gurion to A. Ben-Gurion, October 5, 1937, cited in Shabtai Tveth, *Ben-Gurion and the Palestine Arabs* (Oxford: Oxford University Press, 1985).

139. Black and Morris, *Israel's Secret Wars*; Bill and Springborg, *Politics in the Middle East*; Benny Morris, *The Birth of the Palestinian Refugee Problem, 1947–48* (Cambridge: Cambridge University Press, 1988). See also Nur Masalah, *Expulsion of the Palestinians: The Concept of Transfer in Zionist Political Thought, 1882–1948* (Washington, DC: Institute for Palestine Studies, 1992), 128; Benny Morris, *Righteous Victims: A History of the Zionist-Arab Conflict, 1881–1999* (New York: Alfred Knopf, 1999), 140, 142, 168–69, cited in Mearsheimer and Walt, "The Israeli Lobby and U.S. Foreign Policy," 9.

140 For a delightful article, see Isaac Congedo, "The Case of Jaffa Oranges," TED Case Studies Number 778, 2005. www.american.edu/ted/jaffa.htm.

India

141. For a text of the NPT, see www.fas.org/nuke/control/npt/text/npt2.htm.

142. For an exposition of India's rhetorical stance on the NPT and other nonproliferation regimes, see Ashley J. Tellis, *India's Emerging Nuclear Posture: Between Recessed Deterrent and Ready Arsenal* (Santa Monica, CA: RAND, 2001), and George Perkovich, *India's Nuclear Bomb: The Impact of Global Proliferation* (Berkeley, CA: University of California Press, 1999).

143. William Walker, "India's Nuclear Labyrinth," *The Nonproliferation Review* (Fall 1996): 65.

144. In case you don't believe me, see "Scientist as shamans," *HIMAL South Asia,* July 2002, available at http://www.himalmag.com/2002/july/southasiasphere.htm; Peter Popham, "Why can't Hindus and Muslims get along together? It's a long story," *The Independent* (London) June 1, 1998. Also see Indialine Expeditions, "Rajasthan Treasure Trail," www.indialine.com/travel/tours/tour38.html."

145. U.S. Central Intelligence Agency, *The World Factbook,* www.cia.gov/cia/publications/factbook/geos/su.html.

146. United Nations Development Program, *Human Development Report 2006—Beyond Scarcity: Power, Poverty and the Global Water Crisis,* www.hdr.undp.org/hdr2006/statistics.

147. C. Christine Fair, "Learning to Think the Unthinkable: Lessons from India's Nuclear Test," *India Review* 4, no. 1 (January 2005).

148. Tellis, *India's Emerging Nuclear Posture;* Perkovich, *India's Nuclear Bomb.*

149. For the best exposition as to why the United States should do this, see Ashley J. Tellis, *India as a New Global Power: An Action Agenda for the United States* (Washington, DC: Carnegie Endowment for International Peace, 2005).

150. Estimates of dowry-related deaths are difficult to come by because they tend not to be collected at the national level. The National Crime Records Bureau in 2000 reported that there were 6,995 dowry deaths during that year alone—and that only includes the ones that are discovered. See Chander Mehra, "The Dowry Disease," *India Currents,* February 16, 2004, www.indiacurrents.com/news/view_article.html?article_id =f6cd875a86ebab4d41a 175032d332c26; Cecilia Dugger, "Kerosene, Weapon of Choice for Attacks on Wives in India," *New York Times,* December 26, 2000, www.query.nytimes.com/gst/fullpage.html?res=9F02E0DD1338F935A15751C1A9669 C8B63; UNICEF, www.unicef.org/newsline/00pr17.htm; Carol S. Conrod, "Chronic Hunger and the Status of Women in India," The Hunger Project, June 1998, www.thp .org/reports/indiawom.htm.

151. See Ashley J. Tellis, C. Christine Fair, and Jamison and Jo Medby, *Limited Conflicts Under the Nuclear Umbrella—Indian and Pakistani Lessons from the Kargil Crisis* (Santa Monica, CA: RAND, 2001).

152. See Sumit Ganguly, *The Crisis in Kashmir: Portents of War, Hopes of Peace* (Cambridge: Woodrow Wilson Center Press and Cambridge University Press, 1997); Alexander Evans, "The Kashmir Insurgency: As Bad as It Gets," *Small Wars and Insurgencies* 11, no. 1 (Spring 2000); Robert Wirsing, *India, Pakistan, and the Kashmir Dispute: On Regional Conflict and Its Resolution* (New York: St. Martin's Press, 1994); Navnita Chadha Behera, *Demystifying Kashmir* (Washington, DC: Brookings Institution Press, 2006).

153. If you doubt this tale, check out Hemali Chhapia's piece on the phenomena, "Coaching for Copying Too," *The Times of India*, February 25, 2007.

Pakistan

154. Veena Das, "National Honor and Practical Kinship: Unwanted Women and Their Children," in Faye D. Ginsburg and Rayne Rapp, *Conceiving the New World Order: The Global Politics of Reproduction* (Berkeley, CA: University of California Press, 1995), 212–33.

155. Richard Hough, quoted by Akbar S. Ahmed in *Jinnah, Pakistan and Islamic Identity: The Search for Saladin* (London: Routledge, 1997), 142.

156. Sumantra Bose, *Kashmir: Roots of Conflict, Paths to Peace* (Boston: Harvard University Press, 2005); Behera, *Demystifying Kashmir;* Victoria Schofield, *Kashmir in Conflict: India, Pakistan and the Unending War* (London: I. B. Taurus, 2003); Wirsing, *India, Pakistan, and the Kashmir Dispute;* Lawrence Ziring. *Pakistan in the Twentieth Century: A Political History* (Oxford: Oxford University Press, 1997); Ganguly, *The Crisis in Kashmir.*

157. Douglas Frantz with David Rohde, "A Nation Challenged: Biological Terror; 2 Pakistanis Linked To Papers On Anthrax Weapons, *New York Times,* November 28, 2001.

158. "Remarks [of the U.S. Ambassador to Bangladesh]: Bangladesh Liberation War Museum," October 28, 2004, http://dhaka.usembassy.gov/10.28.04_bd_liberation_war_museum .html.

159. Federation of American Scientists, "Pakistan Nuclear Weapons: A Brief History of Pakistan's Nuclear Program," www.fas.org/nuke/guide/pakistan/nuke/index.html; Andrew Koch and Jennifer Topping, "Pakistan's Nuclear Weapons Program: A Status Report," *Nonproliferation Review* (Spring–Summer 1997): 109–13; "Pakistan Nuclear Forces: 2006," in Shannon N. Kile, Vitaly Fedchenko, and Hans M. Kristensen, "World nuclear forces," *SIPRI Yearbook 2006: Armaments, Disarmament and International Security* (Oxford: Oxford University Press, 2006).

160. For more tales of this odd couple, see George Crile, *Charlie Wilson's War: The Extraordinary Story of How the Wildest Man in Congress and a Rogue CIA Agent Changed the History of Our Times* (New York: Grove Press, 2003).

161. Federation of American Scientists, "Pakistan Nuclear Weapons"; Lawrence Livermore National Laboratory, "Monitoring Clandestine Nuclear Tests," www.llnl.gov/str/ Walter.html.

162. Coll, *Ghost Wars;* Lawrence Wright, *The Looming Tower: Al-Qaeda and the Road to 9/11* (New York: Knopf, 2006).

163. Jai Singh, "Pakistan's top talk diva: actually a dude," *Passport* (A blog by Foreign Policy), blog.foreignpolicy.com/node/448.

164. Syed Shoaib Hasan, "'Censors End' Drag Artist's Show, *BBC News,* June 15 2007. news.bbc.co.uk/2/hi/south_asia/6757323.stm.

Part III: The Dashers of Democracy

165. "Rice names 'outposts of tyranny,'" *BBC News Online,* January 19, 2005, http://news.bbc.co.uk/1/hi/world/americas/4186241.stm.

Cuba

166. See Gardner testimony in "Communist Threat to the United States through the

Caribbean," Hearings before the Subcommittee to Investigate the Administration of the Internal Security Act and Other Internal Security Laws of the Committee on the Judiciary, United States Senate, Eighty-Sixth Congress, August 27, 1960, www.latin americanstudies.org/us-cuba/gardner-smith.htm.

167. Thomas Hugh, *Cuba: The Pursuit for Freedom* (New York: Harper Collins, 1971), 650.

168. For more on that absurd meeting and a photo of their famed handshake, see N. Ravi, "Memorable Meeting: Manmohan," *The Hindu*, September 19, 2006, www.hindu.com/2006/09/19/stories/2006091905340100.htm.

169. Fabian Escalante, *Executive Action: 634 Ways to Kill Fidel Castro (Secret War)* (Melbourne, AU: Ocean Press: 2007); Duncan Campbell, "638 ways to kill Castro," *The Guardian*, August 3, 2006, www.guardian.co.uk/cuba/story/0,1835930,00.html.

170. Richard Luscombe, "World's Longest Serving Leader Gets 100% Approval," *The Scotsman*, March 8, 2003, www.thescotsman.scotsman.com/index.cfm?id=282192003.

171. Escalante, *Executive Action;* Campbell, "638 ways to kill Castro."

172. Campbell, "638 ways to kill Castro."

173. Geoff Simons, *Cuba: From Conquistador to Castro* (Chippenham, Wiltshire, UK: Antony Rowe Ltd., 1996).

174. Anita Snow, "CIA Plot to Kill Castro Detailed," *Washington Post,* June 27, 2007, www.washingtonpost.com/wp-dyn/content/article/2007/06/27/AR2007062700190.html.

175. Amnesty International, *Cuba: "Essential Measures"? Human Rights Crackdown in the Name of Security*, June 3, 2003, www.amnesty.org/library/Index/ENGAMR250172003.

176. "The Castropedia: Fidel's Cuba in facts and figures." *The Independent,* July 30, 2007, www.news.independent.co.uk/world/americas/article2160411.ece.

177. Human Rights Watch, "Cuba Country Summary," January 2007, www.hrw.org/englishwr2k7/docs/2007/01/11/cuba14886.htm.

178. Amnesty International, "Death Penalty: Executions Fall as Pressure Grows for Universal Moratorium," press release, April 27, 2007, www.amnesty.org/library/Index/ENGACT500132007.

179. See their Web site, www.ohchr.org/english/bodies/hrcouncil.

180. Human Rights Watch, "Cuba Country Summary."

181. Ibid.

182. U.S. Department of State, Office of the Coordinator for Counterterrorism, *Country Reports on Terrorism,* April 30, 2007, www.state.gov/s/ct/rls/crt/2006.

183. See U.S. Department of State, *Country Reports on Terrorism,* especially chapter 3, "State Sponsors of Terrorism Overview," April 30, 2007, state.gov/s/ct/rls/crt/2006/82736.htm.

184. C. Christine Fair, "India and Iran: New Delhi's Balancing Act," *Washington Quarterly* 30, no. 3 (Summer 2007).

185. U.S. Department of State, *Country Reports on Terrorism,* chapter 3, "State Sponsors of Terrorism Overview."

186. Hernando Calvo Ospina, "Cuba Exports Health," *Le Monde Diplomatique*, August 2006, www.mondediplo.com/2006/08/11cuba.

187. Even the United States Congressional Research Services acknowledges him as a terrorist. They also note his four accomplices, three of whom are U.S. citizens. See Mark P. Sullivan, *Cuba: Issues for the 110th Congress* (Washington, DC: Congressional Research Service, January 2007).

188. See "The Good Terrorist," *The Economist*, April 26, 2007, www.economist.com/world/la/displaystory.cfm?story_id=9079907.

189. Human Rights Watch, "Cuba Country Summary."

190. Amnesty International, *Cuba: "Essential Measures?"*

191. Amnesty International, *Report 2007: State of the World's Human Rights* (London: Amnesty

International, 2007), www.thereport.amnesty.org/eng/Regions/Americas/Cuba.

192. The text in this section draws from Three Guys From Miami, *Cook Cuban* (Salt Lake City, UT: Gibbs Smith, 2004); Beatriz Llamasm, *A Taste of Cuba* (Northampton: Interlink Books, 2005): Joyce Lafray, *Cuba Cocina: The Tantalizing World of Cuban Cooking* (New York: William Morrow Cookbooks, 2005).

193. World Food Programme, "Where We Work—Cuba," www.wfp.org/country_brief/indexcountry.asp?country=192.

Burma

194. U.S. Department of State, Bureau of Democracy, Human Rights, and Labor, "Burma" in *International Religious Freedom Report 2006*, September 15, 2006, www.state.gov/g/drl/rls/irf/2006/71335.htm; U.S. Department of State, Bureau of Public Affairs; *Burma: A Human Rights Disaster and Threat to Regional Security*, September 16, 2006, www.state.gov/r/pa/scp/2006/72840.htm; Human Rights Report, "Burma: Events of 2006," in *World Report 2007*, www.hrw.org/englishwr2k7/docs/2007/01/11/burma14865.htm.

195. Choe Sang-Hun, "Burma's Protest Crackdown Shatters Uneasy Coexistence: Monks Feeling Wrath of Junta," *International Herald Tribune*, October 24, 2007, www.boston.com/news/world/asia/articles/2007/10/24/burmas_protest_crackdown_shatters_uneasy_coexistence.

196. U Gambira, "What Burma's Junta Must Fear," *Washington Post*, November 4, 2007, www.washingtonpost.com/wp-dyn/content/article/2007/11/02/AR2007110201783.html?hpid =opinionsbox1.

197. Sang-Hun, "Burma's Protest Crackdown Shatters Uneasy Coexistence."

198. Matthew McClearn, "Stranger in a Strange Land," *Canadian Business* 75, no. 3 (February 18, 2002).

199. Jose Manuel Tesoro and Dominic Faulder, "Changing of the Guard: SLORC fixes its name—and purges some faces," Asiaweek.com, November 28, 1997, www.asiaweek.com/asiaweek/97/1128/nat4.html.

200. See Black and Harmston, "Burma: the tyranny continues."

201. Jonathan Head, "Burma discusses version of democracy," *BBC News*, October 23, 2006, http://news.bbc.co.uk/1/hi/world/asia-pacific/6076346.stm.

202. Author fieldwork in June 2006. Also see Human Rights Watch, "Rohingya Refugees from Burma Mistreated in Bangladesh," March 27, 2007, www.hrw.org/english/docs/2007/03/27/bangla15571.htm.

203. United National Development Program, *Human Development Report Statistics*, www.hdr.undp.org/hdr2006/statistics.

204. Mike Thompson, "Burma's Forgotten Rohingya," *BBC News*, March 3, 2006, http://news.bbc.co.uk/2/hi/asia-pacific/4793924.stm.

205. Amy Kazmin, "Burma relocates ministries to remote compound," *Financial Times*, November 7, 2005, www.ft.com/cms/s/1e89b472-4fc9-11da-8b72-0000779e2340.html; "A Capital Move," *The Economist*, November 10, 2005, www.economist.com/display story.cfm?story_id=5139038.

206. Author interviews in June 2006.

207. Discussion of cuisines in this section draws from Vatcharin Bhumichitr, *Vatch's Southeast Asian Cookbook* (New York: St. Martin's Griffin, 2000); Susan Chan, *Flavors of Burma* (New York: Hippocrene, 2003); Mi Mi Khaing, *Cook and Entertain the Burmese Way* (Yangon: Daw Khin Myo Chit, n.d.).

208. Clive Parker, "Forcing the Issue on Myanmar Labor," *Asia Times*, March 1, 2007, www.atimes.com/atimes/Southeast_Asia/IC01Ae01.html; Philip Shenon, "Burma Using Forced Labor on Tourist Projects," July 16, 1994, *New York Times*, http://ibiblio

.net/obl/reg.burma/archives/199407/msg00073.html.

209. U.S. Central Intelligence Agency, *The World Factbook—Burma,* November 7, 2007, www
.cia.gov/library/publications/the-world-factbook/geos/bm.html; "Burma leader's lavish lifestyle aired," *BBC News Online,* November 2, 2006, http://news.bbc.co.uk/2/hi/
asia-pacific/6109356.stm.

210. Khin Maung Soe, "The Underground Revolution," Cell #5, Room #7, Insein Prison,
November 1975, www.aappb.org/article9.html.

211. To find where you can get this yummy beverage, check out www.myanmarbeer.com.
Of course, you are an enemy of freedom if you do.

China

212. For an English version of this fine document, see www.english.people.com.cn/
constitution/constitution.html.

213. For a catalogue of China's "layers of enforcement," see Human Rights Watch, *China
Country Summary,* January 2007, www.hrw.org/englishwr2k7/docs/2007/01/11/
china14867.htm.

214. See Human Rights Watch, "China: Beijing Must Disclose Execution Numbers; Death
Penalty Reform Welcomed but Does Not Go Far Enough," November 1, 2006,
www.hrw.org/english/docs/2006/11/01/china14487.htm.

215. Louisa Lim, "Cases of Forced Abortions Surface in China," *National Public Radio Morning
Edition,* April 23, 2007, www.npr.org/templates/story/story.php?storyId=9766870.

216. This list was mostly derived from U.S. Department of State, Bureau of Democracy,
Human Rights, and Labor, "China (includes Tibet, Hong Kong, and Macau): Country
Reports on Human Rights Practices—2005," March 8, 2006, www.state.gov/g/drl/rls/
hrrpt/2005/61605.htm. Additional sources added where appropriate. Sarcasm added
by the author.

217. U.S. Department of State, Thomas J. Christensen, Deputy Assistant Secretary for East
Asian and Pacific Affairs, Statement before the House Committee on Foreign Affairs,
Subcommittee on Asia, the Pacific, and the Global Environment "U.S.-China Rela-
tions," March 27, 2007, www.state.gov/p/eap/rls/rm/2007/82276.htm.

218. *The Economist,* "China Factsheet," May 8, 2007, www.economist.com/countries/
China/profile.cfm?folder=Profile-FactSheet, and "United States Factsheet," May 30,
2007, www.economist.com/countries/USA/profile.cfm?folder=Profile-FactSheet.

219. See discussions offered by C. Fred Bergsten, Director, Institute for International Eco-
nomics, "The U.S. Trade Deficit and China," Statement before the Hearing on U.S.-
China Economic Relations Revisited, Committee on Finance, United States Senate,
March 29, 2006, www.finance.senate.gov/hearings/testimony/2005test/
032906CBtest.pdf; Albert Keidel, *China's Currency: Not the Problem* (Washington, DC:
CEIP, June 2005).

220. David Barboza, "China Yields to Inquiry on Pet Food," *New York Times,* April 24, 2007,
www.nytimes.com/2007/04/24/business/worldbusiness/24pets.html.

221. David Barboza, "China Makes Arrest in Pet Food Case," *New York Times,* May 4, 2007,
www.nytimes.com/2007/05/04/business/worldbusiness/04food.html.

222. Rick Weiss, "Tainted Chinese Imports Common: In Four Months, FDA Refused 298
Shipments," *Washington Post,* May 20, 2007, www.washingtonpost.com/wp-dyn/
content/article/2007/05/19/AR2007051901273.html.

223. Ibid.

224. Heather Burke, "Mattel Recall of Chinese Toys Will Cost $30 Million,"
Bloomberg.com, August 2, 2007, www.bloomberg.com/apps/
news?pid=20601080&sid=aZoSR1ZU8t MA&refer=asia.

225. "US recalls 440,000 lead-tainted Chinese-made toys," *AFP,* October 31, 2007,
www.afp.google.com/article/ALeqM5hHzPR1q6hHEAAqpt1rOsS8HRiaqw.

226. International Institute for Strategic Studies, *The Military Balance 2007* (London: IISS, 2007).

227. Keith Crane, Roger Cliff, Evan S. Medeiros, James C. Mulvenon, and William H. Overholt, *Modernizing China's Military: Opportunities and Constraints* (Santa Monica, CA: RAND, 2005); Evan S. Medeiros, "Analyzing China's Defense Industries and the Implications for Chinese Military Modernization: Testimony presented to the U.S.-China Economic and Security Review Commission on February 6, 2004" (Santa Monica, CA: RAND, 2004).

228. Erik Baard and Rebecca Cooney, "China's Execution, Inc.: The People's Republic Has Long Been Suspected of Selling Organs from Prisoners. Now One New York Doctor Knows the Rumors Are True," *Village Voice,* May 2–8, 2001, www.villagevoice.com/news/0118,baard,24344,1.html.

229. Michael Swaine, "Assessing the Meaning of the Chinese ASAT Test," CEIP Web Commentary, February 7, 2007, www.carnegieendowment.org/publications/index.cfm?fa=view&id=19006&prog=zch.

230. U.S. Department of State, "U.S.-China Relations"; Nuclear Threat Initiative, "China Profile," January 2007, www.nti.org/e_research/profiles/China/index.html.

231. Nuclear Threat Initiative, "China Profile: Nuclear Overview," January 2007, www.nti.org/e_research/profiles/China/Nuclear/index.html; Nuclear Threat Initiative "China Profile."

232. For allegations of Chinese espionage, see *United States House of Representatives Select Committee on U.S. National Security and Military/Commercial Concerns with the People's Republic of China,* unclassified version, May 1999, www.house.gov/coxreport. For a rebuttal that discounts the impact of Chinese espionage, see Joseph Crincione, "Cox Report and the Threat from China," June 17, 1999 (Washington, DC: Carnegie Endowment for International Peace, 1999).

233. Nuclear Threat Initiative, "China Profile."

234. Nuclear Threat Initiative, "China Profile"; Shirley A. Kan, *China and Proliferation of Weapons of Mass Destruction and Missiles: Policy Issues* (Washington, DC: Congressional Research Service, January 31, 2007).

235. Kan, *China and Proliferation of Weapons of Mass Destruction and Missiles.*

236. Ibid.

237. Ibid.; Gary Milhollin, "The Pitfalls of Nuclear Trade with China: China's export record and its refusals speak of the need for US safeguards," *Boston Sunday Globe,* February 22, 1998, www.wisconsinproject.org/pubs/editorials/1998/pitfalls.html.

238. Kan, *China and Proliferation of Weapons of Mass Destruction and Missiles.*

239. William Schneider," Re-evaluating U.S. Debt." *The Atlantic Online,* October 25, 2005, www.theatlantic.com/doc/prem/200510u/nj_schneider_2005-10-25.

240. This text in this section draws from Fuchsia Dunlop, *Revolutionary Chinese Cookbook: Recipes from Hunan Province* (London: Ebury Press, 2006); Graham Earnshaw, *On Your Own in China,* section on Guongdon, aka Canton, www.earnshaw.com/china/ch08.html; Francine Halvorsen, *The Food and Cooking of China* (New York: John Wiley & Sons, 1996); Lucille Liang, *Chinese Regional Cooking* (New York: Sterling Publishing, 2002); Eileen Yin-Fei Lo, *The Chinese Kitchen* (New York: William Morrow, 1999); Nina Simonds, *Classic Chinese Cuisine* (Boston: Houghton Mifflin, 1994).

241. Calum MacLeod, "China Makes Ultimate Punishment Mobile," *USA Today,* June 15, 2006, www.usatoday.com/news/world/2006-06-14-death-van_x.htm.

242 Baard and Cooney, "China's Execution Inc."

243. U.S. Central Intelligence Agency, *The World Factbook—China,* November 1, 2007, www.cia.gov/library/publications/the-world-factbook/geos/ch.html html.

244. Therese Hesketh and Zhu Wei Xing, "Abnormal sex ratios in human populations: Causes and consequences," *Proceedings of the National Academy of Sciences of the United*

States of American (PNAS) 103 (2006): 13271-75

245. Earnshaw, *On Your Own in China*.

246. For more information about who lives the longest and where, see United Nations Development Program, *Human Development Report 2007/08,* November 2007, www .hdrstats.undp.org/indicators/89.html.

247. A. J. Baker, R. J. Moulton, V. H. MacMillan, and P. M. Shedden, "Excitatory Amino Acids in Cerebralspinal Fluid Following Traumatic Brain Injury in Humans," *Journal of Neurosurgery* 79(3) (September 1993): 369-72; S. A. Lipton and P. A. Rosenberg, "Excitatory Amino Acids as a Final Common Pathway for Neurologic Disorders," *New England Journal of Medicine* 330(9) (March 1994): 613-22; A. H. Dickenson, "Gate Control Theory of pain stands the test of time," *British Journal of Anaesthesia* 88(6) (June 2002): 55-57.

248. Some sources doubted that this was "Beijing style," while others suggested it was. Either way, it's delicious.

Part IV: The Great Satan Barbecue

U.S.A.

249. David F. Schmitz, *The United States and Right-Wing Dictatorships, 1965–1989* (Cambridge: Cambridge University Press, 2006).

250. Estimates calculated by Jeffrey S. Passel, in United States Government Accountability Office, *GAO-06-770 Illegal Immigration: Border-Crossing Deaths Have Doubled Since 1995* (Washington, DC: U.S. GAO, August 2006), www.gao.gov/new.items/d06770.pdf. See also Jeffrey S. Passel and Roberto Suro, *Rise, Peak, and Decline: Trends in U.S. Immigration 1992–2004* (Washington, DC: Pew Hispanic Center, September 27, 2005), www.pewhispanic.org/files/reports/53.pdf.

251. Alkman Granitsas, "Americans Are Tuning Out the World: When the world comes to their shore, U.S. citizens are increasingly less interested in foreign affairs," *Yale Global,* November 24, 2005.

252. The U.S. has the fourth-highest per capita gross national income (GNI) when calculated in "purchasing power parity" or "international dollars" and tenth using the "Atlas method," measured in American greenbacks, according to World Bank, "GNI per capita 2006, Atlas method and PPP," World Development Indicators database," September, 14 2007, www.siteresources.worldbank.org/DATASTATISTICS/Resources/GNIPC.pdf.

253. This chart presents many of the countries in Pew, but some are not included. Spain, Egypt, Jordan, Nigeria, India, and China were excluded due to too few years or because there were no data for 1999-2000. Of these, in 2006 only two states had majorities positively disposed towards the United States (62 percent of Nigerians and 56 percent of Indians). Only 23 percent of Spaniards, 30 percent of Egyptians, 15 percent of Jordanians, and 47 percent of the Chinese liked the United States.

254. Craig Cohen and Derek Chollet, "When $10 Billion Is Not Enough: Rethinking U.S. Strategy toward Pakistan," *Washington Quarterly* 30, no. 2 (Spring 2007): 7-19.

255. The survey queried 28,389 citizens in Argentina, Australia, Brazil, Canada, Chile, China, Egypt, France, Germany, Great Britain, Greece, Hungary, India, Indonesia, Italy, Kenya, Lebanon, Mexico, Nigeria, Philippines, Poland, Portugal, Russia, South Korea, Turkey, United Arab Emirates, and the United States between November 3, 2006, and January 16, 2007. See also WorldPublicOpinion.Org, "Israel and Iran Share Most Negative Ratings in Global," March 2007, www.worldpublicopinion.org/pipa/pdf/mar07/BBC_ViewsCountries_Mar07_pr.pdf.

256. George W. Bush, "Address to a Joint Session of Congress and the American People," September 20, 2001, www.whitehouse.gov/news/releases/2001/09/20010920-8.html.

257. "Usama bin Ladin's speech on the eve of the U.S. 2004 general elections," November 1, 2004, http://english.aljazeera.net/NR/exeres/79C6AF22-98FB-4A1C-B21F-2BC3 6E87F61F.htm.

258. For a fascinating take on globalization (and jihad), see Benjamin R. Barber, *Jihad vs. McWorld: Terrorism's Challenge to Democracy* (New York: Ballantine Books, 1995). For a not-so-funny take on the health impacts of eating supersize McDonald's meals every day for thirty days, see Morgan Spurlock's flick *Super Size Me* (2003).

259. Rachel Shields, "Americans celebrate a national symbol as the Big Mac turns 40," *The Independent,* August 25, 2007, http://news.independent.co.uk/world/americas/article2893894.ece; "The Big Mac turns 40, Gets a Museum," *USA Today*, August 24, 2007, www.usatoday.com/news/nation/2007-08-24-big-mac-at-40_N.htm.

260. Freedom House, "Freedom in the World 2007 Sub-Scores," www.freedomhouse.org/template.cfm?page=372.

261. Pew Global Attitudes, "America's Image in the World."

262. Ibid.

263. You can buy a T-shirt from Contepl8 T-Shirts, http://contempl8.net/they-hate-us-for-our-freedom.htm.

264. WorldPublicOpinion.org, "World View of US Role Goes from Bad to Worse."

265. Gallup Organization, cited by WorldPublicOpinion.org, "US Role in the World," August 3, 2007, www.americans-world.org/digest/overview/us_role/hegemonic_role.cfm.

266. Greg Palast, "1 Million Black Votes Didn't Count in the 2000 Presidential Election: It's Not Too Hard to Get Your Vote Lost—If Some Politicians Want It to be Lost," *San Francisco Chronicle,* June 20, 2004. www.sfgate.com/cgi-bin/article.cgi?file=/chronicle/archive/2004/06/20/ING2976LG61.DTL.

267. Michael Powell and Peter Slevin, "Several Factors Contributed to 'Lost Voters' in Ohio," *Washington Post,* December 15, 2004, www.washingtonpost.com/wp-dyn/articles/A64737-2004Dec14.html.

268. Ibid

269. "Usama bin Laden's speech on the eve of the U.S. 2004 general elections."

270. "The Solution—A Video Speech from Usama bin Laden Addressing the American People on the Occasion of the Sixth Anniversary of 9/11."

271. United Nations Development Program, *Human Development Report 2006*, www.hdr.undp.org/hdr2006/statistics.

272. Eric Klinenberg, "Breaking the News," *Mother Jones* 49 (March/April 2007), www.motherjones.com/news/feature/2007/03/breaking_the_news.html; also see International Federation of Journalists, "Media Concentration," www.ifj.org/default.asp?Issue=OWNER&Language=EN. For a contrarian view from the Heritage Foundation, see James Gattuso, "The Myth of Media Concentration: Why the FCC's Media Ownership Rules Are Unnecessary," Heritage Foundation #284, May 29, 2003, www.heritage.org/Research/InternetandTechnology/wm284.cfm.

273. Cornelia Dean, "Scientific Savvy? In U.S., Not Much," *New York Times,* August 30, 2005, www.nytimes.com/2005/08/30/science/30profile.html.

274. Steven Kull, Clay Ramsay, and Evan Lewis, "Misperception, the Media, and the Iraq War," *Political Science Quarterly* 118, no. 3 (2003–2004): 569–98.

275. Ibid.

276. Ibid

277. Ibid

278. CBS News, "Poll: Creationism Trumps Evolution," November 22, 2004, cbsnews.com/stories/2004/11/22/opinion/polls/main657083.shtml.

279. David Masci, "Twenty Years after a Landmark Supreme Court Decision, Americans Are

Still Fighting about Evolution," Pew Forum on Religion and Public Life, June 13, 2006, www.pewforum.org/docs/?DocID=222.

280. Jon D. Miller, Eugenie C. Scott, and Shinji Okamoto, "Public Acceptance of Evolution," *Science,* vol. 213, no. 5788 (August 11, 2006): 765–66, http://richarddawkins .net/article,706,Public-Acceptance-of-Evolution,Science-Magazine-Jon-D-Miller-Eugenie-C-Scott- Shinji-Okamoto.

281. Pew Forum on Religion and Public Life, "Many Americans Uneasy with Mix of Religion and Politics," August 24, 2006, www.pewforum.org/docs/index.php?DocID=153.

282. Michael A. Fletcher, "Bush Hails Progress Toward 'Culture of Life': Limits on Abortion, Stem Cell Use Cited," *Washington Post,* January 25, 2005, www.washingtonpost.com/ wp-dyn/articles/A32959-2005Jan24.html. Also see the White House, "Promoting a Culture of Life: The Accomplishments," November 5, 2003, www.whitehouse.gov/ infocus/achievement/chap15.html.

283. See Freedom from Religion Foundation, "What Does the Bible Say About Abortion?" nontract #7, 2007, www.ffrf.org/nontracts/abortion.php.

284. Amnesty International, "Death Penalty Statistics 2006," April 2007, www.amnestyusa .org/document.php?id=ENGACT500122007&lang=e. Population data to calculate per capita executions is taken from the CIA *World Factbook,* www.cia.gov/library/ publications/the-world-factbook/index.html.

285. Death Penalty Information Center, "Number of Executions by State and Region Since 1976," updated September 28, 2007, www.deathpenaltyinfo.org/article.php?scid =8&did=186. Also see Death Penalty Information Center, *Innocence and the Crisis in the American Death Penalty* (Washington DC: Death Penalty Information Center, 2004), www.deathpenaltyinfo.org/article.php?scid=45&did=1150. For those of you who think I am being biased, go to www.prodeathpenalty.com to get a dose of those who spend their time defending the practice.

286. Richard C. Dieter, *A Crisis of Confidence: Americans' Doubts About the Death Penalty* (Washington, DC: Death Penalty Information Center Report, 2007), www.deathpenaltyinfo .org/CoC.pdf.

287. Death Penalty Information Center, "Number of Executions by State and Region Since 1976," updated September 28, 2007, www.deathpenaltyinfo.org/article.php?scid =8&did=186. Also see Death Penalty Information Center, *Innocence and the Crisis in the American Death Penalty* (Washington DC: Death Penalty Information Center, 2004), www.deathpenaltyinfo.org/article.php?scid=45&did=1150. For those of you who think I am being biased, go to www.prodeathpenalty.com to get a dose of those who spend their time defending the practice.

288. Thanks to Clay Ramsay for suggesting the title for this chapter while lunching over a plate of chicken mole in DC with our wonderful spouses.

289. Glenn C. Loury, "Ghettos, Prisons and Racial Stigma," April 4, 2007, www.econ.brown.edu/fac/Glenn%5FLoury/louryhomepage/teaching/Ec%20137/ Ec%20137%20spring07/LECTURE%20I.pdf; Roy Walmsley, "Global Incarceration and Prison Trends," *Forum on Crime and Society,* vol. 3, nos. 1 and 2 (December 2003): 65–78; Alan El sner, "America's Prison Habit," *Washington Post,* January 24, 2004, cited by Loury.

INDEX

ABOUT THE AUTHOR

Chris Fair is a Washington, D.C.-based analyst of South Asian political and military affairs. Her friends and colleagues disavow this gustatory castigation, cautioned her against writing it, and hope that she sells enough books to support her gym habits because she won't be employed in D.C. again! Prior to ruining her professional career with this lengthy, opinionated missive of dubious culinary or political insights, she wrote widely on a variety of topics that were obscure and of little interest to most folks.

Fair has lived, studied, traveled, worked, and otherwise eaten her way through the Middle East and South and Southeast Asia. She lives bunkered down in an undisclosed location with her beloved spouse who now feels he must wear high-velocity bullet-repellent evening wear. She is a graduate of the University of Chicago, where she earned a master's degree from the Harris School of Public Policy and a PhD in South Asian languages and civilizations. She also holds a BS in biological chemistry from the University of Chicago and sometimes wonders why she didn't remain a chemist.